HTML5 for iOS and Android
A Beginner's Guide

About the Author

Robin Nixon has worked with and written about computers since the early 1980s (his first computer was a Tandy TRS 80 Model 1 with a massive 4KB of RAM!). During this time he has written in excess of 500 articles for many of the UK's top computer magazines. *HTML5 for iOS and Android: A Beginner's Guide* is his eighth book.

Robin lives with his wife Julie who is a trained nurse, five children, and three disabled foster children on the southeast coast of England, where he works full time as a book author.

Also by Robin Nixon

Learning PHP, MySQL, and JavaScript (O'Reilly, 2009)
ISBN 978-0596157135

Ubuntu: Up and Running (O'Reilly, 2010)
ISBN 978-0596804848

Plug-in PHP (McGraw-Hill Professional, 2010)
ISBN 978-0071666596

Plug-in JavaScript (McGraw-Hill Professional, 2010)
ISBN 978-0071738613

Plug-in CSS (McGraw-Hill Professional, 2010)
ISBN 978-0071748766

About the Technical Editor

Jim McLeod resides in south Florida with his lovely wife of 11 years, Paula. His love of computer languages began in the early '80s with CP/M and he has been exploring that field ever since. His favorite hobby is scuba diving; he got his PADI Instructor's certificate in 2000 in Ft. Lauderdale and has introduced many people to the wonderful undersea world.

HTML5 for iOS and Android
A Beginner's Guide

Robin Nixon

New York   Chicago   San Francisco
Lisbon   London   Madrid   Mexico City
Milan   New Delhi   San Juan
Seoul   Singapore   Sydney   Toronto

The *McGraw·Hill* Companies

Cataloging-in-Publication Data is on file with the Library of Congress

McGraw-Hill books are available at special quantity discounts to use as premiums and sales promotions, or for use in corporate training programs. To contact a representative, please e-mail us at bulksales@mcgraw-hill.com.

HTML5 for iOS and Android: A Beginner's Guide

1234567890 QFR QFR 10987654321

ISBN 978-0-07-175633-4
MHID 0-07-175633-7

Sponsoring Editor   Roger Stewart

Editorial Supervisor   Janet Walden

Project Manager   Aloysius Raj, Newgen Publishing and Data Services

Acquisitions Coordinator   Joya Anthony

Technical Editor   Jim McLeod

Copy Editor   William McManus

Proofreader   Claire Splan

Indexer   Claire Splan

Production Supervisor   James Kussow

Composition   Newgen Publishing and Data Services

Illustration   Newgen Publishing and Data Services

Art Director, Cover   Jeff Weeks

Cover Designer   Jeff Weeks

For Julie.

Contents at a Glance

Contents

Acknowledgments

I would like to thank Roger Stewart for commissioning and editing this book, and Joya, Jim, Melinda, Aloysius, and everyone else who has helped to create it, and without whom it would not be the same. This is my fourth book for McGraw-Hill and the process has been just as enjoyable as it was for all the others.

Introduction

HTML5 for iOS and Android: A Beginner's Guide provides everything you need to know to develop web and stand-alone apps for Apple iOS and Google Android devices using the latest technologies such as HTML5 and CSS3. It assumes that you have no prior programming knowledge and teaches you the basics of both of these technologies, as well as the supporting technologies of JavaScript, MySQL, and PHP.

Although iOS requires apps to be written using Objective C and Android requires the use of Java, the code you need for each is supplied on the companion website so that you do not have to learn these two languages.

Instead, you can create advanced websites, web apps, and stand-alone apps using web technologies, which can then run in iOS and Android devices as if they are native apps.

What This Book Provides

Part I of this book, comprising Chapters 1 to 8, first takes you through the basic principles of HTML 4.01 in Chapter 1 and then introduces HTML5 in Chapter 2 via a fun and comprehensive tutorial packed with plenty of examples and screen shots. Then, Chapter 3 introduces CSS and explains it in detail, after which Chapter 4 covers the power of the latest version of CSS, version 3.

With the HTML and CSS technologies firmly under your belt, Chapters 5 through 7 teach you both the JavaScript and PHP languages from scratch in such a way that you'll be using them to write your own programs in next to no time. Then, to support PHP, Chapter 8 introduces the MySQL database program so that you have access to both the client and server sides of the Ajax communication protocol that is behind so much of today's web infrastructure.

Part II, comprising Chapters 9 through 11, shows you how to leverage your new-found knowledge to create mobile friendly websites and web apps. Part III introduces the iOS and Android SDKs (software development kits), and shows you how to take the web apps in Part II and turn them into stand-alone apps that you can distribute in the Apple and Google app stores.

What Is and Isn't Included

This book includes everything you need to know to create the best-looking websites, web apps, and stand-alone apps for all Apple iOS and Google Android devices using standard web technologies.

This book doesn't include tutorials on using the powerful but immensely complicated Objective C and Java languages used by iOS and Android, because the software on the companion website lets you drop standard HTML websites and web apps into a ready-supplied "wrapper" that communicates directly with the smart devices' operating systems for you.

Of course, for maximum speed, such as that required in fast-action racing games, you will need to resort to writing native apps, but you can use the information in this book for anything that doesn't need to run quite so fast. And because the techniques described use standard web technology, they are quick and easy to implement.

Code License

You are free to use any of the code in this book in your own projects, and you may modify it as necessary without attributing this book—although attribution is always appreciated.

Companion Website

A companion website (at *http://html5formobile.com*) accompanies this book, where all examples and the "wrapper" code needed are freely available to download. You can also visit *www.mhprofessional.com/computingdownload* for the accompanying code and examples for this and other McGraw-Hill Professional books.

Part I

The Core Technologies

A number of core technologies are covered in this book, including HTML, CSS, JavaScript, PHP, and MySQL. You will learn how to use them to create websites, web applications, and even downloadable apps for iOS and Android devices. Of course, you probably won't use all of these technologies together at any one time, but you are sure to use combinations of some of them for most of your mobile apps.

And you don't have to already know any of these languages, because everything you need to learn is clearly explained in Part I of this book, which includes a crash-course introduction to each technology—with sufficient information to build sophisticated web and mobile apps, such as the eBook application shown in the screen grab in Figure 1. This app was written entirely using the information in this book and runs as an app on all iOS and Android devices, and also works as a website for all other browsers.

In Chapters 1 and 2 you will learn how to use standard HTML and the latest HTML5 features to their best effect. Chapters 3 and 4 fully explain Cascading Style Sheets (CSS), including the latest CSS3 properties such as transitions. Chapters 5 and 6 describe JavaScript programming, along with details on how to incorporate popular JavaScript frameworks. Chapters 7 and 8, the final two chapters in Part I, cover the server side of things by introducing PHP and MySQL, with which you can manage the server side of Ajax handshaking—the process of transferring information between a web client and server in the background, without the user being aware.

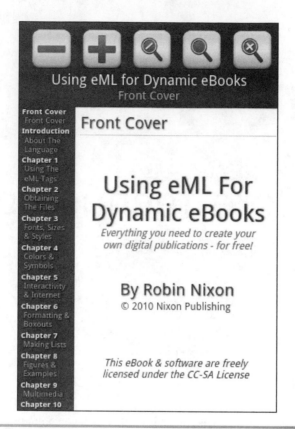

Figure 1 An eBook application written using the information in this book

Once you have completed this part of the book, you will have a thorough grounding in the technologies used throughout the remainder of the book, and you will be able to tweak or improve the examples and even write your own powerful websites and mobile apps.

NOTE

If you are interested, you can download the application in Figure 1 for free via the Apple App Store or the Android Market; just type **eml ebook** for your search term. Or, you can go to *nixonpublishing.com* for the online version.

Chapter 1

Introduction to HTML

Key Skills & Concepts

- HTML tags and attributes
- Incorporating style sheets and JavaScript
- Headings and paragraphs
- Font face, emphasis, and color
- Embedding images and hyperlinking
- Tables, lists, and forms
- Using `<div>` and `<span>` tags
- Framesets and iframes

HTML stands for HyperText Markup Language and is the combination of text and tags that forms the basic structure of all web pages. In this primer I explain the most commonly used HTML 4.01 tags and provide examples of how to use them.

If you are already comfortable with HTML, you can safely skip this chapter, although you may wish to browse the summary of HTML 4 tags in Table 1-2 as a quick refresher before moving on to the new ones introduced in HTML5 (detailed in the next chapter).

Why HTML?

In the pioneer days of the Internet it was possible to connect to and transfer data between the computers connected to the Internet, and there were a number of methods for doing this, such as GOPHER, a system of menus and related documents; TELNET, a method of logging into another computer; and many others.

But what the inventor of the World Wide Web, Sir Tim Berners-Lee, realized was that it would be much more efficient if each document could link to other relevant documents via a single key press or mouse click, using what came to be known as *hyperlinks*. And so HTML was created, making use of angle brackets to contain tags, such as `<a href='http://example.com'>click here</a>` to create a hyperlink, `<b>emphasis</b>` to enable bold text, and so on.

Over the years HTML has been enhanced, and the version supported by most modern browsers up until approximately 2010 is HTML 4.01. Since that date, HTML5 has been achieving growing support, and the open source WebKit browser engine, upon which the Apple iOS and Safari browsers and the Google Android and Chrome browsers are built, is one of the earlier adopters. But before looking at what HTML5 has to offer, let's first see what can be done with HTML 4.

NOTE

When referring to HTML 4, it is common practice to place a space after the acronym HTML. But with HTML5 that space is generally omitted—something to remember when conducting web searches.

HTML Tags

HTML tags start with the < symbol and end with a >. So, for example, the tag <i> tells web browsers to display text following the tag in italics. Most tags are then closed by repeating the tag name but prefacing it with a / character so that, for example, </i> turns off the application of italics to text.

There is an exception to the way some tags are closed, such as with the line break tag, <br>. Since a line break is a single entity, it does not require closing, but to comply with the more strict version of HTML known as XHTML (eXtensible HTML), self-closing tags such as this should still have the closing / character, but placed directly before the final >, like this: <br />. Doing so ensures that your web pages are readable by a wider number of web browsers and clients and are more readily translated to XML (eXtensible Markup Language), the format used by many RSS (Really Simple Syndication) readers.

Tag Attributes

HTML is more than a few simple markup tags, though, because many tags support (or require) the use of *attributes*, items of data (also known as arguments) that provide additional information to the browser.

Attributes consist of an attribute name followed by the = sign and then the attribute data, which must be in either single or double quotation marks. For example, the following is the first part of an anchor in which href is the attribute and the data is supplied between the single quotes:

```
<a href='http://google.com'>
```

There are numerous types of attributes, and different tags support different attributes. But there is a small group of attributes supported by all tags:

- **id** This attribute is used to give a name to the object referred to by the tag so that it can be accessed using Cascading Style Sheets (CSS) or JavaScript. For example, <h1 id='MainHeader'> provides the name or id of 'MainHeader' to the <h1> tag. Nothing happens to the contents of the tag (also known as an object) unless either CSS or JavaScript acts upon it to, for example, apply a particular font styling.

- **class** This attribute lets you supply a group name that may apply to this and other objects. For example, <p class='indent'> applies the class name 'indent' to the <p> tag, which might be used by a style sheet to indent the first line of all objects using it.

- **style** This attribute lets you apply a CSS style to an object by putting it within the quotation marks. For example, to apply the Arial font to a paragraph object, you could use the style attribute like this: `<p style='font-family:Arial'>`.

- **title** With this attribute, any object may be given a title, which most browsers will use to display as a tooltip when the mouse passes over it. For example, the following anchor displays the tooltip `'Go to the Home page'` when moused over: `<a href='/' title='Go to the Home page'>`

Where relevant, the attributes available or required by each tag are explained in the following sections.

The Composition of an HTML Document

There are a number of items you need to put at the start of an HTML web page before you get down to the nitty-gritty of the page itself. This includes things such as detailing the document type to use, the title of the page, meta tags, styles, and more.

The <!DOCTYPE> Tag

So that you can tell browsers exactly how you would like your web page to be displayed—for example, whether to support only strictly formatted HTML—you should start your web pages with a `<!DOCTYPE>` tag, which stands for document type declaration.

There are a number of different arguments available for this tag, which are listed at *doctype.org* and fully explained at *wikipedia.org/wiki/Doctype*. However, in this book all examples use the Transitional type, which requires the following two lines at the start of every document:

```
<!DOCTYPE HTML PUBLIC "-//W3C//DTD HTML 4.01 Transitional//EN"
    "http://www.w3.org/TR/html4/loose.dtd">
```

Tweak for Internet Explorer

Because Microsoft Internet Explorer (IE) places local documents in a trusted security zone, when you open a web page containing any active content such as JavaScript, you have to click a couple of different things to confirm that you wish to grant the web page access to your computer. Obviously, this is quite annoying when you are simply testing a document prior to uploading it to the Internet or using it in an app. For example, Figure 1-1 shows some local active content being accessed, and even after the message and the options menu have been displayed, yet another will appear if you click Allow Blocked Content, asking you to confirm.

Fortunately, there's a simple solution, which is to tell IE that the document was saved from the Internet (even though it wasn't), so that it then automatically assigns the correct security restrictions without being prompted. Therefore, all the examples in this book incorporate the following IE-only tag:

```
<!-- saved from url=(0014)about:internet -->
```

Because it is within comment tags (see the "Using Comments" section, later in this chapter), all browsers other than IE will ignore this line.

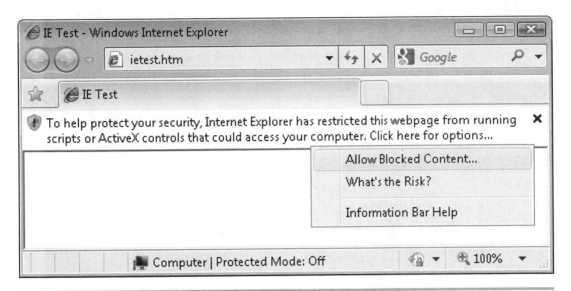

Figure 1-1   How Internet Explorer reacts to dynamic content on a local drive

The <html> Tag

With the first three important lines in place, the next thing a web page requires is an `<html>` tag, which tells the browser where the HTML content starts. This will be closed later with an `</html>` tag.

Any content outside of these tags will be treated simply as text by most browsers unless it is within other tags or comments. Many browsers are forgiving and do their best to display a page well, even with missing or misplaced `<html>` or other tags. But it's best to get things in the right order to ensure that all browsers display your content well.

Within a section denoted by `<html>` and `</html>` tags, there are generally two other types of tag, the `<head>` and `<body>` tags.

The <head> Tag

The section of a web document within `<head>` and `</head>` tags is for placing information about the document, such as its title, any metadata, style sheet information, and so on, as described next.

Creating a Document Title

To define the title of a web document, you place it within `<title>` and `</title>` tags, like this:

```
<title>Rob's Place Chat</title>
```

It is important to choose a title that clearly states what a page is about so that search engines can correctly index the page, and so that visitors can bookmark the page and easily find it again.

Supplying Metadata

Metadata is additional data about a document, and there are many different types of metadata. For example, you can tell a document to replace itself with another one after a given time span, like this:

```
<meta http-equiv='refresh' content='10;url=http://othersite.com' />
```

This particular line will replace the current page with the one at *othersite.com* after ten seconds, and is a type of command sometimes used for quick redirects when a page moves location (although server settings are a better way to manage this for permanent redirects).

Meta tags can be placed outside of the `<head>` section if you wish, but it is generally more meaningful to place them within it, where they're also easy to locate by other people who may update your pages.

Setting the Viewport   In this book the viewport of the browser is generally set to a default width of 980 pixels using the following `<meta>` tag:

```
<meta name='viewport' content='width=980' />
```

What this does is tell mobile devices such as Apple and Android phones that the web page is 980 pixels wide and therefore the view into it can be correctly applied by them. The value of 980 pixels has been chosen because it has become a standard width that mobile browsers handle very well.

Including Style Sheets

You can load style sheets into a web document in a couple of different ways. You can embed a section of CSS within `<style>` and `</style>` tags, or you can use the `<link>` tag to load them in from a separate file, like this:

```
<link rel='stylesheet' href='styles.css' type='text/css' />
```

In Chapter 3 you will see how CSS rules work and how you will format these rules for inclusion by either of these methods.

Inserting JavaScript

Frequently, you will want to load in any JavaScript used by your web pages as quickly as possible to allow it to begin its functioning as soon as the page is ready. In general, therefore, the best place to put it is inside `<script>` and `</script>` tags within the `<head>` section of a web page.

As is often the case with HTML, there are a couple of ways you can do this. You can embed the JavaScript code directly within `<script>` and `</script>` tags, or you can place it within a separate file that you load in separately, as in the following example, which loads the file *ProgramCode.js*:

```
<script src='ProgramCode.js'></script>
```

Chapter 5 explains the use of JavaScript in more detail.

CAUTION

Don't attempt to self-close the first `<script>` tag by placing a / directly prior to the ending >, like this: `<script src='...' />`. Although some browsers may allow this, it is not recommended because many browsers require that all `<script>` tags must have a matching `</script>` tag.

Including Other Files

Often you'll want to tell the browser about other files. For example, in this book some examples are given an icon that will be displayed if they are saved (or bookmarked) to a mobile device as an app. This is achieved in the following manner, which tells the browser to use the file *appicon.png* as the app or bookmark thumbnail:

```
<link rel='apple-touch-icon' href='appicon.png' />
```

Thoughtfully, Android devices also recognize this command (even though it has the word *apple* in it), so it defines the icon for both Apple and Android devices.

NOTE

See Part III for more information about creating thumbnail icons for a wide range of devices, including the iPod Touch, iPhone, iPad, and Android phones and tablets.

Summary of the Web Document Header Lines

To summarize the tags introduced so far, each web document (as used in this book) requires a `<!DOCTYPE>` tag, followed by a comment line to enable Internet Explorer to load in dynamic pages from a local computer without popping up dialog boxes, followed by the opening `<html>` tag, and then the `<head>` and `</head>` tags and their contents.

Therefore, many examples in this book will begin with HTML similar to this:

```
<!DOCTYPE HTML PUBLIC "-//W3C//DTD HTML 4.01 Transitional//EN"
   "http://www.w3.org/TR/html4/loose.dtd">
<!-- saved from url=(0014)about:internet -->
<html>
   <head>
     <title>The Web Page's Title</title>
     <meta name='viewport' content='width=980' />
     <link rel='stylesheet' href='styles.css' type='text/css' />
     <link rel='apple-touch-icon' href='appicon.png' />
     <script src='ProgramCode.js'></script>
   </head>
   <body>
```

The final tag in this example opens up the body section of the document, explained next.

The <body> Tag

The <body> section of HTML is where you place all the things that the web browser should display. At its simplest, you can place plain text between the <body> and </body> tags and the browser will display it for you.

However, no matter how many spaces, carriage returns, or other characters you place within this text, browsers will ignore them and just display the text in one long string. So let's look at how you can format this text to make it start to look more interesting.

Using Comments

Probably the simplest formatting tags for HTML are < ! - - and - ->. Anything you place within them will be ignored by browsers, and therefore they are referred to as comment tags, since they are most useful for leaving comments in a web page to remind you (and other people who will maintain the page) about anything unusual in it.

Here's a typical one-line comment:

```
<!-- Created by Joe Smith, January 27th 2012 -->
```

Comments can contain as few or as many lines as you like and are also useful for quickly removing from display a section of HTML that you might want to restore at a later date.

Text Formatting

HTML 4.01 has almost 100 different tags available, and it is beyond the scope of this book to detail them all. However, there are a number of tags that are used much more frequently than others, so they are explained here, starting with the basic formatting tags.

Headings

To specify headings in a web document, you use the tags <h1> through <h6> and their closing counterparts </h1> through </h6>.

<h1> headings are the highest level and generally display the largest or boldest text. Subheadings and sub-subheadings (and so on) continue with <h2>, <h3>, and so on to <h6> headings, which usually are very small. You will rarely find documents that use more than the first four levels of headings, but the extra two are there if you need them.

Here are two example headings using these tags:

```
<h1>This is a main heading</h1>
<h2>This is a subheading</h2>
```

In Figure 1-2 you can see the default six levels of headings as displayed by Internet Explorer, along with some standard-sized plain text, which, interestingly, is actually larger than the fifth and sixth level headings, although not boldfaced.

By using these tags logically throughout a document, rather than directly specifying font faces and sizes (or other attributes) inline, you can then separately apply different CSS rules to each tag to totally change the look and feel of your headings with just a few simple statements. You'll see the power of this when you get to Chapter 3.

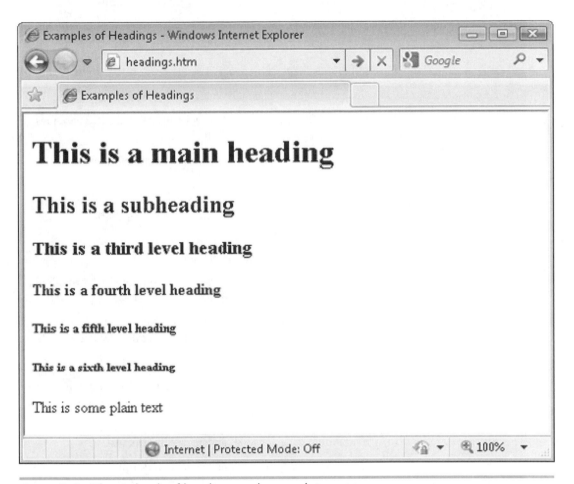

Figure 1-2 The six levels of headings and some plain text

Paragraphs

HTML paragraphs are contained within <p> and </p> tags. Without them, paragraphs would run together, making them hard to read. By default, though, the <p> tag creates a sensible amount of space between each paragraph.

As you'll see in Chapter 3, once a web document is split up into paragraphs with these tags, you can further enhance the way they display by using CSS, such as by indenting the first line of each paragraph, using drop caps, and so on.

Changing Text Emphasis

Here are some of the main tags you can use to give emphasis to text. Some of them are *deprecated*, which means that the developers of HTML intend to remove them at some point in the future, usually because a better method of achieving the same effect has been introduced.

For the deprecated tags, I have also included the recommended alternatives in case you are already in the habit of using them or want to begin using them.

- **<b> ... </b>**   Text within these tags will appear in boldface.

- **<big> ... </big>**   Text within these tags will be bigger than text outside them.

- **<center> ... </center>**   Text within these tags will appear centered. These tags are deprecated and you are recommended to use CSS in their place.

- **<del> ... </del>**   Text within these tags will appear with a strikethrough line through it.

- **<em> ... </em>**   Normally, text within these tags is displayed in italics, so using them is the same as using <i> ... </i>, but it is possible to style these tags differently from <i> ... </i> by using CSS.

- **<i> ... </i>**   Text within these tags will appear in italics.

- **<s> ... </s>**   Text within these tags will appear with a strikethrough line through it. The tags are deprecated and you are recommended to use either CSS or <del> ... </del> tags in their place.

- **<small> ... </small>**   Text within these tags will be smaller than text outside them.

- **<strike> ... </strike>**   These are the same as <s> ... </s>.

- **<strong> ... </strong>**   Normally, text within these tags is displayed in boldface, so using them is the same as using <b> ... </b>, but it is possible to style these tags differently from <b> ... </b> by using CSS.

- **_{...}**   Text within these tags will appear as subscript text.

- **^{...}**   Text within these tags will appear as superscript text.

- **<u> ... </u>**   Text within these tags will appear underlined. These tags are deprecated and you are recommended to use CSS in their place.

Changing Font Face and Color

There are also a variety of ways you can change the font face and color with HTML tags, although they are all deprecated and you are recommended to use CSS instead. However, since they are still in use on millions of websites, you need to know about these tags, if only so that you can update any code you are required to maintain.

- **<font> ... </font>**   Text within these tags is changed according to the arguments supplied for the following attributes:

  - **color='...'**   The color of the text is changed to the value in the quotation marks. This value may be a color name (see "Named Colors," following this list) or a color number (see "Coloring By Numbers," also following this list).

- **face='...'**   The font face of the text is changed to the value in the quotation marks. This value should be the name of a font that is available to the browser. If the font is not found, the browser will select a replacement.

- **size='...'**   The font size of the text is changed to the value in the quotation marks. This should be a value between 1 and 7 (from smallest to largest font size, with a default of 3). The value may be preceded with a + or − symbol to indicate a relative rather than absolute change of size.

- **<basefont> ... </basefont>**   These tags have the same attributes as the <font> tag and are used to change the default font values for an entire document. In particular, if the size is changed, then any use of the <font> tag with + or − values will change the font's size relative to that of the base font. Headings are not affected by this tag, and on some browsers tables do not use this tag's values either.

Additionally, you can change the background color of the <body> tag or of table cells using the bgcolor='...' attribute with either a named or numeric value, as described next.

Named Colors   There are 16 color names you can use with the color attribute: aqua, black, blue, fuchsia, gray, green, lime, maroon, navy, olive, purple, red, silver, teal, white, and yellow.

Some browsers support many more color names, but those names are not part of the HTML 4.01 standard; if you need a wider choice of colors, you should use hexadecimal color numbers, described next, which allows very precise color selection.

Coloring by Numbers   Instead of providing a color name to the color attribute, you can supply a color number, which comprises a # symbol followed by six hexadecimal digits, representing the three primary colors: red, green, and blue.

For example, the value #000000 specifies the color black because it assigns values of 00 to red, 00 to green, and 00 to blue. On the other hand, a value of #ffff00 specifies the color yellow because it assigns values of ff to red, ff to green, and 00 to blue (on a computer, combining red and green results in the color yellow).

Even though the <font> and <basefont> tags may be deprecated and are not recommended to be used, the color names and numbers are still supported and can be used within CSS rules.

NOTE

The value 00 is zero in both decimal and hexadecimal notation, and the value ff in hexadecimal is 255 in decimal. Therefore, there are 256 different shades of each primary color available, resulting in a palette of over 16 million possible color combinations (256×256×256).

Font Faces The fonts available to a browser depend on those installed on its underlying operating system. Therefore, you are allowed to specify more than one font name in a `font='...'` attribute by separating them with commas. This means that you can use any of the strings in Table 1-1 for the argument value, and the browser will display the text in the font you choose (or one similar).

I have chosen to enclose these font strings in double quotes so that any font names within them that contain spaces can then be enclosed in single quotes. By doing this, these same strings can also be used in CSS rules, where they will also ensure that browsers display text in a font as close to your choosing as possible.

So, for example, to change to the Courier New font, you would use the following HTML, which will fall back to the system's standard monospace font if the font isn't available:

```
<font face="'Courier New', monospace">
```

`"Arial, sans-serif"`
`"'Arial Black', sans-serif"`
`"'Arial Narrow', sans-serif"`
`"'Avant Garde', sans-serif"`
`"Bookman, 'Bookman Old Style', serif"`
`"'Century Gothic', sans-serif"`
`"Copperplate, 'Copperplate Gothic Light', serif"`
`"'Comic Sans MS', cursive"`
`"Courier, monospace"`
`"'Courier New', monospace"`
`"Garamond, serif"`
`"'Gill Sans', 'Gill Sans MT', sans-serif"`
`"Georgia, serif"`
`"Helvetica, sans-serif"`
`"Impact, fantasy"`
`"'Lucida Grande', 'Lucida Sans Unicode', sans-serif"`
`"'Lucida Console', monospace"`
`"Palatino, 'Palatino Linotype', serif"`
`"Tahoma, sans-serif"`
`"Times, serif"`
`"'Times New Roman', serif"`
`"Trebuchet, sans-serif"`
`"Verdana, sans-serif"`

Table 1-1 Recommended Strings to Use for Changing Font Face

Embedding Images

After text, images are probably the next most common elements of a web page, and they are embedded using the `<img>` tag, which supports a range of attributes—some of which are described next and shown in Figure 1-3.

- `src='...'` The value inside the quotes tells the browser where to fetch the image from. If it is preceded with the string `http://`, then the image will be downloaded from the website at the domain following the `http://`. Otherwise the image is assumed to be on the current website (or on the local disc) and is loaded from there.

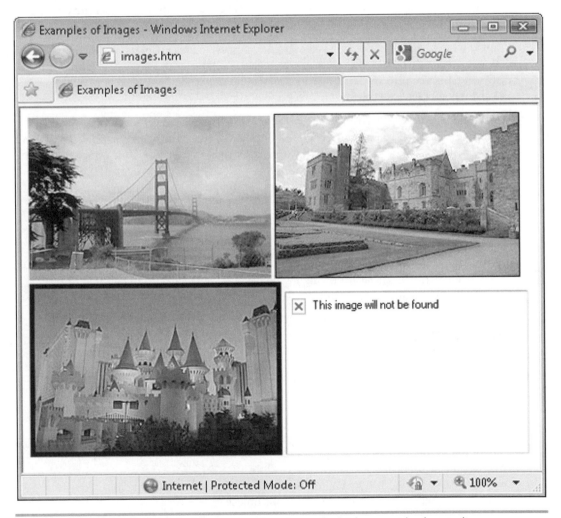

Figure 1-3 Four images with differing borders (one of which cannot be located)

- **alt='...'** Some browsers either do not display images or have had their display disabled, so you can use this attribute to provide alternate text describing the image. This is also useful in cases where an image is slow or fails to load, as shown by the fourth image in Figure 1-3, in which the alternate text is displayed due to the image not being found.

- **width='...'** and **height='...'** By default, web browsers look up an image's dimensions and display it using them. But sometimes you may wish to display an image using a different width and height, which you can specify using one or both of these attributes. If only one attribute is used, the browser computes the other dimension such that the image will stay in proportion. Another reason to specify an image's width and height is to ensure page layout is correctly aligned even before the image is loaded. By specifying these values in advance, the browser will allocate the space required for the image right away.

- **border='...'** Using this attribute, you can specify the width of border (if any) to apply to an image. It accepts the value 0 or any positive number. Unless modified by CSS, if an image has a border and is placed with an anchor, the border color will change when the mouse passes over it. The three images that could be loaded in Figure 1-3 have no border, a 1-pixel border, and a 5-pixel border, respectively.

- **align='...'** With this attribute, you can position an image vertically by aligning it within the current line using any of these values: top, middle, bottom, absmiddle, or absbottom. You can also align it to the left or right of the current line using the values left or right.

For example, to load in the image *pic.jpg* from the current folder, specify its width and height, provide some alternative text and align it to the left of the current line, you might use the following HTML:

```
<img src='pic.jpg' width='320' height='240' alt='Photo' align='left' />
```

Any text or other elements following the image will then be placed to the right of the image and wrap around it.

Ask the Expert

Q: After aligning an element to the left or right, how can I resume normal alignment for subsequent elements?

A: Once text or other HTML elements flow past the bottom of an aligned object, the left or right alignment is cancelled. To clear the alignment of an object before this, you can use one of the following <br /> tag variants, which will (in order) clear left alignment, right alignment, or both types: <br clear='left' />, <br clear='right' />, or <br clear='all' />. When alignment is cleared, subsequent elements will be forced to display below and not alongside the object.

Creating Links

It is possible to attach a hyperlink anchor to almost any element of a web document using the `<a>` tag, which supports three main attributes:

- **href='...'** The value between the quotes is the item to which the anchor is linked. If it is preceded with the string `http://`, then the destination is likely external; otherwise it is assumed to be on the current website (or on the local disc). A typical link looks like this:

```
<a href='http://google.com'>Visit Google</a>
```

- **target='...'** Using this attribute, you can specify what element the target document should be loaded into. This value will usually be the name of an existing `<frame>` or `<iframe>` tag, or may be the special name `'_blank'` to open the target in a new window (or tab, depending on your browser settings). For more about frames, see the section "Frames" later in this chapter.

- **name='...'** This attribute provides a named destination for a link within a page. For example, as well as linking to other pages on your (or other) websites, you can link to specific locations within any web page too. When such links are followed, the browser automatically scrolls down to the relevant section. To use this feature, first create an in-page anchor such as the following:

```
<a name='jumptohere'></a>
```

Now you can hyperlink to this section as follows:

```
<a href='#jumptohere'></a>
```

Or, if the anchor is in a different document from the current one, you might link to it like this:

```
<a href='http://othersite.com/doc.htm#jumptohere'></a>
```

Ask the Expert

Q: Can you point me to a website that illustrates the use of in-page anchors?

A: The Wikipedia website (*wikipedia.org*) is a great place to see both standard and in-page anchors in use because it contains millions of internal cross references, and probably a similarly large number of external ones too.

For example, try following the links in the Contents box of any Wikipedia entry to see how in-page anchors work. Interestingly, typing "html anchor" into the Wikipedia Search box results in you being taken directly to an in-page anchor section of

(continued)

Wikipedia's article on the subject, as shown here:

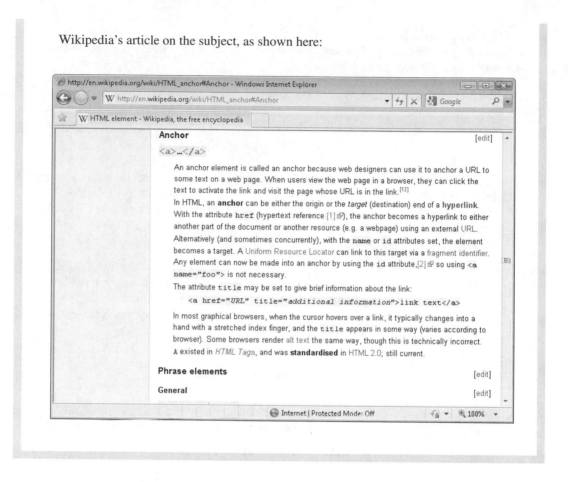

Tables

In recent times tables are often looked on with disdain by users of CSS, who explain how they can get much more precise positioning with CSS. But the fact remains that tables are still great for, well, displaying tables of data.

Also, when you need to put together a quick and simple web page design, tables can get the job done quicker. Then, once you are happy with a design, you can convert it to CSS (if you so choose).

The `<table>` tag supports a number of attributes, of which the main ones are as follows:

- **`align='...'`** This attribute supports values of `left`, `right`, or `center` to align the table according to the surrounding text, although the attribute is now deprecated and use of CSS is recommended instead.

- **`bgcolor='...'`** Using this attribute, you can set the background color of a table. However, CSS is recommended for this as the attribute is now deprecated.

- **border='...'**   With this attribute, you can specify a border around the table of 0 or any positive number of pixels.

- **cellpadding='...'**   This attribute specifies the number of pixels of space between cell walls and their content, which can be a value of 0 or any higher number.

- **cellspacing='...'**   This attribute specifies the number of pixels of space between cells and the outer table border, which can be a value of 0 or any higher number.

- **height='...'** and **width='...'**   With these attributes, you can specify the width and height of a table. When unspecified, the browser will resize the table to the best fit for its contents.

The <table> tag is quite interesting in that it requires the use of further HTML tags nested within it to define the rows and columns of a table. Here are the main ones you are likely to use:

- **<caption> ... </caption>**   These tags display a caption the same width as the table.

- **<tr> ... </tr>**   These tags create a table row and are usually the next level of tags immediately after the <table> tag.

- **<td> ... </td>**   With these tags, you can create individual cells (or columns) within a table row.

- **<th> ... </th>**   You use these tags in the same manner as <td> and </td> to signify to the web browser that the content of the cell is a heading.

If you've never seen these tags before, then creating tables might seem rather complicated, but it really isn't. For example, here's how to put together a simple table detailing the market share of the major web browsers as it stood in August 2010 (according to Wikipedia), and which produces the table shown in Figure 1-4:

```
<table border='1'>
   <caption>
      <i>Web Browser Market Share August 2010</i>
   </caption>
   <tr>
      <th>Browser</th>
      <th>Share</th>
   </tr>
   <tr>
      <td>Internet Explorer</td>
      <td>51.34%</td>
   </tr>
   <tr>
      <td>Mozilla Firefox</td>
      <td>30.82%</td>
   </tr>
```

```
<tr>
    <td>Google Chrome</td>
    <td>10.70%</td>
</tr>
<tr>
    <td>Apple Safari</td>
    <td>5.16%</td>
</tr>
<tr>
    <td>Opera</td>
    <td>1.40%</td>
</tr>
<tr>
    <td>Others</td>
    <td>0.58%</td>
</tr>
</table>
```

You are not restricted to only text and numeric data within table cells; you can place any HTML elements you like within them, such as images, buttons, iframes, and even other tables.

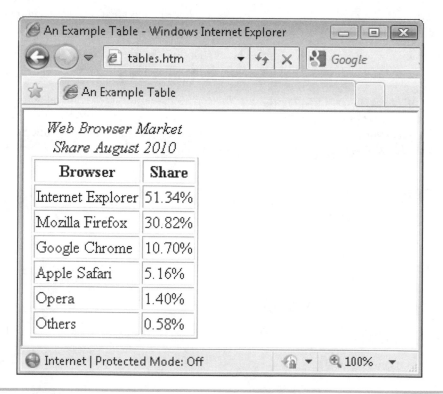

Figure 1-4   Displaying a table using a few simple HTML tags

Lists

When it comes to displaying lists and sublists, HTML really excels, supporting a wide variety of types, as shown in Figure 1-5, in which one of each type of list is displayed.

There are two main types of lists supported by HTML: ordered and unordered. Ordered lists use the `<ol>` tag, and each element in them is prefaced by a number, which increments after each item. Unordered lists use the `<ul>` tag, and all elements are prefaced by one of three different types of symbols.

These tags support the use of attributes to modify the way they display:

- `start='...'` By default, ordered lists start with the number 1 and each additional item in the list is prefaced by the next number in sequence, but you can choose any other starting value, either positive, negative, or zero. This attribute is not used by unordered lists, which always display the same character before each item.

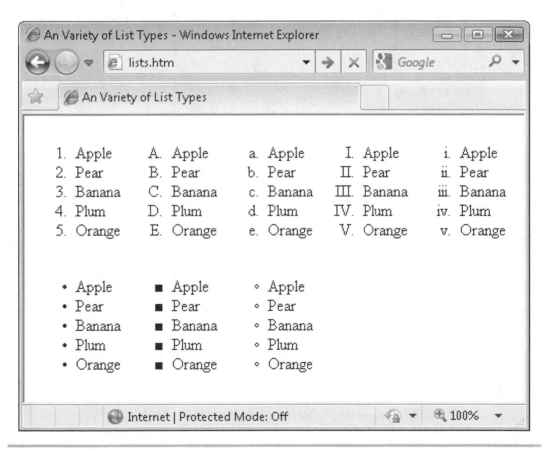

Figure 1-5   HTML supports many different types of list.

- **type='...'** Ordered lists preface each list item with a digit by default, but you can change this behavior to displaying upper- or lowercase letters or upper- or lowercase Roman numerals by giving this attribute a value of one of the following: 'A', 'a', 'I', or 'i', respectively. Unordered lists require any of three words as values for this attribute, 'disc', 'square', or 'circle', the default being the same as specifying 'disc'.

Each element within a list is enclosed within `<li>` and `</li>` tags. For example, the following displays the first list shown in Figure 1-5:

```
<ol>
   <li>Apple</li>
   <li>Pear</li>
   <li>Banana</li>
   <li>Plum</li>
   <li>Orange</li>
</ol>
```

And here's an example of an unordered list prefaced with squares, as shown in the seventh list in Figure 1-5:

```
<ul type='square'>
   <li>Apple</li>
   <li>Pear</li>
   <li>Banana</li>
   <li>Plum</li>
   <li>Orange</li>
</ul>
```

Lists may also have sublists, as shown here:

```
<ul>
   <li>Apple</li>
   <ul>
      <li>Bramley</li>
      <li>Cox</li>
      <li>Golden Delicious</li>
   </ul>
   <li>Pear</li>
   <li>Banana</li>
   <li>Plum</li>
   <li>Orange</li>
</ul>
```

NOTE

In the case of nested unordered lists, by default each sublevel of list is prefaced with a different character, starting with a disc, then a square, and finally a circle character before starting again with a disc for any further levels, and so on.

There is also another type of list supported by HTML, known as a definition list, and it uses the `<dl>` tag. With it, in place of prefacing list elements with symbols, a word or phrase is used (called the *term*), which is then defined in the list element part (called the definition).

For example, here's how you might create a definition list for different food types:

```
<dl>
    <dt>Apple</dt>
    <dd>A fruit with red, yellow, or green skin</dd>
    <dt>Cabbage</dt>
    <dd>Any of several forms of a European vegetable</dd>
    <dt>Peanut</dt>
    <dd>The underground pod of the peanut vine</dd>
</dl>
```

This example will display as follows:

```
Apple
        A fruit with red, yellow, or green skin
Cabbage
        Any of several forms of a European vegetable
Peanut
        The underground pod of the peanut vine
```

Forms

The means by which users are generally invited to submit data to a website is posting via a web form. In Chapter 7 you'll see how you can use PHP on a web server to interpret such posted data, but this section explains how you collect the data in the first instance.

The `<form>` and `</form>` tags enclose a web form and support a number of attributes, of which these are the main two:

- **method='...'**   There are two values accepted by this attribute: `'post'` or `'get'`. When you select `'post'`, all the form data is sent to the web server invisibly, but when using `'get'`, the data is appended to an HTML request following a ? symbol in what is known as a *query string*. This can result in messy-looking URLs but, among other possibilities, it does enable a form to be posted to a local JavaScript program rather than a web server.

- **action='...'**   This attribute should contain the URL to which the form is to be submitted. If the form is sent using a `'get'` request, then a ? followed by the form data will be tacked onto this value.

Figure 1-6 shows a range of form elements all on a single page, each of which is described in the following sections.

The <input /> Tag

Like the `<table>` tag, the `<form>` tag uses additional tags within it. As you might imagine, there are many different tags available, such as `<input />`, which is probably the most

Figure 1-6 The main elements you can include in a `<form>` tag

common. It accepts a number of arguments, of which the first is `type='...'`, which may have any of the following values:

- **`'text'`** This value creates an input field suitable for entering text. You can change the width of the input field with the `size='...'` attribute and limit the number of characters allowed with the `maxlength='...'` attribute.

- **`'password'`**   This value creates an input field suitable for entering passwords in that all typed characters are replaced with the * character when displayed, but are properly stored internally. You can change the width of the input field with the `size='...'` attribute and limit the number characters allowed with the `maxlength='...'` attribute.

- **`'radio'`**   Each form may have any number of radio buttons, each created by giving this value to the `type='...'` attribute of an `<input>` tag, but only one can be active at a time. When another radio button is clicked, the previously selected one is deselected. Radio buttons are round.

- **`'checkbox'`**   You use this attribute value to create check boxes, which are like radio buttons but are square and more than one may be selected at a time.

- **`'hidden'`**   Sometimes in a web form you may wish to pass a value that the user shouldn't see, such as an identifying token or other data. You can do so by passing this value, in which case you also have to provide the value to be posted in the `value='...'` attribute (see the next section).

- **`'submit'`**   This attribute value creates a button that will submit the form. By default, the button is labeled Submit or Submit Query.

The value='...' Attribute

The `<input />` tag may also have additional attributes, of which the main one is `value='...'`, which you can use to prepopulate a field with default data, and is particularly useful when used in conjunction with the `type='hidden'` attribute for posting tracking or other hidden data.

The <textarea> Tag

This tag creates a multiline area in which the user can enter data in a more freeform style. It is suitable for submitting user bios or other information that will not fit in a single-field input.

To specify the number of rows and columns to display, you can use the `rows='...'` and `cols='...'` attributes. The tag is closed with the `</textarea>` tag.

The <select> Tag

With this tag you can create a drop-down list of items from which the user can select one. To use it you must give the tag a name so that posted data can be identified with it, and then you place all the options within `<option>` and `</option>` tags, like this:

```
<select name='chocolate'>
    <option value='plain'>Plain</option>
    <option value='dark'>Dark</option>
    <option value='milk' selected='selected'>Milk</option>
    <option value='white'>White</option>
</select>
```

Whichever chocolate is chosen, the value in lowercase (out of `'plain'`, `'dark'`, `'milk'`, or `'white'`) will be posted, accompanying the field name of `'chocolate'`.

Did you see the `selected='selected'` attribute in the third option of the example? It specifies that this particular option will be selected by default unless the user changes it.

The <button> Tag

This tag displays a clickable button, but I do not recommend its use because Internet Explorer will submit the contents between the `<button>` and `</button>` tags, while other browsers submit the contents of its `value='...'` attribute. Therefore, it is tricky to use consistently, unless you attach to its click events with JavaScript.

The <label> Tag

This tag is especially handy for use with radio buttons or check boxes (which are small) because you can place a radio button or check box next to some explanatory text and surround both with `<label>` and `</label>` tags, enabling the user to click either the text or the radio button/check box to activate it.

Here's an example that is commonly used:

```
<label>
    <input type='checkbox' name='agree' value='yes' />
    I agree to these terms and conditions.
</label>
```

This example displays as follows, and clicking any part of it will check or uncheck the box:

☐ I agree to these terms and conditions.

Bringing a Form Together

Following is the HTML that was used to create the screen grab in Figure 1-6. Because this is purely intended to demonstrate how the different inputs look and work, no attributes have been provided to the `<form>` tag, so the form does not submit, or submits to itself but the data posted is ignored. Also, the `<pre>` tag (which uses a monospace font and *does* display whitespace) simply is used to align all the elements without the need for additional styling.

```
<form><pre>
   Input type: text       <input type='text'     name='f1' size='26' />
   Input type: password   <input type='password' name='f2' size='26' />

   Input type: radio      <input type='radio'    name='f3' value='1' />1
   Input type: radio      <input type='radio'    name='f3' value='2' />2

   Input type: checkbox   <input type='checkbox' name='f4' value='1' />1
   Input type: checkbox   <input type='checkbox' name='f4' value='2' />2

   Input type: hidden      <input type='hidden'   name='f5' />

   Textarea:               <textarea name='f6' rows='3' cols='20'>
                           </textarea>
```

```
Select:                        <select name='f7'>
                                   <option value='1'>First option</option>
                                   <option value='1' selected='selected'>
                                   Second option</option>
                                   <option value='3'>Third option</option>
                               </select>

Button:                        <button name= 'f8' value='f8'>Button </button>

Label:                         <label><input type='checkbox' name='agree'
                               value='yes' /> I agree to the terms</label>

Input type: submit             <input type='submit' />
</pre></form>
```

TIP

To try out this or other example HTML files from this book without having to type them in, you can download them from the companion website at *html5formobile.com*.

The <div> and <span> Tags

The <div> and <span> tags were created to help with combining elements into groups, in a similar manner to placing them into a table cell, and their main purpose is to enable the contained elements to be manipulated ensemble from style sheets.

The <div> tag creates what is called a *block element* in that, by default, its width stretches all the way to the browser's right edge, forcing any following elements onto the line below. Therefore, all block elements created by <div> tag have four sides and are rectangular.

On the other hand, the <span> tag creates an inline element that flows with the text, and therefore it is particularly suited for applying styles to sections of text.

In Chapter 3 you will see how both these containers help with applying CSS rules, each in its own way.

Frames

The final remaining major HTML 4.01 tags relate to placing content in frames. The first way to do this, and the least recommended, is to split a web page into multiple parts and then place them all in frames within the <frameset> tag, like this:

```
<frameset cols='20%, *, 20%'>
   <frame src='header.htm' />
   <frame src='body.htm' />
   <frame src='footer.htm' />
</frameset>
<noframes>
   <!-- Alternative content goes here -->
</noframes>
```

NOTE

The `<noframes>` and `</noframes>` tags in the example display alternative content to users whose browser doesn't support frames. Although all modern mainstream browsers do support frames, some specialist ones, such as audio browsers for blind people or text-only browsers, may benefit from the use of these tags.

This results in a top frame that takes up 20 percent of the browser height and is pulled in from the file *header.htm*. Then there's the main frame, which (due to the * argument in the `cols='...'` attribute) will expand to fit whatever space there is after the fixed-size frames are in place. It is loaded in from the file *body.htm*. And finally the footer frame is loaded in from *footer.htm* and placed in the bottom 20 percent of the web page.

The problem with this method is that the entire web page is composed of frames and there is no content on the page itself. This is obviously not ideal and is not good for ranking in search engines, which will not find such a page very interesting.

Instead, I recommend that when you need a frame, you use an `<iframe>` tag, as shown in Figure 1-7, because you can drop a frame of any width and height anywhere in a document as easily as if it were an image, like this:

```
<!-- Various HTML content here -->
    <iframe src='framecontent.htm' width='200' height='200'></iframe>
<!-- More HTML content here -->
```

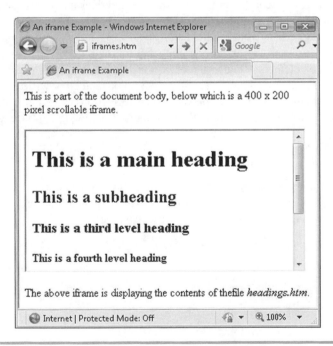

Figure 1-7 Displaying one page within another using the `<iframe>` tag

The Complete Set of HTML 4.01 Tags

For completeness and to act as a refresher, or to give you pointers on what you can do with HTML if you are new to it, Table 1-2 lists all the HTML 4.01 tags, along with short descriptions. It also tells you whether a tag is deprecated and therefore might be removed from future versions of HTML—in which case, for long-term stability of your web sites, you should use the alternative indicated in the table.

Tag or Tags	Description	Deprecated/Alternative
`<!-- ... -->`	A comment	
`<!DOCTYPE>`	Document type	
`<a> ... </a>`	Anchor for a link	
`<abbr> ... </abbr>`	Abbreviation	
`<acronym> ... </acronym>`	Acronym	
`<address> ... </address>`	Author contact details	
`<applet> ... <applet>`	Embedded applet	Yes, use `<object>` instead
`<area />`	Area within an image map	
`<b> ... </b>`	Bold text	
`<base />`	Default link address or target	
`<basefont />`	Default font, color, or size	Yes, use CSS instead
`<bdo> ... </bdo>`	Text direction	
`<big> ... </big>`	Big text	
`<blockquote> ... </blockquote>`	Long quotation	
`<body> ... </body>`	Document body	
` `	Line break	
`<button> ... </button>`	Clickable button	
`<caption> ... </caption>`	Table caption	
`<center> ... </center>`	Centered text	Yes, use CSS instead
`<cite> ... </cite>`	Citation	
`<code> ... </code>`	Computer code text	
`<col />`	Attributes for table columns	
`<colgroup> ... </colgroup>`	Group of table columns	

Table 1-2 All HTML 4.01 Tags *(continued)*

Tag or Tags	Description	Deprecated / Alternative
`<dd> ... </dd>`	Definition list description	
`<del> ... </del>`	Deleted text	
`<dfn> ... </dfn>`	Definition term	
`<dir> ... </dir>`	Directory list	Yes, use `<ul>` instead
`<div> ... </div>`	Block section of a document	
`<dl> ... </dl>`	Definition list	
`<dt> ... </dt>`	Definition list term	
`<em> ... </em>`	Emphasized text	
`<fieldset> ... </fieldset>`	Border around form elements	
`<font> ... </font>`	Font name color and size	Yes, use CSS instead
`<form> ... </form>`	Form	
`<frame />`	Frameset frame	
`<frameset> ... </frameset>`	Set of frames	
`<h1> ... </h1>` - `<h6> ... </h6>`	Headings	
`<head> ... </head>`	Document header	
`<hr />`	Horizontal rule	
`<html> ... </html>`	HTML document	
`<i> ... </i>`	Italic text	
`<iframe> ... </iframe>`	Inline frame	
`<img />`	Image	
`<input />`	Input field	
`<ins> ... </ins>`	Inserted text	
`<isindex> ... </isindex>`	Searchable index	Yes, use `<input>` instead
`<kbd> ... </kbd>`	Keyboard text	
`<label> ... </label>`	Label for an input element	
`<legend> ... </legend>`	Caption for a fieldset element	
`<li> ... </li>`	List item	
`<link />`	Link to supporting file	
`<map> ... </map>`	Image map	
`<menu> ... </menu>`	Menu list	Yes, use `<ul>` instead

Table 1-2 All HTML 4.01 Tags *(continued)*

Tag or Tags	Description	Deprecated / Alternative
`<meta />`	Document metadata	
`<noframes> ... </noframes>`	Alternative content for frames	
`<noscript> ... </noscript>`	Alternative content for scripts	
`<object> ... </object>`	Embedded object	
`<ol> ... </ol>`	Ordered list	
`<optgroup> ... </optgroup>`	Group of list options	
`<option> ... </option>`	Option in a select list	
`<p> ... </p>`	Defines a paragraph	
`<param />`	Parameter for an object	
`<pre> ... </pre>`	Preformatted text	
`<q> ... </q>`	Defines a short quotation	
`<s> ... </s>`	Strikethrough text	Yes, use `<del>` or CSS instead
`<samp> ... </samp>`	Computer code	
`<script> ... </script>`	Script (generally JavaScript)	
`<select> ... </select>`	Select drop-down list	
`<small> ... </small>`	Defines small text	
`<span> ... </span>`	Inline section of a document	
`<strike> ... </strike>`	Strikethrough text	Yes, use `<del>` or CSS instead
`<strong> ... </strong>`	Strong text	
`<style> ... </style>`	Style information	
`<sub> ... </sub>`	Subscript text	
`<sup> ... </sup>`	Superscript text	
`<table> ... </table>`	Table	
`<tbody> ... </tbody>`	Group table body cells	
`<td> ... </td>`	Table cell	
`<textarea> ... </textarea>`	Multiline text input	
`<tfoot> ... </tfoot>`	Group table footer cells	
`<th> ... </th>`	Table header	
`<thead> ... </thead>`	Group table header cells	

Table 1-2   All HTML 4.01 Tags *(continued)*

Tag or Tags	Description	Deprecated / Alternative
`<title> ... </title>`	Document title	
`<tr> ... </tr>`	Table row	
`<tt> ... </tt>`	Teletype text	
`<u> ... </u>`	Underlined text	Yes, use CSS instead
`<ul> ... </ul>`	Unordered list	
`<var> ... </var>`	Variable text	

Table 1-2 All HTML 4.01 Tags

Summary

If you are new to HTML, I recommend that you play with the example files (available for download on the companion website, *html5formobile.com*) to ensure that you have a good feel for what's possible with it.

But newcomer or not, this chapter will have brought you up to speed on using HTML 4.01, and now that you are ready, in the next chapter we'll take a good look at all the new goodies that are provided by HTML5.

Chapter 2

What's New in HTML5

Key Skills & Concepts

- The HTML5 canvas
- Geolocation
- Enhanced form handling
- Pattern matching and inputting times and dates
- Local storage
- Embedding media
- Audio and video codecs
- Microdata, Web Workers, and web applications

Even though this is a book about HTML5 for mobile devices running iOS and Android, because HTML5 is a specification that's still under development and is not expected to be complete before 2012 or 2013, it's important for you to know about all the tags (both current and future), and how they work on other platforms and browsers.

The reason is that you are very unlikely to want your HTML5 web pages, web apps, and device apps to work only on iOS and Android, because being HTML they will also display on most other devices too, and I'm sure you won't want to miss an opportunity to offer your creations on them.

Therefore, this chapter dwells more on what HTML5 can do generally, rather than just what it can do for iOS and Android. Of course, where something is specific to one of these operating systems, it is mentioned, but you should consider the following to be a summary of the current state of play of HTML5 overall. Later in the book we'll see how to apply these features to mobile devices, particularly once you get to Chapter 9, the first chapter in Part II.

So, without further ado, here's what you can expect from HTML5.

NOTE
When an older browser comes across an HTML5 tag that it doesn't recognize, it simply ignores the tag, in the same way as it would if you were to use made-up tag names such as `<madeupnametag>` and `</madeupnametag>`. However, the browser *does* display any text or HTML between such tags.

Canvas

The `<canvas>` element was introduced by Apple to the WebKit rendering engine (the power behind the default iOS and Android web browsers, and also used by Apple Safari and Google

Chrome) to provide a means of drawing graphics from within a web page, without having to load a plug-in such as Java or Flash. It was later standardized and has since been adopted by Opera, and Gecko-based browsers (as used in the Mozilla Firefox browser), and is also included in Google Chrome and Microsoft Internet Explorer 9.

A *canvas* is a region within a web page that can be drawn on using JavaScript. To create a canvas, you use HTML such as the following, which creates a 320×240-pixel canvas with the ID 'mycanvas':

```
<canvas id='mycanvas' width='320' height='240'>
   This section is displayed on browsers that don't support canvas
</canvas>
```

As there can be more than one canvas in a web page, it is necessary to provide an ID for each canvas so that the drawing commands know which canvas they should apply to.

In Figure 2-1 you can see the result of drawing a sequence of circles and squares at graduated levels of brightness on a Chrome browser canvas, and overlaying them with some text.

Because drawing on a canvas requires the use of the JavaScript programming language, full details on how to do this are provided in Chapter 6. In the meantime, if you want to see the source code for this screen grab, please refer to the file *canvas.htm* in the *examples.zip* file available at the companion website, *html5formobile.com*.

Geolocation

The geolocation feature of HTML5 returns the location (or as close as can be determined) of a visitor to the web page, as shown by the example in Figure 2-2, in which the location has been returned of a user standing near the Eiffel Tower in Paris. If a location is returned, it is displayed as a map in an iframe; otherwise an error message is given. This web page is available as *geolocation.htm* in the *examples.zip* file on the companion website.

Because the website visitor's location can then be sent to a web server via a form, or using Ajax, by default all browsers prevent this information from being revealed, unless the visitor gives permission.

Each browser behaves a little differently, but they all offer the same security controls: the first time you visit a website that asks for your location, the web browser asks you whether you wish to provide this information. If you do, there's usually also a box you can check to always allow that website access. If you grant access and don't check the box, then your location will be provided only this one time; next time you visit the website, you will be prompted again. But if you do check the box, you will not be prompted again by that website, which will then always be able to determine where you are.

Similarly, if you don't wish to reveal your whereabouts to a website, you can disallow access, and can normally also check a box to always prevent access to your location to the current website.

To obtain a browser's location, you must make some JavaScript calls, so the details of doing so are provided in Chapter 6.

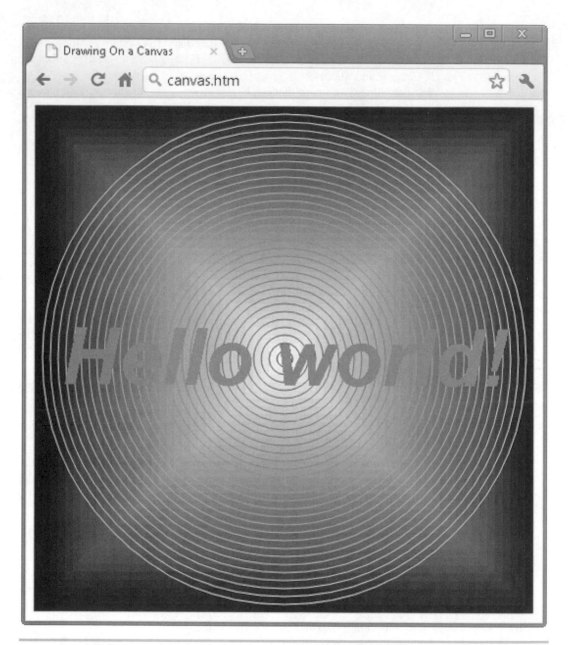

Figure 2-1   Drawing text and concentric squares and circles on a canvas

Figure 2-2 Looking up a user's location is easy with HTML5's geolocation feature

Ask the Expert

Q: How does a web browser determine my location?

A: Your location can be determined in various ways. First, your IP address can reveal which country you are in, and programs that do this can often get close to your locality. Normally, there's nothing you can do about this because all websites need to know your IP address in order to send you data. However, there are third-party services that will act as a proxy for you, replacing your IP address with theirs when you're communicating with a web server.

(continued)

> With HTML5 geolocation, if Wi-Fi is enabled on your computer, locator programs are able to collect more precise location information by scanning your locally accessible Wi-Fi hotspots to pinpoint your location, using databases containing millions of hotspot names and MAC addresses, along with their locations.
>
> Also, if you are using a mobile device, triangulation of the mobile antenna masts you can connect to reveals your location quite accurately, or if your computer has GPS (Global Positioning System) functionality, this can reveal your exact location to within just a few feet.

Forms

Web forms are probably one of the most important and most used parts of the Internet, so it's good to see the number of enhancements that are supplied by HTML5, many of which previously had to be written in rather complicated JavaScript in order to work on all browsers.

In all, there are almost 20 new attributes and over a dozen new input types to enhance your web forms.

Form Attributes

As you will see from the following discussion, HTML5 is still very much an evolving specification that browsers are implementing only piecemeal. Therefore, support for the new features is inconsistent across browsers, and some browsers lack any support. And it's not always the older versions of browsers that haven't yet caught up with the specification; as of this writing, all of the latest versions of all the main browsers omit at least three of these attributes, and some as many as ten.

Nevertheless, over the next few years, most browsers will implement more and more of the HTML5 specification, and therefore the information you need for using these features is presented here.

The autocomplete Attribute

This attribute can be applied to the `<form>` tag or any of the `color`, `date`, `email`, `password`, `range`, `search`, `telephone`, `text`, or `url` types of the `<input>` tag. Valid arguments for this attribute are `'on'` (the default) and `'off'`.

When autocomplete is set to `'on'`, any fields with IDs that have previously had an input entered will remember its value and offer it as a suggested value, saving you from having to enter it again.

When autocomplete is set to `'off'`, this behavior is disabled. When applied to a `<form>` tag, the attribute affects all relevant fields within a form. When applied to an `<input>` tag, only that field is affected. Here are two examples of using the attribute:

```
<form action='prog.php' method='post' autocomplete='on'>
    <input type='text' name='field1' autocomplete='off' />
</form>
```

This feature is supported by the latest versions of all major browsers.

The autofocus Attribute

The autofocus attribute can be applied to any <input> tag to give its field automatic focus when a page loads. This has the effect of placing the cursor in an input field, ready for the user to type, or selecting any other type of field, ready for user action, and is activated like this:

```
<input type='text' name='field' autofocus='autofocus' />
```

This feature is supported by the latest versions of all major browsers except Internet Explorer, but it is safe to use in your web pages because IE still runs perfectly well anyway—it just doesn't provide the extra usability of autofocusing any fields.

The form Attribute

With this attribute, it is not necessary for you to place <input> tags within the form to which they apply. Instead, as long as you give a form an ID, you can specify that form as the argument for a form attribute.

For example, the following code opens and then closes a form with the ID form1, only after which is the <input> tag attached to it:

```
<form id='form1' action='prog.php' method='post'>
   <input type='submit' />
</form>

<input type='text' name='field' form='form1' />
```

This feature is currently available only in the Opera browser and therefore I recommend you do not use it until the other major browsers follow suit.

The formaction Attribute

This attribute is a form override that lets you change the action attribute to a different destination. For example, in the following code, the form will not post to the program prog.php as specified in the <form> tag, but will instead post to prog2.php:

```
<form action='prog.php' method='post'>
   <input type='text' name='field' />
   <input type='submit' formaction='prog2.php' />
</form>
```

This attribute can be particularly useful when you wish to provide more than one submit button, each with a different destination program to which the form should submit.

Form overrides work with either of the submit or image types of the <input> tag, but are currently supported only by the Opera browser. Therefore, I do not recommend using them until the other main browsers catch up.

The formenctype Attribute

This attribute is a form override that lets you change the encoding type of a form (the enctype attribute), in a similar manner to the formaction override. (This attribute currently works on Opera only and therefore its use is not recommended at this time.)

The formmethod Attribute

This attribute is a form override that lets you change the posting method (the `'post'` or `'get'` argument of the `method` attribute), in a similar manner to the `formaction` override. (This attribute currently works on Opera only.)

The formnovalidate Attribute

This attribute is a form override that lets you change the `novalidate` attribute, in a similar manner to the `formaction` override. (This attribute currently works on Opera only.)

The formtarget Attribute

This attribute is a form override that lets you change the `target` attribute, in a similar manner to the `formaction` override. (This attribute currently works on Opera only.)

The height and width Attributes

These attributes can be applied to the `image` type of the `<input>` tag to change its height and width. This feature is available in the latest versions of all major browsers. You use the attributes like this:

```
<input type='image' src='image.png' height='20' width='60' />
```

The list Attribute and <datalist> and <option> Tags

Some input fields support lists, and this attribute can be used to reference them. For example, the following code uses this attribute, along with the new `<datalist>` tag, to offer a selection of URLs from which to choose:

```
Choose a web page: <input type='url' name='links' list='sites' />
<datalist id='links'>
    <option label='Google' value='http://google.com' />
    <option label='Yahoo!' value='http://yahoo.com' />
    <option label='Bing'   value='http://bing.com'   />
    <option label='Ask'    value='http://ask.com'    />
</datalist>
```

This feature works a bit like the `autocomplete` attribute, except that you define the list of suggested choices that appears when the input is given focus.

Currently the feature is supported only by the Opera browser, but you can still use it in your web pages because other browsers will simply not display the list of suggestions. Over time, as other browsers adopt this attribute, your web forms that use it will become quicker to fill in for most visitors.

The min Attribute

This attribute is used to specify a minimum value for input types that contain numbers or dates. I don't recommend you rely on this type of validation yet, though, since only Chrome and the Opera browser support its use, of which here is an example:

```
<input type='time' name='deliver' value='09:00' min='09:00' />
```

The max Attribute

This attribute is used to specify a maximum value for input types that contain numbers or dates, and is also only supported by Chrome and the Opera browser. Here's how you might use it, in conjunction with the `min` attribute:

```
<input type='time' name='deliver' value='09:00' min='09:00'
  max='17:00' />
```

The multiple Attribute

This attribute allows you to accept multiple values for an `<input>` tag that uses either the `email` or `file` type. It works in the latest versions of all major browsers except for Internet Explorer and Opera. You enable it like this:

```
<input type='file' name='images' multiple='multiple' />
```

Then, when the browse dialog box pops up, multiple files can be selected at a time (normally in conjunction with the CTRL key). On browsers that don't yet support this feature, only single files can be selected.

The novalidate Attribute

This attribute specifies that a form should not be validated when it is submitted. It accepts a value of `'true'` or `'false'`. It is not yet implemented in any major browser and therefore should not be used.

When browsers do support it, the attribute will be applicable to the `<form>` tag and any of the `color`, `date`, `email`, `password`, `range`, `search`, `telephone`, `text`, or `url` types of the `<input>` tag. You use it like this:

```
<input type='text' name='field' novalidate='true' />
```

Once this attribute is implemented, you may well choose to use it all the time, at least until the validation features in HTML5 are much better than those currently on offer. If you are looking for reliable in-browser form validation, there are many libraries available, such as the open source tool at *livevalidation.com*.

The pattern Attribute

This attribute lets you specify a regular expression with which an input field should be evaluated. It can be applied to any `<input>` tag that uses any of the `email`, `password`, `search`, `telephone`, `text`, or `url` types. For example, to allow only alphanumeric characters, the dash character, and the underline character in a field, you might use the following HTML:

```
<input type='text' name='username' pattern='[\w\-]{6,16}' />
```

The pattern '[\w\-_]{6,16}' tells the browser to accept only the following:

- **\w** The letters a–z and A–Z, the digits 0–9, and the underline character
- **\-** The dash character
- **{6,16}** Between 6 and 16 characters, inclusive

However, currently this feature works only with the Opera and Chrome browsers and therefore cannot be relied upon for in-browser validation, and for it to work, the !DOCTYPE of a web page must be as follows (rather than one of the HTML 4.01 document types):

```
<!DOCTYPE HTML>
```

I would also add that Chrome simply refuses to submit a form when a pattern doesn't match—giving you no idea why—while Opera says "[input] is not in the format this page requires!" In my view this is really sloppy validation and not much use to anyone. Therefore, I recommend ignoring this feature until such time as it is available on all browsers, and has matured to the point of actually informing users what they need to enter.

The placeholder Attribute

This attribute lets you place a helpful hint in any blank input field, with which you can help explain to users what they should enter. You use it like this:

```
<input type='text' name='username' size='35'
    placeholder='Enter your 6-16 character username' />
```

The size attribute value of 35 ensures that there's enough room for the placeholder text, which, as long as nothing has yet been entered into a field, is displayed in a light color, as shown in Figure 2-3.

As soon as the field is given focus, the prompt disappears, ready for text to be input. This attribute can be applied to any of the email, password, search, telephone, text, and url types of the <input> tag.

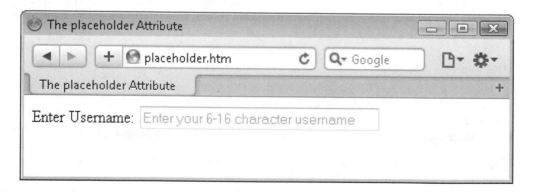

Figure 2-3 Displaying a placeholder in the Apple Safari web browser

The attribute is available in the latest versions of all major browsers except Internet Explorer and Opera. However, it is safe to use as it is simply ignored by these browsers.

The required Attribute

The `required` attribute is used to ensure that a field has been completed before a form is submitted. You use it like this:

```
<input type='number' name='age' required='required' />
```

For this to work, the `!DOCTYPE` of a web page must be as follows (rather than using any HTML 4.01 document types):

```
<!DOCTYPE HTML>
```

As with many other validation features, it is currently available only in the Chrome and Opera web browsers and therefore is not reliable for in-browser validation of all web forms.

The step Attribute

This attribute is used to specify a step value for input types that contain numbers or dates, and also is supported only by Chrome and the Opera browser. Here's how you might use it in conjunction with the `min` and `max` attributes:

```
<input type='time' name='deliver' value='09:00' min='09:00'
   max='17:00' step='3600' />
```

The `step` attribute's `value` can be any positive integer, and is measured in seconds in the case of time references. The result of using the preceding HTML in Opera is shown in Figure 2-4. By clicking the up and down arrow icons next to the spin box, or by using the UP and DOWN keyboard keys, it is possible to scroll through the hours to make a selection.

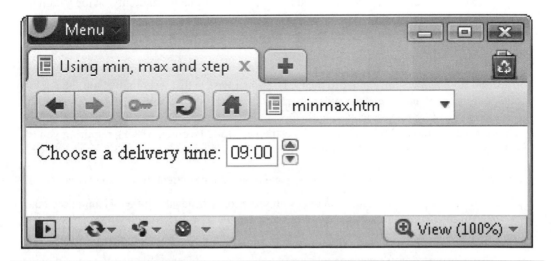

Figure 2-4 Using the `min`, `max`, and `step` attributes in the Opera web browser

Form Input Types

Over the years, web developers have discovered that they require many more types of input on their websites than the simple selection types supported by HTML 4.01. In fact, there are now 16 new types of input available in HTML5.

What these new input types provide is tighter control over user input, along with built-in validation. The only drawback is that these input types are not widely implemented in browsers other than Opera. Nevertheless, you can still use all of the new input types, even on unsupported browsers, because they revert to regular text fields if not supported by the browser.

Of course, this means that you can't yet rely on validation on browsers other than Opera, but if you use these types, then over time, as other browsers catch up, your forms will automatically become easier to complete by most visitors.

When using any of these types, you must use the following HTML5 document type for them to work:

```
<!DOCTYPE HTML>
```

NOTE

Apple iOS devices are partially aware of these input types in the sense that they will change the keyboard type presented to you accordingly. For example, the `email` input type will ensure that an @ symbol is included in the main set of characters, the `number` type ensures that number keys are visible, and the `tel` type displays a telephone keypad. No other enhancements are currently made. None of the Android devices I have checked provide even this small amount of extra input assistance.

The color Input Type

Eventually this input type will call up a color picker so that you can simply click the color of your choice, but right now it restricts you to entering a color name, and only on the Chrome browser. You use it like this:

```
Enter your preferred color <input type='color' name='favcolor' />
```

The date and time Input Types

Date and time pickers are similar to the `color` input type in that, eventually, you'll be able to click one of them and a calendar will pop up, from which you can select a date or time.

Currently these pickers work only in Opera and Chrome, but Chrome's implementation is somewhat silly in that, by default, it calls up the year 1582 (see Figure 2-5), requiring you to enter a fixed date into the `value` field—which is dumb because:

- It's trivial for the browser to seed the date and time with the current details, so why not do so?

- Unless you create the input field on a web server or with JavaScript, you cannot seed the current date yourself and will have to enter a default start date, which will not change as time passes.

Also, Chrome doesn't pop up any type of picker, and you can only click the up and down arrow icons (or press the UP and DOWN keys) to change a selection.

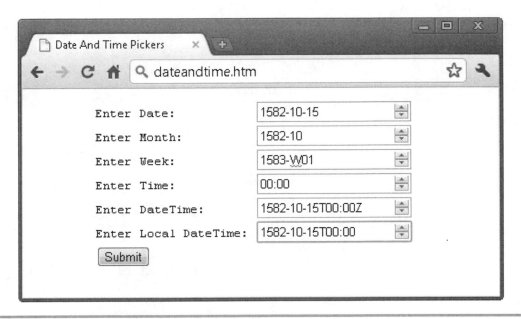

Figure 2-5 Date pickers in Google Chrome are not yet bug free.

On the other hand, Opera always pops up a calendar for making a selection, as shown in Figure 2-6.

You will be confronted with a dilemma if you use any pickers other than the `time` picker, because whereas Opera will work fine by default, Chrome will require you to enter a date such as `2012-06-07` into the `value` field, or it will display dates hundreds of years in the past. However, if you enter such a date, then Opera will use that value as its seed, not the current date.

So my advice? Ignore the date and time picker features until they mature and work properly on all the main browsers; in the meantime there are plenty of JavaScript date picker libraries you can find via search engines.

NOTE
The HTML for the example used in Figures 2-5 and 2-6 is in the file *dateandtime.htm*, available in the downloadable *examples.zip* file at the *html5formobiles.com* website.

The date Input Type   This input type selects a date and is used like this:

```
<input type='date' name='thedate' />
```

The returned value will be of the form `YYYY-MM-DD`. If you wish to ensure it works properly with Chrome, you need to use HTML such as this (although Opera will also then use the seeded date as the default):

```
<input type='date' name='thedate' value='2012-03-17' />
```

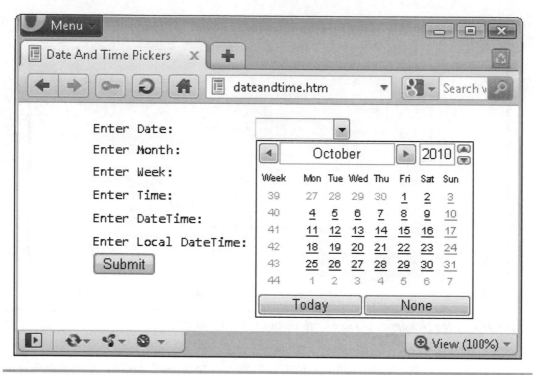

Figure 2-6 Opera makes excellent use of date pickers.

The month Input Type This input type selects a month and is used like this:

```
<input type='month' name='themonth' />
```

The value returned is of the form YYYY-MM. Until it's fixed, remember to seed the input value attribute for Chrome to work correctly.

The time Input Type This input type returns a time in the 24-hour form HH:MM. You use it like this:

```
<input type='time' name='thetime' />
```

The week Input Type This input type returns the week in the form YYYY-WNN (for example, 2011-W06). You use it like this:

```
<input type='week' name='theweek' />
```

Until it's fixed, remember to seed the input value for Chrome to work correctly.

The datetime Input Type   This input type returns the date and time in UTC (Coordinated Universal Time), which will be almost the same as Greenwich Mean Time, give or take a second. The returned value will be of the form YYYY-MM-DDTHH:MMZ (for example, 2011-10-15T15:35Z). You use it like this:

```
<input type='datetime' name='dateandtime' />
```

Until it's fixed, remember to seed the input value for Chrome to work correctly.

The datetime-local Input Type   This input type returns the user's local date and time. The returned value will be of the form YYYY-MM-DDTHH:MM (for example, 2011-10-15T15:35). You use it like this:

```
<input type='datetime-local' name='localdateandtime' />
```

Until it's fixed, remember to seed the input value for Chrome to work correctly.

The email Input Type

This validation type is currently supported only by Chrome and Opera, and ensures that only email addresses that are in a valid format can be entered. You use it like this:

```
<input type='email' name='emailaddress' />
```

The number Input Type

This validation type is currently supported by Chrome and Opera only, and ensures that only numbers can be entered. You use it like this:

```
<input type='number' name='age' />
```

On both browsers, the default value can be changed by clicking the small up and down arrow icons next to the input, or by using the UP and DOWN keys.

The range Input Type

This input type causes a range widget to be displayed that you can slide to select any value between a minimum and maximum, and with a specified start and step value, as shown in Figure 2-7.

It works on the latest versions of Opera, Chrome, and Safari and is used like this:

```
<input type='range' name='num' min='0' max='255'
   value='128' step='1' />
```

In other browsers, a plain-text input field is displayed, into which the user directly enters a number.

The search Input Type

By specifying the search type, browsers are supposed to tailor the input box to provide features such as search suggestions (in a similar way to Google Search), an icon with

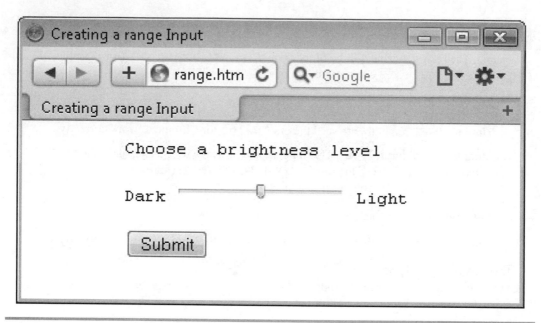

Figure 2-7 Creating a range widget in Safari

which to empty the field, and possibly styling changes to alert you to the type of input. However, currently this has been implemented only on Safari and Chrome, and the only enhancements are an × icon for clearing the input and a rounded input field (on OS X Safari only). But there's no harm in you using this input type right now as other browsers simply display a text field, and when they support the feature in the future, your web pages will already be enhanced for it.

You use the attribute like this:

```
<input type='search' name='searchphrase' />
```

The tel Input Type

This input type informs the browser that a telephone number is to be expected. Currently, it is used only by iOS devices when the field is selected to bring up a telephone number keypad in place of a keyboard, as shown in Figure 2-8 and produced by this HTML:

```
Telephone<br /><input type='tel' name='phone' />
```

The url Input Type

As with the tel input type, this one is also there to tell the browser about the type of data to be expected. In the case of the iPhone and other iOS devices, this type ensures that the ., /, and .com buttons are displayed.

Figure 2-8 Entering data into a `tel` input type on an iPhone

Other browsers may also offer enhancements for this type in the future, which is created with the following HTML:

```
<input type='url' name='webpage' />
```

Local Storage

You are probably quite familiar with *cookies*, small units of data that are stored locally by your browser. They contain information that is helpful to using a website, such as your login details (to save you from having to reenter them each visit), and are often also used somewhat more intrusively to track your surfing habits.

Local storage is similar to cookies, but it supports storing much larger amounts of data and also supplies a local database engine to make saving and retrieving data much easier. The primary benefit is more powerful web apps, with more data residing on your computer rather than on servers somewhere else in the world. For example, a website that manages your TV viewing could store all your favorite programs in a local database, so that when you open the app it only has to check a website of listings to see when these programs are on next, and on which channels. This takes a strain off the web server by leaving the data distributed among users.

Another benefit is that such local databases can be accessed from a local web page using JavaScript, meaning that the data can be used by the app even where there is no Internet connection (in the preceding example, as long as the TV listings have also been downloaded).

So, as you can see, local storage holds tremendous potential for creating mobile device apps purely from HTML and JavaScript, and therefore local storage is one of the key aspects of this book.

In conjunction with the Objective C (for iOS) and Java (for Android) wrappers available on the companion website (*html5formobile.com*) and documented in Part II, you will be able to make professional-looking, slick, lightning-fast apps that you can then also use as websites with minimum modification. In the future, it may also be possible to create wrappers that enable your web apps to also run on other mobile operating systems such as Windows Phone 7, MeeGo, and Blackberry OS.

Don't worry, though. You won't have to learn either of these languages, because in Part III I will walk you step by step through placing your web apps in ready-made wrappers that you can download from the companion website. However, because you need to use JavaScript to access local storage, details on doing so are provided in Chapter 6.

Media

Probably the most popular part of the HTML5 specification (other than the `<canvas>` tag) is the built-in ability of HTML5 browsers to play media without requiring any plug-in such as Flash, QuickTime, or Microsoft Media Player.

Of course, the technology is still young and the file formats supported are constantly evolving and vary by browser for patent reasons, but this section explains all you need to know to embed media using HTML5.

Codecs

The term *codec* stands for enCOder/DECoder and describes the functionality provided by software that encodes and decodes media such as audio and video. In HTML5, there are currently a number of different sets of codecs available, depending on the browser used:

- **H.264** This is a patented, proprietary video codec for which playback is free for the end user, but which may incur royalty fees for all parts of the encoding and transmission process. Consequently, Safari and Internet Explorer support it, but browsers that use only open source or that do not have the financial ability to license it do not.

- **Theora**   This is a video codec that is unencumbered by patents and free of royalty fees at all levels of encoding, transmission, and playback. This codec is supported by Chrome, Firefox, and Opera.

- **VP8**   This video codec is similar to Theora but is owned by Google, which has published it as open source, making it royalty free. It is supported by Chrome, Firefox, and Opera.

- **AAC**   This audio codec, which stands for Advanced Audio Encoding, is the one used by Apple's iTunes Store. Like H.264, it is a proprietary, patented technology and is supported by Safari, Chrome, and Internet Explorer.

- **MP3**   This audio codec, which stands for MPEG Audio Layer 3, has been available for many years, and although the term is often (incorrectly) used to refer to any type of digital audio, it is a proprietary, patented technology that is supported by Safari, Chrome, and Internet Explorer.

- **PCM**   This audio codec, which stands for Pulse Code Modulation, stores the full data as encoded by an analog-to-digital converter, and is the format used for storing data on audio CDs. Because PCM does not use compression, it is called a *lossless* codec and its files are generally many times larger than AAC or MP3 files. It is supported by Safari, Firefox, and Opera.

- **Vorbis**   Sometimes referred to as Ogg Vorbis because it generally uses the .ogg file extension, this audio codec is unencumbered by patents and royalty free. It is supported by Chrome, Firefox, and Opera.

These audio and video codecs are usually contained in one of three wrapper or container types: MP4, OGG, and WebM. Table 2-1 shows the complete list of container types and codecs used by the main browsers.

Browser	Container(s)	Video	Audio
Apple iOS	MP4	H.264	AAC, MP3, PCM
Apple Safari	MP4	H.264	AAC, MP3, PCM
Google Android (Pre v. 3)	—	—	—
Google Chrome*	MP4, OGG, WebM	Theora, VP8	AAC, MP3, Vorbis
Microsoft Internet Explorer	MP4	H.264	AAC, MP3
Mozilla Firefox*	OGG, WebM	Theora, VP8	PCM, Vorbis
Opera	OGG, WebM	Theora, VP8	PCM, Vorbis

* See Note on next page.

Table 2-1   Video and Audio Support in the Most Popular Browsers and Devices

NOTE

Microsoft has released plug-ins for Chrome and Firefox to enable the playback of H.264 video, so if you want users of these browsers to be able to access your H.264 content, you can point them to the following URLs for downloading and installing the plug-ins:

interoperabilitybridges.com/wmp-extension-for-chrome
interoperabilitybridges.com/html5-extension-for-wmp-plugin

The best way you can keep up to date on HTML5 implementation is to visit the website *html5test.com* using a target browser and operating system. It will then report on exactly which HTML5 features have been implemented, as shown in Figure 2-9, in which an iPhone 4 is being tested, and Figure 2-10, in which an Android 2.1 device is displaying the website.

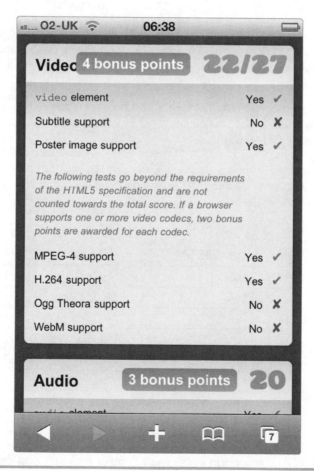

Figure 2-9 Testing an iPhone 4's implementation of HTML5 video

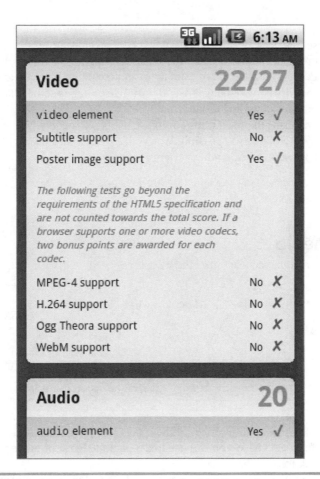

Figure 2-10 An Android 2.1 device being tested for HTML5 video support

Ask the Expert

Q: I'm confused by all these different standards. What does it all mean to me as a web developer?

A: The upshot is that, unfortunately, there is no single combination of container and codecs that will work on all HTML5 browsers, and therefore content that must be viewable on them all currently requires encoding into at least two different formats.

(continued)

But worse than that, if you want to play media on an Android device, then you're heading for problems, because while the `<audio>` tag is recognized, no audio formats are supported in all versions of Android up to and including 2.2. Version 3 of Android, however, reportedly fixes the bug. Also, the `<video>` tag is somewhat buggy on Android, but it can be worked around.

Hopefully, during the life of this edition of the book, the dust will settle a little and a single standard will evolve (possibly WebM due to Google's backing) that can play on all HTML5 browsers and operating systems.

Playing Media

To play HTML5 media, you use either the `<audio>` or the `<video>` tag, like this:

```
<audio src='music.aac'>
   Only non-HTML5 Browsers display what appears here
</audio>
```

Or like this:

```
<video src='video.mp4' width='320' height='240'>
   Only non-HTML5 Browsers display what appears here
</video>
```

Any HTML you place within either of these tags will be ignored on HTML5 browsers, but all others will process it, so you can use this to include Flash or other ways of displaying media as a fallback for such browsers.

Due to a bug on Android devices, you must add the following JavaScript call to the tag in order for it to play (otherwise the `<video>` tag does nothing):

```
<video src='video.mp4' width='320' height='240'
   onclick='this.play()'>
</video>
```

Unfortunately, this causes the play button to work improperly in other browsers, because when the button is clicked, it sends a second play command, which then acts as a pause—stopping playback again almost instantly. Therefore, you will probably wish to perform some browser detection before using the `<video>` tag, and only attach to the `onclick` event if the browser is found to be Android. Chapter 7 shows you how to do this.

The <source> Tag

When you call up a media file, by default the browser automatically starts downloading the file to determine its type, and then allows playback only if it is a supported format. Because this can waste bandwidth, you can tell the browser more about a file by using the `<source>` tag, as follows, so that the browser won't even try to download the file if it cannot play it:

```
<audio>
    <source='music.aac' type='audio/aac' />
</audio>
```

You can also provide file information for videos, like this:

```
<video width='320' height='240'>
    <source src='movie.mp4' type='video/mp4' />
</video>
```

CAUTION

Due to a bug, Android versions 2.1 and 2.2 refuse to display a video if you use the `type` attribute. Therefore, you need to omit it on that platform. Chapter 7 has details on browser detection and serving up custom HTML in cases such as this.

If you know the codecs used, you can even supply that information within the `type` attribute to further save on bandwidth use in cases where the codec is unrecognized, like this:

```
<video>
    <source src='video.ogv'
            type="video/ogg; codecs='theora, vorbis'" />
</video>
```

To support a range of different browsers, you can use the `<source>` tag multiple times for different encodings of a file, like this:

```
<audio>
    <source src='music.aac' type='audio/aac' />
    <source src='music.mp3' type='audio/mp3' />
    <source src='music.ogg' type='audio/ogg' />
</audio>
```

In this case the browser plays the first file it knows it can play, if any.

Audio and Video Attributes

To control how a media file will play, you can supply a number of different attributes to the `<audio>` or `<video>` tag, to cause playback controls to be displayed, make the media play automatically, and so on.

autoplay   Using this attribute, you can make a file play as soon as enough of it has loaded. You use it like this:

```
<audio src='music.aac' autoplay></audio>
```

controls   When you want to give users access to playback controls, simply include the `controls` attribute, like this:

```
<audio src='music.aac' controls></audio>
```

Of course, you can mix and match these attributes, so the following is quite acceptable:

```
<audio src='music.aac' controls autoplay></audio>
```

height and width   These two attributes are used only with the `<video>` tag for specifying the dimensions to use when displaying it. If omitted, the video displays using the dimensions with which it was encoded. You use the attributes like this:

```
<video src='movie.mp4' height='240' width='320'></video>
```

loop   To make a file loop, you can use the following HTML:

```
<audio src='music.aac' loop autoplay></audio>
```

Usually when you loop music, it's for a background effect, so this example also includes an `autoplay` attribute, but you can use the `loop` attribute on its own too.

poster   This attribute lets you choose an image to display in the same place that a video will play. To display correctly proportioned, it must have the same relative dimensions as the video. You use it like this:

```
<video src='movie.mp4' poster='movie.png'></video>
```

preload   If you wish to speed up access to a media file for your users, you can tell the browser to start loading it as soon as it can, as follows, so that the file will be ready to play immediately when the user clicks the play button:

```
<video src='movie.mp4' preload></video>
```

Or, to explicitly prevent browsers from preloading a file, you can also use the attribute like this:

```
<video src='movie.mp4' preload='none'></video>
```

src   This attribute of the `<audio>`, `<video>`, and `<source>` tags provides the source path and/or filename to the media to be played. It is used like this (as you have seen many times already):

```
<video src='movie.mp4'></video>
```

The <embed> Tag

Although the `<embed>` tag had been supported for a number of years, it was officially deprecated in HTML 4.01—in other words, it was planned to be removed, but left in for the time being. The idea was to replace it with the `<object>` tag, but because hardly anyone took any notice of this and continued using the `<embed>` tag anyway, it has been reinstated in HTML5.

So, now that it's official (again), here's how you can use it to embed a nonstandard object such as a Flash file, for example:

```
<embed src='flashanimation.swf' />
```

The tag is self-closing (using `/>`) and supports the attributes `height`, `width`, `src`, and `type`. Here's how it's used when you select the Embed option for a YouTube video—in this case, Part 1 of the award-winning Dr. Horrible's Sing-Along Blog (as shown in Figure 2-11):

```
<object width="480" height="385">
   <param name="movie" value="http://www.youtube.com/v/apEZpYnN_1g">
   </param>
   <param name="allowFullScreen" value="true"></param>
   <param name="allowscriptaccess" value="always"></param>
   <embed src="http://www.youtube.com/v/apEZpYnN_1g"
      type="application/x-shockwave-flash"
      allowscriptaccess="always"
      allowfullscreen="true" width="480" height="385">
   </embed>
</object>
```

If you use the `<embed>` tag this way with a YouTube video, you will find that it plays well on iOS devices, which communicate with YouTube to play the file using compatible codecs.

On iPads, embedded YouTube videos play from within a web page, while other iOS devices launch a separate video player application, as do some Android devices. When you have finished viewing a video, you can then return from the player using the Done button on iOS or the Back button on Android.

Microdata, Web Workers, and Offline Web Applications

These are three advanced features of HTML5 that are only just beginning to be used. For example, no current browsers incorporate Microdata, and it may be some time before they all do. On the other hand, Web Workers are now supported by Chrome, Firefox, Safari, Opera, and iOS, but cannot run on either Internet Explorer or Android devices. Web applications are the furthest along the way to being used by all browsers, but still, half of all web surfers are locked out of using them because Internet Explorer doesn't yet support this feature.

Therefore, while you don't need to know how to use these features yet, this section explains what they do so that you can be prepared for when they become fully available.

Figure 2-11 Playing a YouTube video on an iPhone

Microdata

Microdata is a subset of HTML designed to make a document have meaning to machines, by providing metadata, just as it has meaning to a reader of the document. What it does is make available the following new tag attributes: itemscope, itemtype, itemid, itemref, and itemprop. Using them, you will be able to clearly define the properties of an item such as a book, providing a range of information that a computer can use to understand, for example, its authors, publishers, contents, and so on.

Web Workers

Normally, to achieve background processing in JavaScript, you need to set up a timer that is constantly called, supplying slices of processor time to one or more functions. These functions must then quickly do a small piece of work and return, in order to not slow down the browser and make it seem sluggish.

Web Workers, however, provide a standard way for browsers to run multiple JavaScript threads in the background that can pass messages to each other, in much the same manner as the threads running in an operating system. You simply call up a new worker script that will sit in the background waiting for messages to be sent to it, which it will then act upon.

On the whole, the aim of this technology is to achieve a speed increase of two to three times that of regular background JavaScript code, although getting to grips with programming them is likely to require a longer rather than shorter learning curve.

Offline Web Applications

The idea of offline web applications is that once you visit a website, the website tells your browser about all the files it uses so that the browser can download them all and you can then run the web application locally, even without an Internet connection. In essence, this is the sort of thing that we will do in Chapter 11, although you will create a bundle by dropping all the files directly into a wrapper, rather than by having a website download them to a device.

There's also a complication with web applications in that they require a web server to be configured with the correct MIME types (originally known as Multipurpose Internet Mail Extensions, but the word "Mail" has since been replaced with "Media") in order for a browser that understands web applications to make use of the feature and fetch the files it needs. For this reason, and because Internet Explorer doesn't yet support web applications, this book ignores this feature and provides a simpler, alternate method of creating web applications that also run as local apps.

Other HTML5 Tags

There are a number of other new HTML5 tags that have not yet been implemented in any browser, and which I therefore won't detail (particularly because their specs could change). But, for the sake of completeness, these tags are `<article>`, `<aside>`, `<command>`, `<details>`, `<figcaption>`, `<figure>`, `<footer>`, `<header>`, `<hgroup>`, `<keygen>`, `<mark>`, `<meter>`, `<nav>`, `<output>`, `<progress>`, `<rp>`, `<rt>`, `<ruby>`, `<section>`, `<summary>`, `<time>`, and `<wbr>`. You can get more information about these and all other HTML5 tags at *dev.w3.org/html5/markup*.

Summary

This chapter has introduced everything you need to know about HTML5 to be able to use it (or at least some of it) right now. However, the specification of HTML5 is probably going to keep on evolving until 2012 or 2013, so some of these details may change, and certainly some of the tags and attributes that are not (or only partially) implemented across all browsers will be gradually included.

Now that you know some of the things HTML5 can do for you, in the next chapter I'll introduce Cascading Style Sheets (CSS). If you already use the technology, I recommend that you at least browse through Chapter 3, as it will serve as a refresher on the subject, prior to Chapter 4 introducing all the new CSS3 tags. Otherwise, if you *are* new to CSS, you should find the chapter has all you need to get started using it.

Chapter 3

Introduction to CSS

Key Skills & Concepts

- The Document Object Model (DOM)
- Using Cascading Style Sheets
- Constructing CSS rules
- The cascade
- Units of measurement
- Fonts and text styles and colors
- Element positioning
- The box model

When HTML was invented, it was based around the Document Object Model (DOM), a means of separating out all the different elements within a web page into discrete objects, each with its own properties and values. This led logically to the introduction of style sheets, enabling a web page's content to be completely separated from its styling. Using style sheets also makes HTML documents easily modifiable by languages such as JavaScript to provide dynamic user interaction.

Because web pages use a DOM, it is easy for you to style every aspect of them with CSS. For example, each heading will be within pairs of tags, such as `<h1>` ... `</h1>`, and thus a single CSS instruction can set the styling of all such occurrences within a document, changing the font used, its size, any font decoration, and so on.

This lets you completely change the design of a page without altering the HTML. Some style settings can even apply dynamic effects to page elements, such as changing their color and other properties when the mouse passes over them, or even create transition effects by using proprietary browser extensions.

How the Document Object Model Works

The DOM separates the different parts of an HTML document into a hierarchy of objects, each of which has its own properties. The term *property* is used to refer to an attribute of an object, such as the HTML it contains, its width and height, and so on.

The outermost object possible is the *window* object, which is the current browser window, tab, iframe, or popped up window. Underneath this is the *document* object, of which there can be more than one (such as several documents loaded into different iframes within a page). And inside a document there are other objects, such as the head and body of a page.

Within the head there can be other objects, such as the title and meta objects, while the body object can contain numerous other objects, including headings, anchors, forms, and so forth. For example, Figure 3-1 shows a representation of the DOM of an example document, with the document title `Hello` a meta tag in the head section, and three HTML elements (a link, a form, and an image) in the body section.

Of course, even the simplest of web pages has more structure than is shown here, but it serves to illustrate how the DOM works; starting from the very outside is the window, inside of which there's a single document, and within the document are the various elements or objects, which connect to each other.

In Figure 3-1, property values are shown with a darker background and in italics. For example, the value `robots` is the value of the property `name`, which is a property of `meta`, and so on. Although it isn't shown in the figure, the meta tag should have another matching property called `content`, which would contain a string specifying which robots may access the web page.

Other properties are `href`, which has a value of `http://google.com` (and is itself a property of `a`, and so on), and `title` which has the value `Hello`. All the other items are objects or object argument names. If the figure were to extend further down and sideways, other objects and properties attached to the ones shown would come into view. A couple of the places where these would appear are shown by unconnected dotted lines, under `type` and `name`.

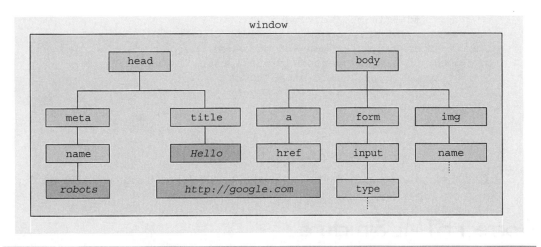

Figure 3-1   Example of a DOM showing head and body sections

Representing this as HTML code, the structure of the head section looks like this:

```
<head>
    <meta name="robots" content="index, follow" />
    <title>Hello</title>
</head>
```

And the body section of HTML might look like this:

```
<body>
    <img src="/images/welcome.jpg" />
    <a href="http://google.com">Visit Google</a>
    or enter your username and password to continue...
    <form id="login" method="post" action="login.php">
        <input type="text" name="name" />
        <input type="password" name="password" />
        <input type="submit" />
    </form>
</body>
```

Remembering that these two sections of HTML are part of the same document, we would bring them together inside an <html> tag, like this:

```
<html>
    <head>
        <meta name="robots" content="index, follow" />
        <title>Hello</title>
    </head>
    <body>
        <img src="/images/welcome.jpg" />
        <a href="http://google.com">Visit Google</a>,
        or enter your username and password to continue...
        <form id="login" method="post" action="login.php">
            <input type="text" name="name" />
            <input type="password" name="password" />
            <input type="submit" />
        </form>
    </body>
</html>
```

Of course, all web pages are different, but they usually follow the same form as this.

Correct HTML Structure

To follow recommended HTML structure and ensure that your documents are readable by the maximum number of browsers and other clients, arguments within tags should be contained in either single or double quotation marks, like this: `<a href='http://yahoo.com'>`; however, nearly all browsers allow you to omit them, like this: `<a href=http://yahoo.com>`.

You should also close every tag, and do so in the right order. For example, you shouldn't close a document by issuing `</html>` followed by `</body>` because the proper nesting of tags would be broken by this reversal. The correct way to close a document is with `</body>`, followed by `</html>`.

Also, for the same reason, you should self-close any tags that do not have a closing version, such as `<img src="..." />` (which doesn't have a matching `</img>` tag), and therefore requires a / character right before the final > to properly close it. In the same way, `<br>` becomes `<br />`, and so on.

By following these rules, your documents are easier for programs to understand, and they also are easier to convert to XML (eXtensible Markup Language), a stricter markup language used for handling data such as RSS (Really Simple Syndication) feeds.

About Cascading Style Sheets

Using CSS, you can apply styles to your web pages to make them look exactly how you want. This works because CSS is connected to the DOM, so that you can quickly and easily restyle any element. For example, if you don't like the default look of the `<h1>`, `<h2>`, and other heading tags, you can assign new styles to override the default settings for the font family and size used, specify whether bold or italics should be set, and change many more properties too.

One way you can add styling to a web page is by inserting the required statements into the head of a web page between the `<head>` and `</head>` tags. So, for example, to change the style of the `<h1>` tag, you might use the following code:

```
<style>
   h1 { color:red; font-size:3em; font-family:Arial; }
</style>
```

Within an HTML page, this might look like the following (see Figure 3-2):

```
<html>
   <head>
     <style>
        h1 { color:red; font-size:3em; font-family:Arial; }
     </style>
   </head>
   <title>Hello World</title>
   <body>
      <h1>Hello there</h1>
   </body>
</html>
```

Figure 3-2 Styling the `<h1>` tag, with the original style shown in the smaller window

Importing a Style Sheet

When you wish to style a whole site, rather than a single page, a better way to manage style sheets is to completely remove them from your web pages to separate files, and then import the ones you need. This lets you have different style sheets for different layouts (such as web and print) without changing the HTML.

There are a couple of different ways this can be achieved, the first of which is by using the CSS `@import` directive, like this:

```
<style>
   @import url("/css/styles.css");
</style>
```

This statement tells the browser to fetch a style sheet with the name *styles.css* from the */css* folder. The `@import` command is quite flexible in that you can create style sheets that themselves pull in other style sheets, and so on. Just make sure that there are no `<style>` or `</style>` tags in any of your external style sheets or they will not work.

Importing CSS from Within HTML

You can also include a style sheet with the HTML `<link>` tag, like this:

```
<link rel="stylesheet" type="text/css" href="/css/styles.css" />
```

This has the exact same effect as the @import directive, except that <link> is an HTML-only tag and is not a valid style directive, so it cannot be used from within one style sheet to pull in another, and also cannot be placed within a pair of <style> . . . </style> tags.

Just as you can use multiple @import directives within your CSS to include multiple external style sheets, you can also use as many <link> statements as you like in your HTML.

Local Style Settings

There's also nothing stopping you from individually setting or overriding certain styles for the current page on a case-by-case basis by inserting style statements directly within HTML, like this (which results in italic blue text within the tags):

```
<div style="font-style:italic; color:blue;">Hello</div>
```

But this should be reserved only for the most exceptional circumstances, as it breaks the separation of content and layout.

Using IDs

A better solution for setting the style of an element is to assign an *ID* to it in the HTML, like this (remembering that you can generally use single and double quotes interchangeably in matching pairs):

```
<div id='iblue'>Hello</div>
```

What this does is state that the contents of the div with the ID "iblue" should have the style applied to it that is defined in the "iblue" style setting. The matching CSS statement for this might look like the following:

```
#iblue { font-style:italic; color:blue; }
```

Note the use of the # symbol, which specifies that only the ID with the name "iblue" should be styled with this statement.

Using Classes

If you would like to apply the same style to many elements, you do not have to give each one a different ID because you can specify a *class* to manage them all, like this:

```
<div class="iblue">Hello</div>
```

What this does is state that the contents of this element (and any others that use the class) should have the style defined in the "iblue" class applied to it. Once a class is applied, you can use the following style setting, either in the page header or within an external style sheet, to set the styles for the class:

```
.iblue { font-style:italic; color:blue; }
```

Instead of using a # symbol, which is reserved for IDs, class statements are prefaced with a . (period) symbol.

Ask the Expert

Q: Are the semicolons used in CSS necessary, or are they optional as with JavaScript?

A: The answer is yes and no. In order to separate multiple CSS statements on the same line, you must place semicolons between them. But if there is only one statement on a line (or in an inline style setting within an HTML tag), then you can omit the semicolon, as you can for the final statement in a group.

To avoid hard-to-find CSS errors, you may prefer to always use a semicolon after every CSS rule so that you can copy and paste the rules, and otherwise modify properties, without worrying about removing semicolons where they aren't strictly necessary, or having to add them where they are required.

CSS Rules

Each statement in a CSS rule starts with a selector, which is the thing upon which the rule is effected. For example, in the following assignment, h1 is the selector that is being given a font size 240 percent larger than the default:

```
h1 { font-size:240%; }
```

Providing a new value to the font-size property of the selector ensures that the contents of all <h1> . . . </h1> pairs of tags will be displayed at a font size of 240 percent relative to the default size. This is achieved by placing one or more assignments within the { and } symbols that follow the selector (in this case, font-size:240%;). The part before the : (colon) symbol is the property, while the part following the colon is the value applied to it.

Lastly, there is a ; (semicolon) to end the statement, which, in this instance, is not required (but would be if another assignment were to follow on the same line). For the sake of avoiding tricky-to-track-down errors, in this book I always include the semicolons even when they are not necessary.

Multiple Assignments

You can create multiple property assignments in a couple of different ways. First, you can concatenate them on the same line, like this:

```
h1 { font-size:240%; color:blue; }
```

This adds a second assignment that changes the color of all <h1> headers to blue. You can also place the assignments one per line, like the following:

```
h1 { font-size:240%;
color:blue; }
```

Or you can space the assignments out a little more, so that they line up below each other in a column at the colons, like this:

```
h1 {
   font-size:240%;
       color:blue;
}
```

This way you can easily see where each new set of rules begins, because of the selector in the first column, and the assignments that follow are neatly lined up with all property values starting at the same horizontal offset. In the preceding example, both semicolons are unnecessary, but if you ever want to concatenate any such groups of statements into a single line, it is very quick to do with the semicolons already in place.

There is no right or wrong way to lay out your CSS, but I recommend that you at least try to keep each block of CSS internally consistent, so that it can be easily understood at a glance.

Comments

It is a good idea to comment your CSS rules, even if you describe only the main groups of statements rather than all or most of them. You can do this in two different ways. First, you can place a comment within a pair of /* . . . */ tags, like this:

```
/* This is a CSS comment */
```

Or you can extend a comment over many lines, like this:

```
/* A Multi
   line
   comment */
```

CAUTION
If you use multiline comments, be aware that you cannot nest more single-line (or any other) comments within them; otherwise, you will get unpredictable errors.

Style Types

CSS offers numerous different style types ranging from the default styles set up by your browser (and any user styles you may have applied), through inline or embedded styles to external style sheets. The styles defined in each type have a hierarchy of precedence, from low to high.

Default Styles

The lowest level of style precedence is the default styling applied by a web browser. These styles are provided as a fallback for when a web page doesn't have any styles. They are intended to be a generic set of styles that will display reasonably well in most instances.

Pre-CSS, the default styles were the only styles applied to a document, and only a handful of them could be changed by a web page (such as font face, color and size, and a few element-sizing arguments).

User Styles

User styles are the next-highest precedence of styles after default styles. They are supported by most modern browsers but are implemented differently by each. If you would like to learn how to create your own default styles for browsing, open a search engine and enter your browser name followed by "user styles" (for example, enter "firefox," "mozilla," "opera," or "ie" followed by "user styles") to find out how. Figure 3-3 shows a user style sheet being applied to Microsoft Internet Explorer. You can open the Accessibility dialog box that is shown by choosing Tools | Internet Options and clicking the Accessibility button on the General tab.

If a user style that is assigned has already been defined as a browser default, it overrides the browser's default setting. Any styles not defined in a user style sheet retain their default values as set up in the browser.

External Style Sheets

The next type of styles are those that are assigned in an external style sheet. These settings override any assigned by either the user or the browser. External style sheets are the recommended way to create your styles because you can produce different style sheets for different purposes—such as for general web use, for viewing on a mobile browser with a smaller screen, for printing purposes, and so on—and then apply just the one needed for each type of media.

Internal Styles

Internal styles, which you create within `<style>` . . . `</style>` tags, take precedence over all the preceding style types. At this point, though, you are beginning to break the separation between styling and content because any external style sheets loaded in at the same time as the internal style sheets will have a lower precedence.

Inline Styles

Lastly, inline styles are where you assign a property directly to an element. They have the highest precedence of any style type, and are used like this:

```
<a href="http://google.com" style="color:green;">Visit Google</a>
```

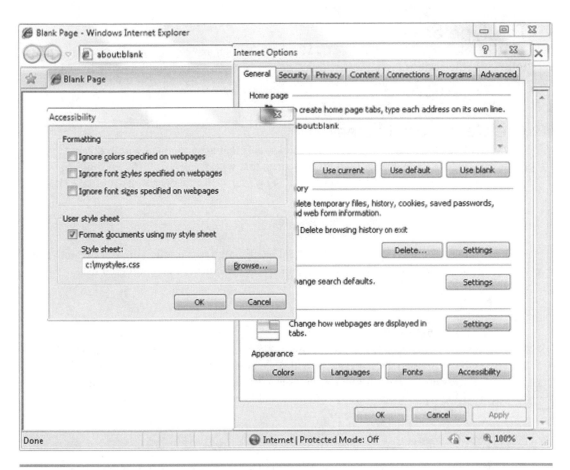

Figure 3-3   Applying a user style sheet to Internet Explorer 8

In this example, the link specified will be displayed in green, regardless of any default or other color settings applied by any other type of style sheet, whether directly to this link or generically for all links.

When you use this type of styling, you are breaking the separation between layout and content, so you are recommended to use it only when you have a very good reason to do so.

Selectors

The means by which you access one or more elements is called *selection*, and the part of a CSS rule that does this is known as a *selector*. As you might expect, there are many different varieties of selector.

The Type Selector

The type selector works on types of HTML elements such as `<p>` or `<i>`. For example, the following rule ensures that all text within `<p>` . . . `</p>` tags is fully justified:

```
p { text-align:justify; }
```

The Descendant Selector

Descendant selectors let you apply styles to elements that are contained within other elements. For example, the following rule sets all text within `<b>` . . . `</b>` tags to red, but *only* if they occur within `<p>` . . . `</p>` tags (like this: `<p><b>Hello</b> there</p>`):

```
p b { color:red; }
```

Descendant selectors can continue nesting indefinitely, so the following is a perfectly valid rule to make the text blue within bold text, inside a list element of an unordered list:

```
ul li b { color:blue; }
```

The Child Selector

The child selector is similar to the descendant selector but is more constraining about when the style will be applied, by selecting only those elements that are direct children of another element. For example, the following code uses a descendant selector that will change any bold text within a paragraph to red, even if the bold text is itself within italics (like this: `<p><i><b>Hello</b> there</i></p>`):

```
p b { color:red; }
```

In this instance, the word "Hello" displays in red. However, when this more general type of behavior is not required, a child selector can be used to narrow the scope of the selector. For example, the following child selector will set bold text to red only if the element is a direct child of a paragraph, and is not itself contained within another element:

```
p > b { color:red; }
```

Now the word "Hello" will not change color, because it is not a direct child of the paragraph.

The ID Selector

If you give an element an ID name (like this: `<div id='mydiv'>`), then you can directly access it from CSS in the following way, which changes all the text in the div to italic:

```
#mydiv { font-style:italic; }
```

Reusing IDs

IDs can be used only once within a document, so only the first occurrence found will receive the new property value assigned by a CSS rule. But in CSS you can directly reference any IDs that have the same name, as long as they occur within different element types, like this:

```
<div id='myid'>Hello</div>
<span id='myid'>Hello</span>
```

Because IDs normally apply only to unique elements, the following rule will apply an underline to only the first occurrence of myid:

```
#myid { text-decoration:underline; }
```

However, you can ensure that CSS applies the rule to both occurrences, like this:

```
span#myid { text-decoration:underline; }
div#myid  { text-decoration:underline; }
```

Or, more succinctly, like this (see the section "Selecting by Group" a bit later in the chapter):

```
span#myid, div#myid { text-decoration:underline; }
```

CAUTION

If you use this form of selection, remember that any JavaScript that also must access these elements cannot easily do so because the commonly used getElementByID() function will return only the first occurrence. To reference any other instances, the programmer would have to search through the whole list of elements in the document, a more tricky task to undertake.

The Class Selector

When you want a number of elements in a page to share the same styling, you can assign to them all the same class name (like this: <span class='myclass'>) and then create a single rule to modify all those elements at once, as in the following rule, which creates a 10-pixel left margin offset for all elements using the class:

```
.myclass { margin-left:10px; }
```

In modern browsers, HTML elements may also use more than one class by separating them with spaces, like this: <span class='thisclass thatclass otherclass'>. Older browsers only allow a single class.

Narrowing Class Scope

You can narrow the scope of action of a class by specifying the types of elements to which it should apply. For example, the following rule applies the setting only to paragraphs that use the class `main`:

```
p.main { text-indent:30px; }
```

In this example, only paragraphs using the class `main` (like this: `<p class="main">`) will receive the new property value. Any other element types that may try to use the class (such as `<div class="main">`) will be ignored.

The Attribute Selector

Many HTML tags support attributes, and using this type of selector can save you from having to use IDs and classes to references those attributes. For example, you can directly reference attributes in the following manner, which sets all elements with the attribute `type="submit"` to a width of 100 pixels:

```
[type="submit"] { width:100px; }
```

If you wish to narrow down the scope of the selector to, for example, only form input elements with that attribute type, you could use the following rule instead:

```
form input[type="submit"] { width:100px; }
```

NOTE
Attribute selectors also work on IDs and classes, so that, for example, `[class="classname"]` performs in exactly the same way as the ID selector `.classname` (except that the latter has a higher precedence). Likewise, `[id="idname"]` is equivalent to using the class selector `.idname`. Classes and ID selectors prepended with # or . can therefore be viewed as shorthand for attribute selectors, but with a higher precedence.

The Universal Selector

The universal (or wildcard) selector matches any element, so the following rule will make a complete mess of a document by giving a green border to all of its elements:

```
* { border:1px solid green; }
```

It's therefore unlikely that you will use the * on its own, but as part of a compound rule, it can be very powerful. For example, the following rule will apply the same styling as the preceding example, but only to all paragraphs that are subelements of the element with the ID `boxout`, and only as long as they are not direct children:

```
#boxout * p { border:1px solid green; }
```

Let's look at what's going on here. The first selector following #boxout is a * symbol, so it refers to any element within the boxout object. The following p selector then narrows down the selection focus by changing the selector to apply only to paragraphs (as defined by the p) that are subelements of elements returned by the * selector. Therefore, this CSS rule performs the following actions (in which I use the terms *object* and *element* interchangeably to refer to the same thing):

1. Find the object with the ID of boxout.

2. Find all subelements of the object returned in step 1.

3. Find all p subelements of the objects returned in step 2 and, since this is the final selector in the group, also find all p subelements and sub-subelements (and so on) of the objects returned in step 2.

4. Apply the styles within the { and } characters to the objects returned in step 3.

The net result of this is that the green border is applied only to paragraphs that are grandchildren (or grand-grandchildren, and so on) of the main element.

Selecting by Group

Using CSS, it is possible to apply a rule to more than one element, class, or any other type of selector at the same time by separating the selectors with commas. So, for example, the following rule will place a dotted orange line underneath all paragraphs, the element with the ID of idname, and all elements using the class classname:

```
p, .idname, #classname { border-bottom:1px dotted orange; }
```

The Cascade

A fundamental characteristic of CSS properties is that they *cascade*, which is why the technology is called Cascading Style Sheets. But what does this mean?

Cascading is a method used to resolve potential conflicts between the various different types of style sheet a browser supports, and apply these sheets in order of precedence by who created them, the method used to create the style, and types of properties selected.

Style Sheet Creators

There are three main types of style sheet supported by all modern browsers. In order of precedence from high to low, they are

1. Those created by a document's author

2. Those created by the user

3. Those created by the browser

These three sets of style sheets are processed in reverse order. First, the defaults in the web browser are applied to the document. Without these defaults, web pages that don't use style sheets would look terrible. The default styles include the font face, size and color, element spacing, table borders and spacing, and all the other standard document features a user would expect.

Next, if the user has created any styles to use instead of the standard ones, they are applied, replacing any of the browser's default styles that may conflict.

Last, any styles created by the current document's author are then applied, replacing any that have been created either as browser defaults or by the user.

Style Sheet Methods

Style sheets can be created in three different ways, or methods. In high to low order of precedence, they are

1. As inline styles

2. In an embedded style sheet

3. As an external style sheet

Again, these methods of style sheet creation are applied in reverse order of precedence. Therefore, all external style sheets are processed first, and their styles are applied to the document.

Next, any embedded styles (within `<style>` ... `</style>` tags) are processed, and any that conflict with external rules are given precedence and override them.

Last, any styles applied directly to an element as an inline style (such as `<div style="...">` ... `</div>`) are given the highest precedence, and override all previously assigned properties.

Style Sheet Selectors

There are three different ways of selecting elements to be styled. Going from highest to lowest order of precedence, they are

1. Referencing by individual ID

2. Referencing in groups by class

3. Referencing by element tags (such as `<p>` or `<b>`)

Selectors are processed according to the number and types of elements affected by a rule, which is a little different from the previous two methods for resolving conflicts. This is because rules do not have to apply only to one type of selector at a time, but instead may reference many different selectors. Therefore, a method is needed to determine the precedence of rules that can contain any combination of selectors. This is done by calculating the specificity of each rule by ordering them from the widest to the narrowest scope of action.

Calculating Specificity

The specificity of a rule is calculated by creating three-part numbers based on the selector types in the preceding numbered list. These compound numbers start off looking like [0, 0, 0]. When processing a rule, each selector that references an ID increments the first number by 1, so that the compound number becomes [1, 0, 0]. If there are three ID references in a particular rule, for example, the compound number becomes [3, 0, 0].

Then the number of selectors that reference a class is placed in the second part of the compound number. If there are five of them, for example, the number becomes [3, 5, 0].

Finally, all selectors that reference element tags are counted, and this number is placed in the last part of the compound number. If there are two such selectors, the final compound number becomes [3, 5, 2], which is all that is needed to compare this rule's specificity with another.

In cases where there are nine or fewer of each type in a compound number, you can convert it directly to a decimal number, which in this case is 352. Rules with a lower number than this will have lower precedence, and those with a higher number will have greater precedence. Where two rules share the same value, the most recently applied one wins.

Using a Different Number Base

Where there are more than nine of a type in a number, you have to work in a higher number base. For example, the compound number [11, 7, 19] doesn't convert to decimal by simply concatenating the three parts. Instead, you can convert the number to a higher base such as base 20 (or higher if there are more than 19 of any type).

To do this, multiply the three parts out and add the results like this, starting with the rightmost number and working left:

```
       20 x 19  =     380
    20x20 x  7  =    2800
 20x20x20 x 11  =   88000
Total in decimal =  91180
```

On the left, replace the values of 20 with the base you are using; then, once all the compound numbers of a set of rules are converted from this base to decimal, it is easy to determine the specificity, and therefore the precedence, of each.

Thankfully, all of this is handled for you by the CSS processor, but knowing how it works helps you to properly construct rules and understand what precedence they will have.

NOTE

If all this precedence calculation sounds rather complicated, you'll be pleased to know that in most cases you can usually get by with this simple rule of thumb: "In general, the fewer elements that are to be modified, the greater the precedence given to a rule."

Some Rules Are More Equal Than Others

Where two or more style rules are exactly equivalent, the most recently processed rule takes precedence. However, you can force a rule to a higher precedence than other equivalent rules by using the !important tag, like this:

```
p { color:#ff0000 !important; }
```

When you do this, all previous equivalent settings are overridden (even ones using !important) and any equivalent rules that are processed later will be ignored. So, for example, the second of the two following rules would normally take precedence, but because of the use of !important in the prior assignment, the second one is ignored:

```
p { color:#ff0000 !important; }
p { color:#ffff00 }
```

Ask the Expert

Q: Can user style sheets for specifying default browser styles use the !important keyword?

A: Yes. If a user has also applied !important to a setting, the user's style setting takes precedence over the same properties specified in the current web page. However, on very old browsers using CSS 1, this feature isn't supported.

The Difference Between Divs and Spans

Both divs and spans are types of containers, but they have different qualities. By default, a div has infinite width (at least to the browser edge), which can be seen by applying a border to one, like this:

```
<div style="border:1px solid green;">Hello</div>
```

A span, however, is only as wide as the text it contains. Therefore, the following line of HTML shows the border only around the word "Hello" and does not extend to the right edge of the browser:

```
<span style="border:1px solid green;">Hello</span>
```

Also, spans follow text or other objects as they wrap around and can therefore have a complicated border. For example, in the following web page, CSS has been used to make the background of all divs yellow and the background of all spans cyan, and to add a border to both, before then creating a few example spans and divs:

```
<html
   <head>
      <title>Div and span example</title>
         <style>
            div, span { border:1px solid black;  }
            div        { background-color:yellow; }
            span       { background-color:cyan;   }
         </style>
   </head>
   <body>
      <div>This text is within a div tag</div> This isn't.
      <div>And this is again.</div><br />
      <span>This text is inside a span tag.</span> This isn't.
      <span>And this is again.</span><br /><br />
      <div>This is a larger amount of text in a div element that
      wraps around to the next line of the browser</div><br />
      <span>This is a larger amount of text in a span element that
      wraps around to the next line of the browser</span>
   </body>
</html>
```

Figure 3-4 shows what this page looks like in a web browser. Although it is printed only in shades of gray (and not colors), the figure clearly shows how divs extend to the right edge of a browser and force following content to appear at the start of the first available position below them.

The figure also shows how spans only take up the space required to hold their contents—without forcing following content to appear below them. For example, in the bottom two examples of the figure, you can also see that when divs wrap around the screen edge, they retain a rectangular shape, whereas spans simply follow the flow of the text (or other contents) within them.

Ask the Expert

Q: What types of content are best suited for placing in a `<div>` tag as opposed to a `<span>` tag?

A: Since `<div>` tags can only be rectangular, they are better suited for containing objects such as images, boxouts, quotations and so on, while `<span>` tags are best used for holding text or other attributes that are placed one after another inline, and that should flow from left to right.

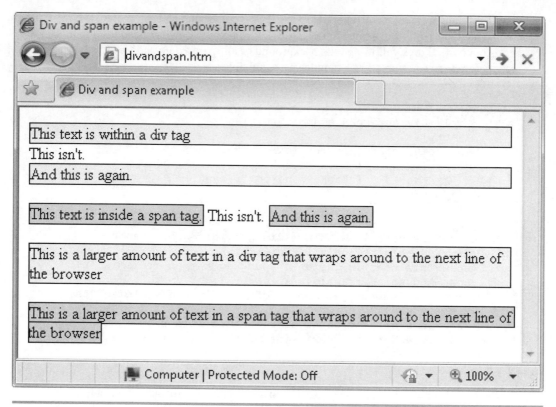

Figure 3-4 A variety of divs and spans of differing widths

Measurements

CSS supports an impressive range of different units of measurement, enabling you to tailor your web pages precisely to specific values, or by relative dimensions. The ones I generally use (and believe you will also find the most useful) are pixels, points, ems, and percent, which are described here along with other units of measurement:

- **Pixels** The size of a pixel (px) varies according to the dimensions and pixel depth of the user's monitor. Because 1 pixel equals the width/height of a single dot on the screen, this measurement is best suited to monitors.

  Example: `#classname { margin:5px; }`

- **Points** A point (pt) is equivalent in size to 1/72 of an inch. The measurement comes from a print-design background and is best suited for that medium, but it is also commonly used on monitors.

  Example: `#classname { font-size:14pt; }`

- **Inches**   An inch (`in`) is the equivalent of 72 points and is also a measurement type best suited for print.

  Example: `#classname { width:3in; }`

- **Centimeters**   Centimeters (`cm`) are another unit of measurement best suited for print. One centimeter is a little over 28 points.

  Example: `#classname { height:2cm; }`

- **Millimeters**   A millimeter (`mm`) is 1/10th of a centimeter (or almost 3 points). Millimeters are another measure best suited to print.

  Example: `#classname { font-size:5mm; }`

- **Picas**   A pica (`pc`) is another print typographic measurement, which is equivalent to 12 points.

  Example: `#classname { font-size:1pc; }`

- **Ems**   An em (`em`) is equal to the current font size and is therefore one of the more useful measurements for CSS since it is used to describe relative dimensions.

  Example: `#classname { font-size:2em; }`

- **Exs**   An ex (`ex`) is also related to the current font size; it is equivalent to the height of a lowercase letter *x*. This unit of measurement is not widely used and is most often used as a good approximation for helping to set the width of a box that will contain some text.

  Example: `#classname { width:20ex; }`

- **Percent**   This unit (`%`) is related to the em in that it is exactly 100 times greater (when used on a font). Whereas 1 em equals the current font size, the same size is 100 in percent. When not relating to a font, this unit is relative to the size of the container of the property being accessed.

  Example: `#classname { height:120%; }`

Fonts

There are four main font properties that you can style using CSS: family, style, size, and weight. Between them you can fine-tune the way text displays in your web pages, when printed, and so on.

Font Family

This property assigns the font to use. It also supports listing a variety of fonts in order of preference from left to right, so that styling can fall back gracefully when the user doesn't have the preferred font installed. For example, to set the default font for paragraphs, you might use a CSS rule such as this:

```
p { font-family: Verdana, Arial, Helvetica, sans-serif; }
```

Where a font name is made up of two or more words, you must enclose the name in quotation marks, like this:

```
p { font-family: "Times New Roman", Georgia, serif; }
```

TIP
Because they should be available on virtually all web browsers and operating systems, the safest font families to use on a web page are Arial, Helvetica, Times New Roman, Times, Courier New, and Courier. The Verdana, Georgia, Comic Sans MS, Trebuchet MS, Arial Black, and Impact fonts are safe for Mac and PC use, but might not be installed on other operating systems such as Linux. Other common but less safe fonts are Palatino, Garamond, Bookman, and Avant Garde. If you use one of the less safe fonts, make sure you offer fallbacks of one or more safer fonts in your CSS so that your web pages will degrade gracefully on browsers without your preferred fonts.

Font Style

With this property, you can choose to display a font normally, in italics, or obliquely. The following rules create three classes (`normal`, `italic`, and `oblique`) that can be applied to elements to create these effects:

```
.normal  { font-style:normal;  }
.italic  { font-style:italic;  }
.oblique { font-style:oblique; }
```

Font Size

As described in the earlier section on measurements, there are a large number of ways you can change a font's size. But these all boil down to two main types: fixed and relative. A fixed setting looks like the following rule, which sets the default paragraph font size to 14 point:

```
p { font-size:14pt; }
```

Alternatively, you may wish to work with the current default font size, using it to style various types of text such as headings. In the following rules, relative sizes of some headers are defined, with the `<h4>` tag starting off 20 percent larger than the default, and with each greater size another 40 percent larger than the previous one:

```
h1 { font-size:240%; }
h2 { font-size:200%; }
h3 { font-size:160%; }
h4 { font-size:120%; }
```

Font Weight

Using this property, you can choose how boldly to display a font. It supports a number of values, but the main ones you will use are likely to be normal and bold, like this:

```
.bold { font-weight:bold; }
```

Managing Text Styles

Regardless of the font in use, you can further modify the way text displays by altering its decoration, spacing, and alignment. There is a crossover between the text and font properties, though, in that effects such as italics or bold text are achieved via the font-style and font-weight properties, while others such as underlining require the text-decoration property.

Decoration

With the text-decoration property, you can apply effects to text such as underline, line-through, overline, and blink. The following rule creates a new class called over that applies overlines to text (the weight of over-, under-, and through lines will match that of the font):

```
.over { text-decoration:overline; }
```

Spacing

A number of different properties allow you to modify line, word, and letter spacing. For example, the following rules change the line spacing for paragraphs by modifying the line-height property to be 25 percent greater, the word-spacing property to 30 pixels, and letter-spacing to 3 pixels:

```
p {
    line-height:125%;
    word-spacing:30px;
    letter-spacing:3px;
}
```

Alignment

There are four types of text alignment available in CSS: left, right, center, and justify. In the following rule, default paragraph text is set to full justification:

```
p { text-align:justify; }
```

Transformation

There are four properties available for transforming text: `none`, `capitalize`, `uppercase`, and `lowercase`. The following rule creates a class called `upper` that will ensure all text is displayed in uppercase when it is used:

```
.upper { text-transform:uppercase; }
```

Indenting

Using the `text-indent` property, you can indent the first line of a block of text by a specified amount. The following rule indents the first line of every paragraph by 20 pixels, although a different unit of measurement or a percent increase could also be applied:

```
p { text-indent:20px; }
```

Colors

Colors can be applied to the foreground and background of text and objects using the `color` and `background-color` properties (or by supplying a single argument to the `background` property). The colors specified can be one of the named colors (such as `red` or `blue`), colors created from hexadecimal RGB triplets (such as `#ff0000` or `#0000ff`), or colors created using the `rgb()` CSS function.

The standard 16 color names, as defined by the W3C (*w3.org*) standards organization, are as follows: `aqua`, `black`, `blue`, `fuchsia`, `gray`, `green`, `lime`, `maroon`, `navy`, `olive`, `purple`, `red`, `silver`, `teal`, `white`, and `yellow`. The following rule uses one of these names to set the background color for an object with the ID of `object`:

```
#object { background-color:silver; }
```

In the following rule, the foreground color of text in all divs is set to yellow (because on a computer display, combining hexadecimal levels of `ff` red, `ff` green, and `00` blue creates the color yellow):

```
div { color:#ffff00; }
```

Or, if you don't wish to work in hexadecimal, you can specify your color triplets using the `rgb()` function, as in the following rule, which changes the background color of the current document to aqua:

```
body { background-color:rgb(0, 255, 255); }
```

TIP

If you prefer not to work in ranges of 256 levels per color, you can use percentages in the `rgb()` function instead, with values from 0 to 100, ranging from the lowest (0) amount of a primary color, through to the highest (100), like this: `rgb(58%, 95%, 74%)`. You can also use floating-point values for even finer color control, like this: `rgb(23.4%, 67.6%, 15.5%)`.

Short Color Strings

There is also a short form of the hex digit string in which only the first byte of each 2-byte pair is used for each color. For example, instead of assigning the color #fe4692, you use #f49, omitting the second hex digit from each pair. This results in almost the same color and is useful where exact colors are not required. The difference between a six-digit and three-digit string is that the former supports 16 million different colors, while the latter supports 4000.

Wherever you intend to use a color such as #803060 (in which the second digit of each pair is zero), this is the direct equivalent of #836 (since the zeros are implied by the shorter version), and you can use either string to create the exact same color.

In this book I use either type according to the color required at the time.

Positioning Elements

Elements within a web page fall where they are placed in the document, but you can move an element by changing its position property from the default of static to one of absolute, relative, or fixed.

An element with absolute positioning is removed from the document, and any other elements that are able to will flow into its released space. You can then position the object anywhere you like within the document using the top, right, bottom, and left properties. It will then rest on top of (or behind) other elements.

So, for example, to move an object with the ID of object to the absolute location of 100 pixels down from the document start and 200 pixels in from the left, you would apply the following rules to it (you can also use any of the other units of measurement supported by CSS):

```
#object {
   position:absolute;
   top:100px;
   left:200px;
}
```

Likewise, you can move the object relative to the location it would occupy in the normal document flow. So, for example, to move object 10 pixels down and 10 pixels to the right of its normal location, you would use the following rules:

```
#object {
   position:relative;
   top:10px;
   left:10px;
}
```

The final positioning property setting lets you move an object to an absolute location, but only within the current browser viewport. Then, when the document is scrolled, the object remains exactly where it has been placed, with the main document scrolling beneath it—a great way to create dock bars and other similar devices. To fix the `object` to the top-left corner of the browser window, you would use the following rules:

```
#object {
    position:fixed;
    top:0px;
    left:0px;
}
```

Figure 3-5 shows a simple dock bar created using a value of `fixed` for the `position` property to align the icons at the screen bottom. With a little JavaScript or proprietary CSS transforms, the icons can be made to resize as the mouse passes over them, as is happening to the second one. You can refer to my books *Plug-in CSS* and *Plug-in JavaScript* (McGraw-Hill), respectively, for CSS and JavaScript plug-ins to handle this and many other handy functions.

Pseudo Classes

There are a number of selectors and classes that are used only within a style sheet and do not have any matching tags or attributes within any HTML. Their task is to classify elements using characteristics other than their name, attributes, or content that cannot be deduced from the document tree. These include pseudo classes such as `first-line`, `first-child`, and `first-letter`.

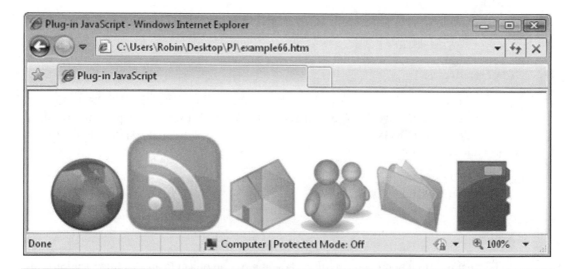

Figure 3-5 Creating a simple dock bar using the `position` property

Pseudo classes are separated from elements using a : (colon) character. For example, to create a class called bigfirst for emphasizing the first letter of an element, you would use a rule such as the following:

```
.bigfirst:first-letter {
   font-size:400%;
   float:left;
}
```

When the bigfirst class is applied to an element, the first letter will be displayed much enlarged, with the remaining text shown at normal size neatly flowing around it (due to the float property), as if the first letter were an image or other object.

Other pseudo classes include hover, link, active, and visited, all of which are useful mostly for applying to anchor elements, as in the following rules, the first of which sets the default color of all links to blue, and the second of which sets the default color of links that have already been visited to light blue:

```
a:link    { color:blue;     }
a:visited { color:lightblue; }
```

The following pair of rules is interesting in that it uses the hover pseudo class so that the rules are applied only when the mouse is placed over the element. In this example, they change the link to white text on a red background, providing a dynamic effect you would normally only expect from using JavaScript code.

```
a:hover {
   color:white;
   background:red;
}
```

Here I have used the background property with a single argument, instead of the longer background-color property.

The active pseudo class is also dynamic in that it effects a change to a link during the time between the mouse button being clicked and released, as with the following rule, which changes the link color to dark blue:

```
a:active { color:darkblue; }
```

Another interesting dynamic pseudo class is focus, which is applied only when an element is given focus by the user selecting it with the keyboard or mouse, as with the following rule, which uses the universal selector to always place a mid-gray, dotted, 2-pixel border around the currently focused object:

```
*:focus { border:2px dotted #888888; }
```

Shorthand Rules

To save space, groups of related CSS properties can be concatenated into a single shorthand assignment. For example, I have already used the shorthand for creating a border a few times, as in the `focus` rule in the previous section, which is actually a shorthand concatenation of the following rule set:

```
*:focus {
    border-width:2px;
    border-style:dotted;
    border-color:#888888;
}
```

When using a shorthand rule, you need only apply the properties up to the point where you wish to change values. So you could use the following to set only a border's width and style, but not its color:

```
*:focus { border:2px dotted; }
```

CAUTION

The order in which the properties are placed in a shorthand rule is very important, and misplacing them is a common way to get unexpected results. Since there are far too many properties to detail in this chapter, if you wish to use shorthand CSS, you need to look up the default properties and their order of application using a CSS manual or search engine. To get started, I recommend the web page at *dustindiaz.com/css-shorthand*.

The Box Model

The fundamental CSS properties affecting the layout of a page are based around the box model; a nested set of properties surround an element, as shown in Figure 3-6.

Virtually all elements have (or can have) these properties, including the document body, whose margin you can (for example) remove with the following rule:

```
body { margin:0px; }
```

Once you have the hang of the box model, you will be well on your way to creating professionally laid-out pages, since these properties alone will make up much of your page styling.

The Margin Property

The margin is the outermost level of the box model. It separates elements from each other and its use is quite smart. For example, assume you have chosen to give a number of elements a default margin of 10 pixels around each. When placed on top of each other, this would create a gap of 20 pixels due to adding the border widths together.

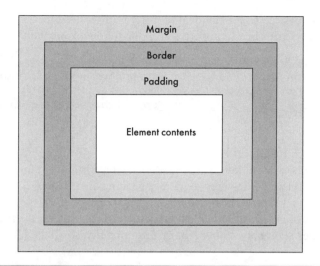

Figure 3-6   The nested levels of the CSS box model

However, to overcome this potential issue, when two elements with borders are directly one above the other, only the larger of the two margins is used to separate them. If both margins are the same width, just one of the widths is used. This way, you are much more likely to get the result you want. But you should note that the margins of absolutely positioned or inline elements do not collapse.

The margins of an element can be changed en masse with the `margin` property, or individually with `margin-left`, `margin-top`, `margin-right`, and `margin-bottom`. When setting the `margin` property, you can supply one to four arguments, which have the effects described in the comments in the following rules:

```
margin:1px;              /* Set all margins to 1 pixel wide           */
margin:1px 2px;          /* Set the top and bottom margins to 1 pixel
                            and the left and right to 2 pixels wide   */
margin:1px 2px 3px;      /* Set the top margin to 1 pixel, the left
                            and right to 2 pixels, and the bottom
                            margin to 3 pixels wide                   */
margin:1px 2px 3px 4px;  /* Set the top margin to 1 pixel, the right
                            to 2 pixels, the bottom to 3 pixels, and
                            the left margin to 4 pixels wide          */
```

The Border Property

The border level of the box model is similar to the margin except that there is no collapsing. The main properties used to modify borders are `border`, `border-left`, `border-top`, `border-right`, and `border-bottom`, and each of these can have other subproperties added as suffixes, such as `-color`, `-style`, and `-width`.

The four ways of accessing individual property settings used for the `margin` property also apply with the `border-width` property, so all the following are valid rules:

```
border-width:1px;              /* All borders                 */
border-width:1px 2px;          /* Top/bottom and left/right   */
border-width:1px 2px 3px;      /* Top, left/right, and bottom */
border-width:1px 2px 3px 4px;  /* Top, right, bottom, and left */
```

The Padding Property

The deepest of the box model levels is the padding, which is applied inside any borders and/ or margins. The main properties used to modify padding are `padding`, `padding-left`, `padding-top`, `padding-right`, and `padding-bottom`.

The four ways of accessing individual property settings used for the `margin` and `border` properties also apply with the `padding` property, so all the following are valid rules:

```
padding:1px;              /* All borders                 */
padding:1px 2px;          /* Top/bottom and left/right   */
padding:1px 2px 3px;      /* Top, left/right, and bottom */
padding:1px 2px 3px 4px;  /* Top, right, bottom, and left */
```

Element Contents

Deep within the box model levels, at its center, lies an element that can be styled in all the ways discussed in this chapter, and that can (and usually will) contain further subelements, which in turn may contain sub-subelements, and so on, each with its own styling and box model settings.

Summary

Although this chapter has covered only a subset of CSS (there are many, many more aspects to the language than could ever be properly discussed in a single chapter), it provides more than enough information to get you off to an excellent start with CSS.

In the next chapter we'll take what you've learned here and show you how to use this new knowledge with CSS3, which supports goodies such as transitions, animations, more fonts, rounded borders, shadows, and a great deal more.

Chapter 4

The CSS3 Enhancements

Key Skills & Concepts

- Background and border styles, colors, and images

- Creating box and text shadows

- Element overflow

- Manipulating colors and changing opacity

- Word wrapping and using columns

- Box sizing and resizing

- Using web fonts

The first implementation of CSS was initially drawn up in 1996 and then released in 1999. By 2001, all new browser releases supported CSS, but even so, the standard was once again revised in 2008. At the same time (beginning in 1998), CSS2 was already being drawn up, and the standard was eventually completed in 2007—but revised again in 2009.

Then there's CSS3, which commenced development in 2001, but some features of which were proposed only as recently as 2009. Therefore, the development process will likely continue for some time before a final recommendation for CSS3 is agreed upon. And even though CSS3 isn't yet complete, people are already beginning to put forward suggestions for CSS4 (and even ideas for HTML6, too).

Because the development of web standards is in a constant state of flux, a book such as this can only summarize the state of play at a given point in time. Therefore, in the following descriptions, where it is noted that certain features are not implemented in particular browsers (or have been applied in a nonstandard way), that may not be the case by the time you read this book. In view of this, I recommend that you also check in with the following websites to keep current with the latest developments:

- *css3.info*   For the latest news on CSS3

- *quirksmode.org*   For the latest browser compatibility issues

- *html5test.com*   To verify which HTML5 features a browser supports

So, bearing in mind the ongoing development of browsing technology, this chapter describes what CSS3 has to offer at the time of writing.

Attribute Selectors

As explained in Chapter 3, selectors are used in CSS to match HTML elements, and there are ten different types of them:

Selector Type	Example
Type	`b { font-weight:bold; }`
Class	`classname { color:blue; }`
ID	`idname { background-color:red; }`
Descendant	`p em { color:cyan; }`
Child	`div > em { color:green; }`
Universal	`* { color:black; }`
Adjacent sibling	`i + b { color:gray; }`
Attribute	`a[href='mysite.com'] { color:red; }`
Pseudo classes	`a:hover { text-decoration:underline; }`
Pseudo elements	`p:first-letter { font-size:300%; }`

With CSS3 three enhancements have been made to attribute selectors so that you can more easily match elements based on the contents of their attributes.

For example, in CSS2 you can use a selector such as a [href='mysite.com'] to match the string "mysite.com" when found in an href attribute, but there's no way to match only a portion of a string. CSS3 comes to the rescue with three new operators: ^, $, and *. Using one of them directly preceding the = symbol, you can match the start, end, or any part of a string, respectively. For example, a [href^='mysite'] will match any href attribute whose value begins with the string "mysite", so that <a href='mysite.com'> will match, but <a href='thisismysite.com'> will not.

To match only at the end of a string, you can use a selector such as img [src$='.jpg'], which will match any img tag whose src attribute ends with ".jpg". For example, <img src='photo.jpg' /> will match, but <img src='fromjpg.png' /> will not.

Or, to match any substring, you can use a selector such as a [href*='google'] to find any links on a page that have the string "google" anywhere within them. For example, <a href='http://google.com'> and <a href='http://googlemail.com'> will both match.

Backgrounds

CSS2 provides a lot of support for backgrounds, but it still has some weaknesses regarding the CSS box model that have now been addressed in CSS3, with two new properties: background-clip and background-origin. With background-origin, you can specify where a background should start within an element, and with `background-clip`, you can specify how to clip the background so that it doesn't appear in parts of the box model where you don't want it to.

To accomplish these results, both properties support the following attributes:

- **`border-box`**   Refers to the outer edge of the border
- **`padding-box`**   Refers to the outer edge of the padding area
- **`content-box`**   Refers to the outer edge of the content area

These properties are used by the latest versions of all major browsers, with the exception of Safari and Firefox, which use their own, nonstandard property names, `border`, `padding`, and `content`, which omit the `-box` suffix.

Also, there's a new `background-size` property, and multiple backgrounds are now supported too.

All of these new features are described in turn in the following sections.

The background-clip Property

This property specifies whether the background should be ignored (clipped) if it appears within either the border or padding area of an element. For example, the following rule states that the background may display in all parts of an element, all the way to the outer edge of the border:

```
background-clip:border-box;
```

To restrict the background from appearing within the border area of an element, you can restrict it to only the section of an element inside the outer edge of its padding area, like this:

```
background-clip:padding-box;
```

Or to restrict the background to display only within the content area of an element, you would use this rule:

```
background-clip:content-box;
```

Figure 4-1 shows three rows of elements displayed in the Safari web browser, in which the first row uses `border-box` for the `background-clip` property, the second row uses `padding-box`, and the third row uses `content-box`.

In the first row, the inner box (an image file that has been loaded into the top left of the element, with repeating disabled) is allowed to display anywhere in the element. You can also clearly see it displayed in the border area of the first box because the border has been set to dotted.

In the second row, neither the background image nor the background shading displays in the border area because they have been clipped to the padding area with a `background-clip` property value of `padding-box`.

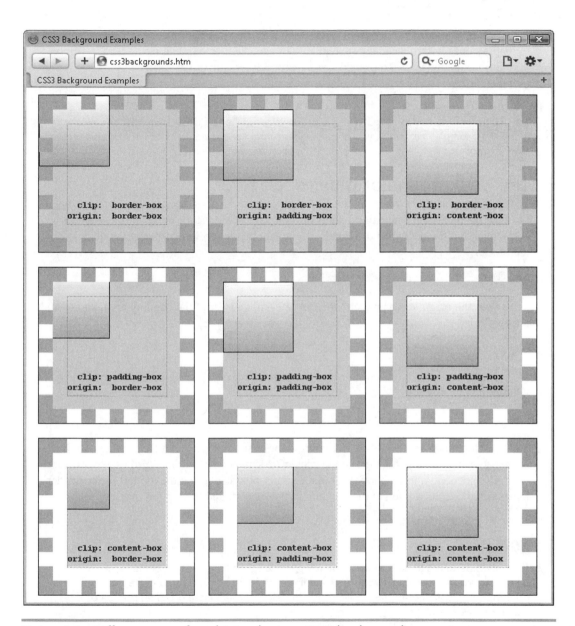

Figure 4-1   Different ways of combining the new CSS3 background properties

Then, in the third row, both the background shading and the image have been clipped to display only within the inner content area of each element (shown inside a light-colored, dotted box), using a `background-clip` property of `content-box`.

NOTE
The CSS and HTML used to create Figure 4-1 are contained in the file css3backgrounds.htm in the file examples.zip, which you can download from the companion website at html5formobile.com.

The background-origin Property

With this property you can also specify where you would like a background image to be located by specifying where the top left of the image should start. For example, the following rule states that the background image's origin is to be the top-left corner of the outer edge of the border:

```
background-origin:border-box;
```

To set the origin of an image to the top-left outer corner of the padding area, you would use this rule:

```
background-origin:padding-box;
```

Or to set the origin of an image to the top-left corner of an element's inner content section, you would use this rule:

```
background-origin:content-box;
```

Looking again at Figure 4-1, in each row the first box uses a `background-origin` property of `border-box`, the second uses `padding-box`, and the third uses `content-box`. Consequently, in each row the smaller inner box displays at the top left of the border in the first box, the top left of the padding in the second, and the top left of the content in the third box.

NOTE
The only differences to note between the rows, with regard to the origins of the inner box in Figure 4-1, are that in rows two and three the inner box is clipped to the padding and content areas respectively, and therefore outside these areas no portion of the box is displayed.

Compatibility Issues

As is often the case in the ever-evolving field of web development, some browsers handle things differently. For example, older versions of the Firefox and Safari browsers have their own property names. The standard property names are `background-clip` and `background-origin`, but on Firefox (and other Gecko-based browsers) they are called `-moz-background-clip` and `-moz-background-origin`, while on older Safari browsers (and others based on the WebKit rendering engine) their names are `-webkit-background-clip` and `-webkit-background-origin`.

Therefore, when you use the `background-clip` property, for example, if you want your CSS rules to apply on as wide a range of browsers as possible, you must use three rules to ensure that the browsers recognize what you want to achieve. You should also take into account that older versions of Firefox and Safari use the nonstandard values of `border`, `padding`, and `content` for these properties, instead of `border-box`, `padding-box`, and `content-box`.

Therefore, to set the `background-clip` property of an element to `border-box` on a variety of platforms, you should issue the following three rules:

```
-moz-background-clip    :border;
-webkit-background-clip:border;
background-clip         :border-box;
```

Likewise, to set an element's `background-clip` property to `padding-box`, you would use these rules:

```
-moz-background-clip    :padding;
-webkit-background-clip:padding;
background-clip         :padding-box;
```

And to set an element's `background-clip` property to `content-box`, you would use these rules:

```
-moz-background-clip    :content;
-webkit-background-clip:content;
background-clip         :content-box;
```

You should approach the `background-origin` property in the same way, so here are the three sets of rules you should use for maximum compatibility:

```
-moz-background-origin    :border;
-webkit-background-origin:border;
background-origin         :border-box;

-moz-background-origin    :padding;
-webkit-background-origin:padding;
background-origin         :padding-box;

-moz-background-origin    :content;
-webkit-background-origin:content;
background-origin         :content-box;
```

Other Issues

Versions of Firefox prior to 4.0 do not support the value of `content-box` when applied to the `background-clip` property. If you use `content-box` on such a browser, the value will be ignored, so the result will be the same as using the `border-box` value—or not using the property at all.

Also, as I write, all versions of Safari up to 5.02, all versions of iOS up to 4.1, and all versions of Android up to 2.2 still accept only the old style name of `-webkit-background-clip` for the `background-clip` property, so make sure you continue to use both the old and new ones for the foreseeable future.

The background-size Property

In the same way that you can specify the width and height of an image when used in the `<img ... />` tag, you can now also do the same for background images on the latest versions of all browsers.

Because the browsers work differently from each other, you need the following set of rules to change the size of a background on all browsers (where *ww* is the width and *hh* is the height):

```
-moz-background-size    :wwpx hhpx;
-webkit-background-size:wwpx hhpx;
-o-background-size      :wwpx hhpx;
background-size         :wwpx hhpx;
```

If you prefer, you can use only one argument, and then both dimensions will be set to that value. Also, if you apply this property to a block-level element such as a `<div>` (rather than one that is inline such as a `<span>`), you can specify the width and/or height as a percentage, instead of as a fixed value.

Using the auto Value

If you wish to scale only one dimension of a background image, and then have the other one scale automatically to retain the same proportions, you can use the value `auto` for the other dimension, like this:

```
background-size:100px auto;
```

This sets the width to 100 pixels, and the height to a value proportionate to the increase or decrease in width.

Multiple Backgrounds

With CSS3 you can now attach multiple backgrounds to an element, each of which can use the previously discussed CSS3 background properties. Figure 4-2 shows an example of this on an

Figure 4-2 This certificate comprises a `<div>` element containing eight different background images.

iPhone. In it, eight different images have been assigned to the background, to create the four corners and four edges of the certificate border.

To display multiple background images in a single CSS rule, you separate them with a comma. For example, here is the CSS that was used to create the background in Figure 4-2—with plenty of whitespace and formatting added to make it clear what is happening:

```
background:url('b1.gif')    top       left    no-repeat,
           url('b2.gif')    top       right   no-repeat,
           url('b3.gif')    bottom    left    no-repeat,
           url('b4.gif')    bottom    right   no-repeat,
           url('ba.gif')    top               repeat-x,
```

```
url('bb.gif')   left      repeat-y,
url('bc.gif')   right     repeat-y,
url('bd.gif')   bottom    repeat-x; }
```

The first four lines place the corner images into the four corners of the element, and the final four lines place the edge images, which are handled last because the order of priority for background images goes from high to low. In other words, where they overlap, additional background images will appear behind already placed images. If they weren't in this order, then the repeating edge images would display over the corners, which would be incorrect.

Using this CSS, you can resize the containing element to any dimensions, and the border will correctly resize to fit, which is a lot easier than using tables or multiple elements to achieve the same effect. What's more, this feature is supported by the latest versions of all major browsers on all platforms.

Incidentally, if the rounded borders supported by the new CSS3 border properties (discussed next) are still not enough for you, you can easily modify or replace the images used in this example to create the exact style of border you require, using a similar single CSS rule.

NOTE
The file used to create Figure 4-2, *css3multiplebg.htm*, is available for download from the companion website, *html5formobile.com*.

Borders

CSS3 also brings a lot more flexibility to the way borders can be presented, by allowing you to change the colors of all four border edges independently, to display images for the edges and corners, to provide a radius value for applying rounded corners to borders, and to place box shadows underneath elements.

The border-color Property

There are two ways you can apply colors to a border. First, you can pass a single color to the property, as follows:

```
border-color:#888;
```

This rule sets all the borders of an element to a mid-gray color. You can also set border colors individually, like this (which sets the border colors to various shades of gray):

```
border-top-color    :#000;
border-left-color   :#444;
border-right-color  :#888;
border-bottom-color:#ccc;
```

You can also set all the colors individually with a single rule, as follows:

```
border-color:#f00 #0f0 #880 #00f;
```

This rule sets the top border color to #f00, the right one to #0f0, the bottom one to #880, and the left one to #00f (red, green, orange, and blue, respectively). You can also use color names for the arguments.

NOTE

The Gecko engine, which powers Firefox, also supports the capability to assign multiple colors to each single edge (allowing cool effects such as gradients), using properties such as -moz-border-top-colors. But since this is not yet supported on any other browsers, there's no point to documenting it here. Hopefully, by the time the next edition of this book is published, all browsers will support this nifty feature.

The border-image Property

On the latest versions of all major browsers, except Internet Explorer, it is possible to display images for the four edges and four corners of an element. Using this feature, you can achieve similar results to those described in the "Multiple Backgrounds" section (a little earlier in this chapter), but you use only a single image comprising all eight elements, such as the one shown in Figure 4-3.

In this image, each of the four corners is separated from the others by a single-pixel edge. Your edges may have more detail than a single pixel's width or height, and your corners can also be smaller or larger.

To attach this image to an element as its border, you use rules such as these:

```
border-width:102px;
-moz-border-image    :url('border.png') 102 102 102 102;
-webkit-border-image:url('border.png') 102 102 102 102;
border-image         :url('border.png') 102 102 102 102;
```

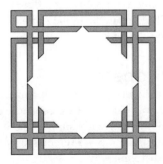

Figure 4-3   A compound image *(border.png)* used for creating borders

The first CSS rule defines the width of the border, which can be a single value if all the images are the same dimensions, or which can list the dimensions in clockwise order from the top to the left. The other lines are three versions of the rule, one for Firefox, one for iOS, Android, Safari, and Chrome, and one for other browsers such as Opera.

In the rules, the URL of the image is followed by four values that represent the number of pixels to use for each of the top, right, bottom, and left corners. Whatever space remains is used for the edges, as shown in Figure 4-4, in which light gray lines divide the eight elements. The area in the central, ninth portion of an image is ignored.

In the case of the *border.png* example, it is 205×205 pixels, with each of the corners being 102×102 pixels, leaving a single pixel width or height for the edge parts. You can also use percent values in place of pixels by adding a % character to them, like this (although I generally recommend using pixels since they are much more precise):

```
border-image:url('border.png') 49.75% 49.75% 49.75% 49.75%;
```

Ask the Expert

Q: So which is better, border images or multiple background images?

A: If you are creating borders on elements that should be visible in all browsers, I recommend you use multiple background images, as they also work in Internet Explorer—which is not the case with border images.

For iOS and Android, however, using the `border-image` property is probably the simpler solution, and it also reduces the number of hits on your server from eight to just one for each border.

You can also use more than 50 percent of an image for any corner, even up to 100 percent; you may find it interesting to try applying different values to the property in the example *css3borderimage.htm* file, available in the *examples.zip* file—downloadable from the companion website at *html5formobile.com*.

The border-radius Property

Prior to CSS3, talented web developers came up with numerous different tweaks and fixes to achieve rounded borders, generally using `<table>` or `<div>` tags. But now, with CSS3, adding rounded borders to an element is really simple, and it works on the latest versions of all major browsers, as shown in Figure 4-5—a screen grab from an Android device, in which a 10-pixel border is displayed in different ways.

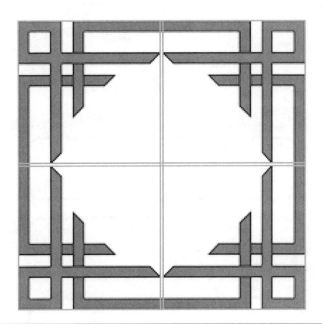

Figure 4-4 The *border.png* image divided into its constituent parts and enlarged for clarity

NOTE

The *css3borderradius.htm* file used to create the screen grab in Figure 4-5 is available from the companion website.

For example, to create a rounded border with a radius of 20 pixels, you could simply use the following rule:

```
border-radius:20px;
```

But it's not quite as easy as that, because although iOS and Android will work fine, some current (and many older) versions of the major browsers use different property names, and if you wish to support them all, you need to also use rules for them such as these (using -moz- and -webkit- prefixes):

```
-moz-border-radius    :20px;
-webkit-border-radius:20px;
```

Or you can specify a separate radius for each of the four corners, like this (applied in a clockwise direction starting from the top-left corner):

```
border-radius:10px 20px 30px 40px;
```

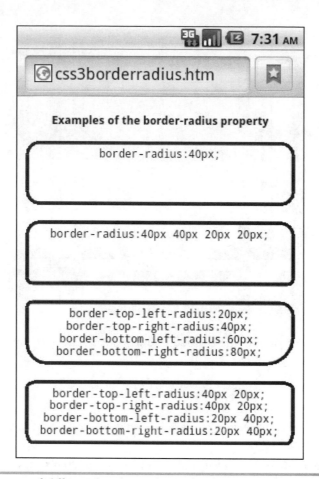

Figure 4-5 A selection of different border-radius styles

If you prefer, you can also address each corner of an element individually, like this:

```
border-top-left-radius     :20px;
border-top-right-radius    :40px;
border-bottom-left-radius  :60px;
border-bottom-right-radius :80px;
```

And, when referencing individual corners, you can supply two arguments to choose a different vertical and horizontal radius—giving more interesting and subtle borders—like this:

```
border-top-left-radius     :40px 20px;
border-top-right-radius    :40px 20px;
border-bottom-left-radius  :20px 40px;
border-bottom-right-radius :20px 40px;
```

The first argument is the horizontal radius, and the second is the vertical radius.

Mozilla Firefox

Although you can place `-moz-` in front of the `border-radius` property to make it work on Firefox, you cannot do so with the individual corner properties such as `border-top-left-radius`. Instead, the Gecko engine used by Firefox provides the following property names:

```
-moz-border-radius-topleft
-moz-border-radius-topright
-moz-border-radius-bottomright
-moz-border-radius-bottomleft
```

TIP

If you are developing just for iOS and Android, you need only use the standard property names, but you should add the alternate property names if you want your code to support most other reasonably recent versions of the major browsers.

The box-shadow Property

Another great way to emphasize an object is to give it a box shadow. To do this, you specify a horizontal and vertical offset from the object, the amount of blurring to add to the shadow, and the color to use, like this:

```
box-shadow:15px 15px 10px #888;
```

The two instances of `15px` specify the vertical and horizontal offset from the element, and these values can be negative, 0, or positive. The `10px` specifies the amount of blurring, with smaller values resulting in less blurring. And the `#888` is the color for the shadow, which can be any valid color value. The result of this rule can be seen Figure 4-6.

You may also add the value `inset` as an argument to this rule and the box shadow will then be displayed inside the object's borders, rather than outside.

However, as with many CSS3 properties, this is sufficient only for the Opera and Internet Explorer browsers. To apply a shadow on iOS, Android, Safari, and Chrome, you should use the following alternative:

```
-webkit-box-shadow:15px 15px 10px #888;
```

And for Firefox and other Gecko-based browsers, you should use

```
-moz-box-shadow:15px 15px 10px #888;
```

If you wish to support all major browsers, then you need to use all three rules.

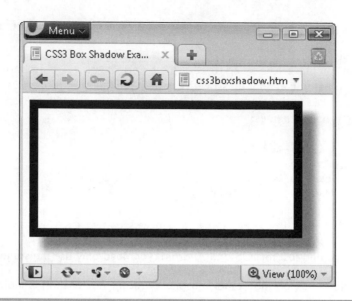

Figure 4-6 A box shadow displayed under an element in Opera

Element Overflow

In CSS2, it is possible to allow or prevent the overflow from an element by setting the `overflow` property to `hidden`, `visible`, `scroll`, or `auto`. But with CSS3, you can now separately apply these values in the horizontal or vertical direction, as shown in Figure 4-7, in which the 16 possible combinations are displayed for content that overflows in both directions.

Figure 4-7 might seem somewhat counterintuitive, because sometimes the `overflow-x` or `overflow-y` property is set to `visible`, but the content of the element doesn't actually display outside of it. According to the W3C specifications, the reason for this is that some combinations with the `visible` argument are not possible; for example, if one property is specified as `visible` while the other is either `scroll` or `auto`, the `visible` value should be changed to `auto`.

There are a few differences in how these properties are implemented, though, because as well as this rule, in Internet Explorer versions 6 through 9, any `visible` property, when combined with `hidden`, is also changed to `hidden`.

Here are some examples of using the properties:

```
overflow-x:hidden;
overflow-x:visible;
overflow-y:auto;
overflow-y:scroll;
```

NOTE

The code used for Figure 4-7 is available as *css3overflow.htm* on the companion website, *html5formobile.com*.

Figure 4-7 Various combinations of the overflow-x and overflow-y properties

Colors

The number of ways in which you can define colors has been greatly expanded with CSS3, and you can now also use CSS functions to apply RGB (red, green, and blue), RGBA (RGB and alpha), HSL (hue, saturation, and luminance), and HSLA (HSL and alpha) colors—the alpha value allows you to specify a color's transparency.

HSL Colors

To define a color with the hsl() function, you must first choose a hue value between 0 and 359 from a color wheel. Any higher color numbers simply wrap around to the beginning again, so the value 0 is red, as are the values 360 and 720. In a color wheel, the primary colors of red, green, and blue are separated by 120 degrees, so that green has the value 120, blue has the value 240, and the numbers between these values represent shades comprising different proportions of the primary colors on either side.

Next you need the saturation level, which is a value between 0 and 100 percent. This specifies how washed out or vibrant a color will appear. Figure 4-8 shows a color wheel displaying both hue and saturation. Because the figure is shown in levels of gray in this book, you cannot see a lot of detail, but if you look closely you should notice a lighter Y shape. This

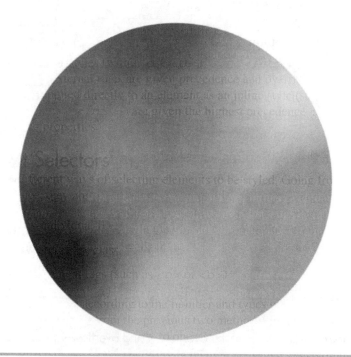

Figure 4-8　A color wheel displaying both hue and saturation

is because red is at the top, green is at the 4 o'clock position, and blue is at 8 o'clock, with the arms and leg of the Y (starting at 10 o'clock) being the colors magenta, yellow, and cyan.

The saturation values commence in the center of the wheel with a mid-gray color (a saturation of 0 percent) and then become more and more vivid as they progress to the outer edge (a saturation of 100 percent). All that's then left is for you to decide how bright you want the color to be by choosing a luminance value of between 0 and 100 percent.

A value of `50 percent` for the luminance gives the fullest, brightest color, and decreasing the value (down to a minimum of `0 percent`) results in making it darker until it displays as black. Increasing the value (up to a maximum of `100 percent`) results in it getting lighter until it shows as white. You can visualize this as being similar to mixing levels of either black or white into the color.

Therefore, for example, to choose a fully saturated yellow color with standard 50 percent brightness, you would use a rule such as this:

```
color:hsl(60, 100%, 50%);
```

Or, for a darker blue color, you might use a rule such as:

```
color:hsl(240, 100%, 40%);
```

You can also use this (and all other CSS color functions) with any property that expects a color, such as `background-color`, and so on.

HSLA Colors

To provide even further control over how colors appear, you can use the `hsla()` function, supplying it with a fourth (or alpha) level for a color, which is a floating-point value between 0 and 1. A value of 0 specifies that the color is totally transparent, while 1 means it is fully opaque.

Here's how you would choose a fully saturated yellow color with standard brightness and 30 percent transparency:

```
color:hsla(60, 100%, 50%, 0.3);
```

Or, for a fully saturated but lighter blue color with 82 percent transparency, you might use this rule:

```
color:hsla(240, 100%, 60%, 0.82);
```

RGB Colors

You probably are more familiar with using the RGB system of selecting a color, as it's similar to using the #nnnnnn and #nnn color formats. For example, to apply a yellow color to a property, you can use either of the following rules (the first supporting 16 million colors, and the second four thousand):

```
color:#ffff00;
color:#ff0;
```

You can also use the CSS `rgb()` function to achieve the same result, but you use decimal numbers instead of hexadecimal (where `255` decimal is `ff` hexadecimal):

```
color:rgb(255, 255, 0);
```

But even better than that, you don't even have to think in amounts of up to 256 anymore, because you can specify percentage values, like this:

```
color:rgb(100%, 100%, 0);
```

In fact, you can now get very close to a desired color by simply thinking about its primary colors. For example, green and blue make cyan, so to create a color close to cyan, but with more blue in it than green, you could make a good first guess at 0 percent red, 40 percent green, and 60 percent blue, and try a rule such as this:

```
color:rgb(0%, 60%, 40%);
```

RGBA Colors

As with the `hsla()` function, the `rgba()` function supports a fourth, alpha argument, so you can, for example, apply the previous cyan-like color with a transparency of 40 percent by using a rule such as this:

```
color:rgba(0%, 60%, 40%, 0.4);
```

The opacity Property

The `opacity` property provides the same alpha control as the `hsla()` and `rgba()` functions, but it lets you modify an object's opacity (or transparency) separately from its color.

To use it, you apply a rule such as the following to an element (which in this example sets the opacity to 25 percent—or 75 percent transparent):

```
opacity:0.25;
```

This property works in the latest versions of all main browsers, including iOS and Android, but if you need backward compatibility with older browser versions, you also need to add the following rule for Safari and Chrome,

```
-webkit-opacity:0.25;
```

the following rule for Firefox,

```
-moz-opacity:0.25;
```

and the following rule (in which the opacity value is multiplied by 100) for releases of Internet Explorer prior to version 9:

```
filter:alpha(opacity='25');
```

Multicolumn Layout

Over the years, one of the most requested features by web developers has been multiple columns, and this request has finally been fulfilled with CSS3—at least for most browsers, including iOS, Android, Safari, Chrome, and Firefox (sadly, Opera and Internet Explorer have yet to catch up).

In browsers that support it, flowing text over multiple columns is as easy as specifying the number of columns, and then (optionally) choosing the spacing between them and the type of dividing line (if any), as shown in Figure 4-9.

The CSS used to create the figure is as follows:

```
text-align           :justify;
font-size            :16pt;
-webkit-column-count:3;
-webkit-column-gap   :1em;
-webkit-column-rule  :1px solid black;
```

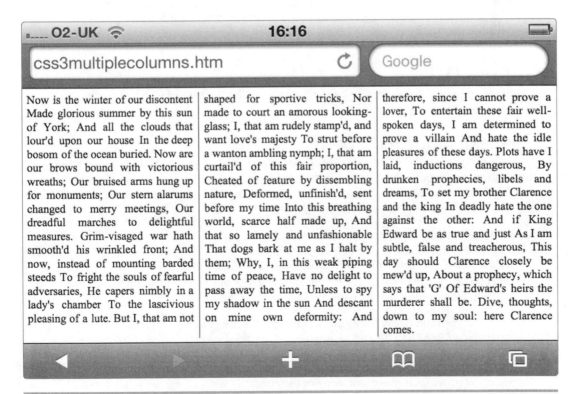

Figure 4-9   A three-column layout displaying text from a Shakespeare play on an iPhone

The first two lines simply tell the browser to right-justify the text and set it to a font size of 16 point. These rules aren't needed for multiple columns, but they improve the text display. The remaining lines set up the element so that text in it will flow over three columns, with a gap of 1 em between the columns, and with a 1-pixel border down the middle of each gap.

For iOS and Android (and Safari and Chrome), this is all you need to do. But if you would like to support Firefox as well, you need to also add the following lines:

```
-moz-column-count:3;
-moz-column-gap  :1em;
-moz-column-rule :1px solid black;
```

Unfortunately, there's nothing you can do yet to achieve this effect in Internet Explorer or Opera, other than splitting content into separate <table> or <div> elements, for example.

NOTE

Is it just me, or do you also hate web page mockups that use the "Lorem Ipsum" Latin text? For me there's nothing better than copying and pasting a good bit of Shakespeare or Dickens instead.

Text Effects

A number of new effects can now be applied to text with the help of CSS3, including text shadows, text overlapping, and word wrapping.

The text-shadow Property

This property is similar to the box-shadow property and takes the same set of arguments: a horizontal and vertical offset, an amount for the blurring, and the color to use. For example, the following rule offsets the shadow by 3 pixels both horizontally and vertically, and displays the shadow in dark gray, with a blurring of 4 pixels:

```
text-shadow:3px 3px 4px #444;
```

The result of this rule looks like the text shown in Figure 4-10.

This property works on iOS, Android, and all major browsers except Internet Explorer. If you wish to also support that browser, you need to add the following rule:

```
filter:progid:DXImageTransform.Microsoft.Shadow(
    color='#888888', Direction=135, Strength=4);
```

While this rule does not produce a proper text shadow (as implemented by the other browsers), it provides a reasonable copy of the effect, as you can see in Figure 4-11.

Me, and my shadow.

Figure 4-10 The CSS3 `text-shadow` property applied to a sentence

Me, and my shadow.

Figure 4-11 Emulating the `text-shadow` property in Internet Explorer

The text-overflow Property

When using any of the CSS overflow properties with a value of `hidden`, you can also use the `text-overflow` property to place an ellipsis (three dots) just before the cutoff to indicate that some text has been truncated, like this:

```
text-overflow:ellipsis;
```

Without this property, truncated text looks like the text shown in Figure 4-12, but with it the result is as shown in Figure 4-13.

Unfortunately, neither Firefox nor Opera supports this property, but iOS, Android, and the latest versions of all other major browsers do.

The word-wrap Property

As an alternative to using the `text-overflow` property and truncating text, when you have a really long word that is wider than the element containing it, you can use the `word-wrap` property with a value of `break-word` to force the long word to always wrap, like this:

```
word-wrap:break-word;
```

For example, in Figure 4-14 the word Antidisestablishmentarianism is too wide for the containing box and, because no overflow properties have been applied, has overflowed its bounds.

But in Figure 4-15, the `word-wrap` property of the element has been assigned a value of `break-word`, so the word has neatly wrapped around to the next line.

This property is supported by all the latest versions of all major browsers.

Cut off in his prin

Figure 4-12 The phrase "Cut off in his prime." is truncated.

Cut off in his p...

Figure 4-13 An ellipsis indicates that the phrase has been truncated.

Antidisestablishmentarianism

Figure 4-14 The word is too wide for its container and has overflowed.

Antidisestablishm entarianism

Figure 4-15 The word-wrap property has been used to force the long word to wrap.

The box-sizing Property

The W3C box model, the default on all browsers other than Internet Explorer 5.5, specifies that the width and height of an object should refer only to the dimensions of an element's content, ignoring any padding or border. But some web designers have expressed a desire to specify dimensions that refer to an entire element, including any padding and border.

To provide this feature, CSS3 lets you choose the box model you wish to use, with the `box-sizing` property. For example, to use the total width and height of an object including padding and borders, you would use this rule:

```
box-sizing:border-box;
```

Or, to have an object's width and height refer only to its content, you would use this rule (the default):

```
box-sizing:content-box;
```

Let's look at what this means in practice by viewing an object that is of known dimensions, such as Figure 4-16—a 200×70-pixel rectangle.

Now compare that with the object shown in Figure 4-17, which has both padding of 10 pixels and a border of 10 pixels, and which is also given the same 200×70 dimensions. In this case, because the value of the `box-sizing` property is `border-box`, everything in the object must fit within the width and height specified.

This means that both the border and the padding are applied *inside* the given width and height, resulting in a reduced content area of just 162×32 pixels—exactly the effect that some web developers dislike.

200 x 70 pixels

Figure 4-16 A rectangle with a width of 200 pixels and height of 70 pixels

Figure 4-17 A 200×70-pixel object displayed using the `border-box` value

Figure 4-18 The object is now displayed using the content-box value.

On the other hand, the object shown in Figure 4-18 uses the content-box value for the box-sizing property, and therefore the padding and border are applied *outside* the fixed content area, which remains at the originally specified 200×70 pixels.

As you can imagine, there's a lot of discussion over which of the box-sizing settings is better, but armed with this property, whichever side of the fence you stand on, you can now build your web pages the way that seems the most intuitive to you.

Browser Compatibility

The standard box-sizing name for this property is not yet used by any browsers other than Opera and Android. Therefore, for this feature to work on iOS devices (as well as Safari and Chrome), you need to also use the following versions of the property name and argument:

```
-webkit-box-sizing:border-box;
-webkit-box-sizing:content-box;
```

If you would like to also support Firefox and Internet Explorer, then you also have to add one or more of the following versions of the property name:

```
-moz-box-sizing:border-box;
-moz-box-sizing:content-box;

-ms-box-sizing:border-box;
-ms-box-sizing:content-box;
```

The resize Property

If you wish to give your users a little more control over the way in which they input information into forms, you can use the resize property to allow them to resize an object to more comfortable dimensions. To apply this feature, use one of the following rules:

```
resize:horizontal;
resize:vertical;
resize:both;
```

The first rule allows users to resize objects only horizontally, the second rule allows only vertical resizing, and the third allows both. When resizing, you can't make an object smaller than its original dimensions, but you can make it any larger size. So, to restrict the scope of this feature, you can use the `max-height` and `max-width` properties, like this:

```
max-height:500px;
max-width:300px;
```

Currently, probably due to the ability of web pages on touch devices to be resized by pinching, this feature is not enabled on either iOS or Android, but it does work on the latest versions of Firefox, Chrome, and Safari, on which browsers a small resize handle is placed at the lower right of any resizable object that you can grab and drag, as shown in Figure 4-19.

The outline-offset Property

If you don't like the way the outline box is applied to an object when it gains focus, you can use the `outline-offset` property to enlarge it, as follows, which (for example) moves all four edges of the outline out from the object by 15 pixels:

```
outline-offset:15px;
```

This works on the latest versions of all browsers except Internet Explorer.

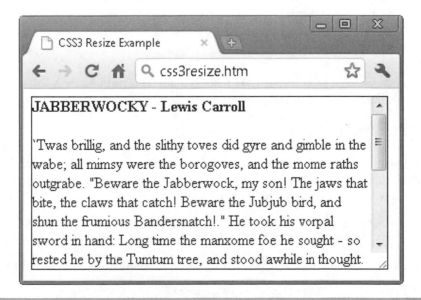

Figure 4-19   This object can be resized using the bottom-right drag handle.

Web Fonts

The use of CSS3 web fonts vastly increases the typography available to web designers by allowing fonts to be loaded in and displayed from across the Web, not just from the user's computer. To achieve this, you declare a web font using the @font-face rule, like this:

```
@font-face {
    font-family:FontName;
    src:url('FontName.otf');
}
```

The url() function requires a value containing the path or URL of a font. On most browsers, you can use either TrueType (.ttf) or OpenType (.otf) fonts, but Internet Explorer restricts you to only TrueType fonts that have been converted to EOT (.eot).

To tell the browser the type of font, you can use the format() function. You use it like this for OpenType fonts:

```
@font-face {
    font-family:FontName;
    src:url('FontName.otf')
    format('opentype');
}
```

For TrueType fonts, you use it like this:

```
@font-face {
    font-family:FontName;
    src:url('FontName.ttf')
    format('truetype');
}
```

However, since IE accepts only EOT fonts, it ignores @font-face rules that contain the format() function.

Google Web Fonts

As long as you are creating an Internet-enabled (rather than stand-alone) app or web page, one of the best ways to use web fonts is to load them in for free from Google's servers. To find out more about this, you should check out *code.google.com/webfonts*, but to show you how easy it is, here's how you load one in using a <link> tag:

```
<link href='http://fonts.googleapis.com/css?family=Lobster&subset=latin'
    rel='stylesheet' type='text/css'>
```

Then to use such a font, just apply it in a CSS rule, like this:

```
h1 { font-family:'Lobster', arial, serif; }
```

Figure 4-20 shows just a few of the over 50 fonts and font variants provided by Google.

Figure 4-20 A selection of Google web fonts displayed on an Android device

Other CSS3 Additions

There are a number of other CSS3 additions that, for one reason or another, I have not mentioned, usually because they are merely a draft proposal, their application is experimental, or their features could be subject to change.

Some examples include style sheets for outputting speech, auto generating of content, and a range of `nav-` properties that will eventually provide a means of specifying the navigation (or tabbing) order of elements on a page.

As and when these and newer goodies become widely available, I will incorporate them into future editions of this book. In the meantime, though, you can keep up to date with the latest browser implementations by visiting the companion website at *html5formobile.com*.

Summary

At this point, you now have all the information you need to understand what's possible with the latest versions of both HTML and CSS. But you're not quite ready to see how to use them to create iOS and Android websites and apps, because there's still the matter of how to manipulate web pages and their properties to achieve dynamic user interaction. To remedy that, the next four chapters show you how to perform server- and client-side programming—along with database management—beginning with a comprehensive introduction to JavaScript.

Chapter 5

An Introduction to JavaScript

Key Skills & Concepts

- Incorporating JavaScript code into a web page
- JavaScript language syntax
- Numeric variables, strings, and arrays
- Operators and built-in JavaScript functions
- Using functions and passing arguments
- The difference between global and local variable scope
- Controlling program flow with conditional expressions
- Creating different types of looping structures
- Basic error handling

JavaScript is the free language built into all modern browsers, including Apple iOS, Google Android, Microsoft Internet Explorer, Mozilla Firefox, Apple Safari, Opera, and Google Chrome. It is the power behind the dynamic HTML used for Web 2.0 websites such as Facebook, Flickr, Gmail, and many others.

Unlike other languages used for creating websites, such as Perl, PHP, and Ruby, which run on a web server, JavaScript runs within the web browser. This makes it the perfect tool for creating dynamic web pages because it can modify HTML elements in real time.

JavaScript is also the technology behind Ajax functionality, in which data is transferred between a web server and web browser behind the scenes, without the user being aware of it.

Ask the Expert

Q: Why is JavaScript so named?

A: JavaScript is a quite different language from Java, but, as part of a marketing deal made between Netscape and Sun Microsystems in 1995, JavaScript was given its name to try and benefit from the general buzz surrounding the Java language. To justify this naming, in JavaScript all Java keywords are reserved, its standard library follows Java's naming conventions, and its Math and Date objects are based on Java 1.0 classes. Also, the trademark name *JavaScript* belongs to Sun (and therefore now Oracle)—but the similarities end there.

Incorporating JavaScript in a Web Page

There are two ways you can include JavaScript code in a web page: either directly within `<script>` and `</script>` tags, or by specifying the name of a file to load in as the `src` argument to a `<script>` tag.

For example, the following is a small JavaScript segment that will pop up a window to say "Hello" by calling the built-in `alert()` function:

```
<script>
   alert("Hello")
</script>
```

On the whole, people tend to put such JavaScript segments near the start of a web page so that it runs sooner rather than later, but you can place JavaScript code anywhere you like in a page, and any output it makes will appear in that section of the page.

The second means of incorporating JavaScript in a page is shown next, in which the file *code.js* is fetched and acted upon as if it were embedded directly in the page:

```
<script src='code.js'></script>
```

In this case, the included file must *not* contain any `<script>` or `</script>` tags, as these have already been provided by the calling `<script>` and closing `</script>` tags.

Using Comments

When you wish to include comments in your code or perhaps prevent one or more lines of code from being executed during debugging, you can use the `/*` and `*/` comment tags, like this:

```
<script>
   /* The line below displays an alert box */
   alert("Hello")
</script>
```

You can include as few or as many characters and even lines of code as you like within these comments. Sometimes, though, you simply want to make a quick comment without having to place comment tags after it as well as before it, which you can do with `//`, the other type of comment tag, like this:

```
<script>
   // The line below displays an alert box
   alert("Hello")
</script>
```

This type of comment automatically closes when the end of a line is reached.

Using Semicolons

In some languages, such as PHP and CSS, you must place a semicolon after every statement, even when there's only one on a line. With JavaScript, you can omit the semicolon for all single-statement lines if you wish, but you *must* place them between multiple statements on a line.

Using semicolons in JavaScript only when they are required is the style I use in this book, although you will find that many programmers use the semicolon everywhere in JavaScript regardless.

JavaScript Variables

If you have never encountered them before, you can think of variables as containers for values, in much the same way as the small glass jars in a spice rack contain different spices, except that variables contain digital values such as numbers and letters.

So, for the following examples, assume you have several small spice jars made out of transparent glass from which you have removed the original labels. Also imagine that you have a pen, some paper, and some sticky labels.

Variable and Object Naming

In JavaScript, variables and object names are case sensitive and may include any of the letters a through z and A through Z, the digits 0 through 9, and the _ and $ characters.

Variable and object names may not begin with a digit, and there is no predefined limit on their length, although shorter names make for more readable code (as long as they are not cryptic).

CAUTION

The $ symbol is often used by special features in JavaScript frameworks (files of helper code to aid with cross-browser compatibility and programming in general), such as jQuery, Script.aculo.us, Prototype, and many others. Therefore, I recommend that you avoid using the $ symbol in your own code when you're also using a framework.

Numeric Variables

Creating a numeric variable is like taking an empty spice jar and placing a small strip of paper in it on which you have written a number. Then you screw the lid on and attach a sticky label (on which you have written the variable's name) to the jar.

For example, to use this analogy to describe creating a variable called age with the value 49, you would write the number 49 on the small piece of paper and pop it in the jar, and then write the word age on a label and attach it to the jar.

The jar now represents the variable age and the piece of paper represents the variable's value. If someone asks you what the value of age is, you simply look through the transparent glass of the jar labeled age to read the value of 49.

Assigning a Value to a Variable

In JavaScript, the equivalent is to assign the value 49 to the variable `age`, like this:

```
<script>
   age = 49
</script>
```

You can read back the value of `age` and pass its value to another variable, which is the equivalent of reading the value from the first jar and then labeling a new jar `copyofage` and placing the copied value into it, like this:

```
<script>
   age       = 49
   copyofage = age
</script>
```

So now both variables `age` and `copyofage` have the value 49.

You can also send the value of a variable directly to a function (a small, ready-made, JavaScript program) to display or otherwise use. For example, the following code passes the value of the `age` variable to the `alert()` function, which pops up a window displaying its value, as shown in Figure 5-1:

```
<script>
   alert(age)
</script>
```

The following example brings all this together into a complete web page that first assigns the value 49 to the variable `age` and then displays it in an alert box (and is the code that was used to create Figure 5-1):

```
<!DOCTYPE html>
<html>
   <head>
      <title>Example</title>
   </head>
```

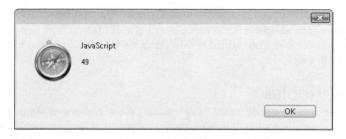

Figure 5-1   Displaying a value in an alert box on a Safari web browser

```
    <body>
      <script>
        age = 49
        alert(age)
      </script>
    </body>
</html>
```

NOTE
Because all JavaScript must be within `<script>` and `</script>` tags, I will omit these tags from all further examples—make sure you put them in if you try out the examples for yourself.

Adding Numeric Values
Adding numbers together, numbers to numeric variable values, and even numeric variable values to other numeric variable values is very easy.

For example, in the following three statements, first the variable `tempval` is assigned the value 40 (the sum of 23 and 17). Then `otherval` is assigned the value in `tempval` (40), plus an additional value of 19—totaling 59. Finally, `result` is assigned the value in `tempval` (40), plus the value in `otherval` (59)—totaling 99.

```
tempval  = 23 + 17           // tempval is assigned the value 40
otherval = tempval + 19      // otherval is assigned the value 59
result   = tempval + otherval // result is assigned the value 99
```

After these three statements, `tempval` has the value 40, `otherval` 59, and `result` 99.

Using Floating-Point Numbers
You can also assign and manipulate floating-point numbers (numbers with a fractional part), as with the following statements, which combine to give the variable `weight` a value of 88.26:

```
weight = 23.56
weight = weight + 64.7
```

NOTE
Note how in the second statement the variable `weight` is used on both sides of the = symbol so that its value is read, added to 64.7, and then the result of the addition is assigned back to `weight`.

String Variables
String variables are a little different from numeric ones in that you assign to a variable a group of characters instead of a number (or, using the analogy, you write a word, phrase, or paragraph on the piece of paper you put in the spice jar).

For example, the following statement assigns a sentence to a variable called `hobbies`:

```
hobbies = 'Swimming, running, movies, books and TV'
```

String Concatenation

Combining strings is called *concatenation* rather than *addition*, but the same + operator is used. For example, the following code displays an alert box containing the string `"I am Spartacus!"`:

```
string1 = 'I am '
string2 = 'Spartacus!'
name    = string1 + string2
alert(name)
```

In our analogy of spice jars, in this example there are a total of three jars in use. The first jar is labeled `string1` and contains a piece of paper that reads `"I am"`, and the second jar is labeled `string2` and contains a piece of paper that reads `"Spartacus!"`. These two jars have then had their values read and concatenated into a single sentence on a new piece of paper, which has been placed in the third jar, labeled `name`.

Escaping Characters

To show that a value is a string (and not a number or operator), it must be enclosed in either single or double quote marks. For example, the following two statements are equivalent:

```
somewhere = 'Over the rainbow'
somewhere = "Over the rainbow"
```

However, this can cause a problem when you wish to actually include one or the other type of quote within a string. One way around this is to enclose the string in the opposite type of quotation marks to the type used inside the string, like this:

```
heyhey = "We're the Monkees!"
```

If the outer double quotes were single quotes, then JavaScript would think that only `'We'` is the string, and that the rest of the statement is an indecipherable syntax error.

Alternately, here's a legal statement that embeds double quotes within single ones:

```
line = 'She said, "What big eyes you have!"'
```

But what happens when you need both single *and* double quotes to be in a string, as in this (illegal) statement?

```
line = 'Rhett Butler: "Frankly my dear, I don't give a damn."'
```

The answer is that you must escape one or more of the quotes by prefacing them with a \, as in this corrected version:

```
line = 'Rhett Butler: "Frankly my dear, I don\'t give a damn."'
```

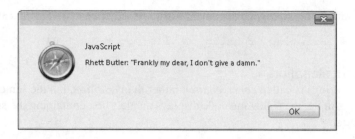

Figure 5-2 Strings can use escaped characters to contain special characters.

In this instance, using an escape character before the double quotes isn't necessary because the containing quotes are single. However, you are allowed to escape any enclosed quotes if you like, and some people prefer to always do this, as follows:

```
line = 'Rhett Butler: \"Frankly my dear, I don\'t give a damn.\"'
```

When you escape characters in a string, it may look messy at first, but JavaScript takes care of it and displays such strings correctly, as shown in Figure 5-2, in which the value assigned to the variable `line` is displayed in an alert box.

Arrays

In JavaScript (and many other languages) there is another type of variable called an *array*. In fact, it is more of a construct than a variable, in that an array is like a collection of spice jars joined together with sticky tape.

For example, suppose you wish to keep track of the goals scored by players on a five-player soccer team, and you know that Andrew has scored 3 goals, Brian has scored 2, Clive has scored 4, David has yet to score, and Edward has scored 1 goal. You could indicate this with the following statements:

```
andrew = 3
brian  = 2
clive  = 4
david  = 0
edward = 1
```

These statements are equivalent to taping five spice jars together to form a single unit containing multiple elements of data—in other words, an array of jars. But this is not optimal coding because five storage types (variables) are used, where only one is required.

NOTE
No capital letters are used for these names because they are variables, and the convention I use in JavaScript programs is to begin variables with a lowercase letter. However, you can use any combination of upper- and lowercase letters in your variable names.

Assigning Numeric Values to an Array

Here's one way you can combine several variables together into a single JavaScript array, in this case called `goals`:

```
goals     = Array()
goals[0]  = 3
goals[1]  = 2
goals[2]  = 4
goals[3]  = 0
goals[4]  = 1
```

The array is created using the `Array()` function, and then five elements are populated with the goals scored by each player (elements 0 through 4). You can equally create an array with this statement, which is the equivalent of using the `Array()` function:

```
goals = []
```

However, the assigning of values to the array in the preceding example is overly complicated, because JavaScript allows you to create an array and assign values to its elements both at the same time, as follows:

```
goals = [3, 2, 4, 0, 1]
```

Once the array has data in it, as long as you know which player represents which of the taped-together jars, you can now easily look up a player's score by placing a value representing an index into the array within square brackets, like this:

```
score = goals[2]
```

Because array elements always start at 0 (not 1), this statement says, "assign to `score` the value in the *third* element of the array `goals`." In this case the value is 4—the number of goals scored by Clive—so `score` now has the value 4.

Assigning String Values to an Array

Just like physically joined-together spice jars, arrays can contain anything you can put in them, which includes strings. This means that the following is a valid way of keeping track of the soccer team's players:

```
players = ['Andrew', 'Brian', 'Clive', 'David', 'Edward']
```

Fetching a string value from an array element is also very easy. For example, the following statement returns the name Clive:

```
name = player[2]
```

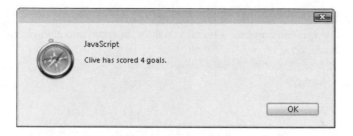

Figure 5-3 Strings and numeric variables combined in an `alert()` call

Therefore, we now have an easy way of connecting players to their goal scoring, as in the following group of five statements (in which I have spaced out the player and goal assignments for clarity):

```
players = ['Andrew', 'Brian',  'Clive',   'David',   'Edward']
goals   = [3,         2,        4,         0,         1       ]

name    = players[2]
score   = goals[2]
alert(name + ' has scored ' + score + ' goals.')
```

Let's look more closely at what is happening here. In the third and fourth statements, the index into the array is the value 2, which actually references the third element of each array (because the first element is at location 0). Therefore, since `player[2]` refers to Clive, then `goals[2]` refers to the number of goals Clive has scored.

These values are placed in the variables `name` and `score`, which are then used within a call to the `alert()` function to display a meaningful sentence, as shown in Figure 5-3.

NOTE
As the fifth statement in the preceding list shows, the argument provided to the `alert()` function consists of a combination of strings and variables, which are concatenated using the + symbol to create a single string that is then displayed.

Associative Arrays
With JavaScript you can further improve on the preceding example by using associative arrays, in which elements within an array are referred to by a name, rather than by an index offset number. What's more, only a single array is required (whereas the previous example required two). For example, the following statement assigns pairs of names and values to the `goals` array:

```
goals = {'Andrew':3, 'Brian':2, 'Clive':4, 'David':0, 'Edward':1}
```

NOTE

Note that curly brackets (not square ones) are required during an assignment when creating associative arrays.

Now you can more easily reference the goals scored by a player, as in the following statement, which assigns the value 2 to the variable `score`:

```
score = goals['Brian']
```

You can also update an element when one of the players scores another goal, like this (which increments the value in the element by 1):

```
goals['David'] = goals['David'] + 1
```

Or, as with any variable assignment, you can provide an absolute value, or the result of any numeric calculation.

Associative Arrays and String Values   Associative arrays can contain strings as well as numeric values, so, for example, the following statement stores the favorite colors of five girls:

```
favcolors = { 'Anne':'pink', 'Bea':'red', 'Cara':'orange',
   'Debbie':'green', 'Elaine':'purple' }
```

Using this structure, you can easily determine Bea's favorite color with the following statement:

```
color = favcolors['Bea']
```

The result of this statement is to assign the string `'red'` to the variable `color`.

NOTE

Associative arrays in JavaScript are not actually arrays; in fact, they are objects. However, you can write values to and read them from objects using the same syntax as with arrays. Therefore, you don't need to concern yourself about the difference between arrays and objects at this point.

Multidimensional Arrays

JavaScript arrays are quite interesting in that their elements may contain other arrays, as well as numbers and strings. This means it's possible to create multidimensional arrays. For example, in the following code I have chosen to create a multidimensional array using the `Array()` function for clarity:

```
tictactoe = Array(
   Array('.', '.', '.'),
   Array('.', '.', '.'),
   Array('.', '.', '.')
)
```

Here, the array `tictactoe` is created, and it then has its first three elements assigned values, each of which is a further array of three elements. The net result of all this is an array of two dimensions comprising a three by three matrix, populated with the string `'.'` in each element.

If you prefer, you can shorten and simplify the creation of multidimensional arrays by avoiding use of the `Array()` function, replacing it with square brackets instead, like this:

```
tictactoe =
[
    ['.', '.', '.'],
    ['.', '.', '.'],
    ['.', '.', '.']
]
```

Or you could also code it more compactly, like this:

```
tictactoe = [['.', '.', '.'], ['.', '.', '.'], ['.', '.', '.']]
```

TIP

I think the short form of array creation (without using the `Array()` function) is better for beginners because it uses the square brackets that will also be used for accessing the array after it is created.

Using this data structure, it is now possible to store the moves of a game of Tic-Tac-Toe, for example, assuming that these are the first three moves:

```
tictactoe[1][1] = 'X'
tictactoe[0][0] = 'O'
tictactoe[1][0] = 'X'
```

To reference a multidimensional array, you use additional pairs of square brackets after the first pair. So, in the preceding statements, Player 1 places an X right in the center of the array (`tictactoe[1][1]`), then Player 2 puts a O in the top-left corner (`tictactoe[0][0]`), after which Player 1 places another X just under Player 2's O (`tictactoe[1][0]`), at which point the game board looks like this:

```
O  .  .
X  X  .
.  .  .
```

Because all array elements support containing other arrays, the number of subdimensions you can create is limited only by the available memory on your computer. So, for example, you might reference an element in a three-dimensional array like this (although such complex arrays are not covered in this book):

```
item = bigarray[7][5][12]
```

Multidimensional Associative Arrays   You may also create multidimensional associative arrays using code such as the following (remember that associative arrays require curly brackets, not square ones):

```
tictactoe =
{
    'row1':{'col1':'.', 'col2':'.', 'col3':'.'},
    'row2':{'col1':'.', 'col2':'.', 'col3':'.'},
    'row3':{'col1':'.', 'col2':'.', 'col3':'.'}
}
```

Then, to assign values to elements, you would use the element names in your code (rather than index numbers), like this:

```
tictactoe['row2']['col2'] = 'X'
tictactoe['row1']['col1'] = 'O'
tictactoe['row2']['col1'] = 'X'
```

In Chapter 6, you'll see how the fact that associative arrays are really objects means they can also be accessed as such, as in the following statements, which are equivalent to the previous three because the . symbol is the divider that JavaScript uses to separate objects and subobjects (or properties):

```
tictactoe.row2.col2 = 'X'
tictactoe.row1.col1 = 'O'
tictactoe.row2.col1 = 'X'
```

Ask the Expert

Q: **Which browser is best for JavaScript development?**

A: I prefer Mozilla Firefox because I browse with it and because it's the most popular browser after Internet Explorer (which is the least-standard browser, even though it's from Microsoft). In Firefox, pressing SHIFT-CTRL-J at any time opens the Error Console, in which all errors, warnings, and messages have their own tabs. It also supports the powerful debugging utility Firebug (available at *getfirebug.com*).

   If your favorite browser is Google Chrome, you'll be interested to know (if you don't already) that it also supports using SHIFT-CTRL-J to bring up a more powerful Error Console, but I generally find all the information I need from the Firefox one. In Opera, you can call up an Error Console via Tools | Advanced | Error Console. In Safari (as long as "Show Develop menu in menu bar" is checked in Preferences | Advanced), you can

(continued)

use CTRL-ALT-C on a PC or ALT-CMD-C on a Mac to bring up an Error Console. And finally, in Internet Explorer you can click the yellow triangle that appears in the bottom-left corner of the browser window whenever there's an error, enabling you to view information about it.

Non-Firefox browsers can also run the light version of Firebug to help with debugging. It runs in all main browsers and is available at *getfirebug.com/firebuglite*.

JavaScript Operators

Now that you've been introduced to numbers, strings, variables, and arrays, it's time to see how to manipulate them using various operators, such as the + symbol, which you have already seen used for both adding numbers and concatenating strings.

Arithmetic Operators

JavaScript supports a number of arithmetic operators, as detailed in Table 5-1, which also shows examples of each operator in use, and the result of performing each example calculation.

The first four operators in this table speak for themselves; they are the standard addition, subtraction, multiplication, and division operators (although on computers, the * symbol is used for multiplication and the / symbol is used for division, rather than the × and ÷ operators that you may have used at school).

If you are unfamiliar with the % operator, it is known as the modulus operator and is used to determine how much is left over after a division operation. For example, if you have seven apples to divide among three children without cutting them up, you can perform the following calculation:

```
remainder = 7 % 3
each      = (7 - remainder) / 3
```

The result of the first statement is the value 1, which is placed into the variable remainder. Then this value is subtracted from the initial number of 7 apples (leaving 6), and this value is then divided by the 3 children, resulting in a value of 2, which is assigned to the variable each. Therefore, each child is given two apples, with one remaining.

The final two operators in the table let you quickly increment or decrement the value in a variable, as in the following example, in which the variable potatoes is assigned the value 99, and is then incremented so that the variable has the value 100:

```
potatoes = 99
++potatoes
```

Operator	Description	Example	Result
+	Addition	1 + 2	3
-	Subtraction	7 − 3	4
*	Multiplication	6 * 9	54
/	Division	21 / 7	3
%	Remainder after division (modulus)	44 / 10	4
++	Increment	++f	f + 1
−−	Decrement	−−g	g − 1

Table 5-1   The Seven JavaScript Arithmetic Operators

If you issue the statement `alert(potatoes)` at this point, you will see the value 100 displayed. You can then, for example, decrement the number of potatoes back to 99, like this (after which another call to `alert(potatoes)` will confirm the value is back to 99):

```
--potatoes
```

You can also place the `++` or `--` operator after a variable to increment or decrement it only *after* its value has been accessed. For example, the following two lines display an alert box with the value 100:

```
potatoes = 99
alert(++potatoes)
```

However, the following lines display only the value 99, because the increment is set to occur after the current value is looked up:

```
potatoes = 99
alert(potatoes++)
```

You can verify that the increment actually occurred by issuing another `alert(potatoes)` statement, which will then display the variable's current value of 100.

Arithmetic Functions

Another way to determine the quotient (or nonfractional part) of a division is with the JavaScript built-in math function `floor()`, which returns only the portion in the result that is before the decimal point, like the following statement (which returns 2):

```
Math.floor(7 / 3)
```

As you might expect, JavaScript comes with several ready-made math functions, as detailed in Table 5-2, which also gives examples of their use and the values returned by the examples.

Function	Returned Value	Example	Result
`Math.abs(p)`	The absolute value of `p`; negative values are changed to positive	`Math.abs(-23)`	`23`
`Math.acos(p)`	The arc cosine of `p`	`Math.acos(0.45)`	`1.10403…`
`Math.asin(p)`	The arc sine of `p`	`Math.asin(0.6)`	`0.64350…`
`Math.atan(p)`	The arc tangent of `p`	`Math.atan(10)`	`1.47112…`
`Math.atan2(p,q)`	The arc tangent of `p/q`	`Math.atan2(10,3)`	`1.27933…`
`Math.ceil(p)`	`p` rounded up to the nearest integer	`Math.ceil(17.24)`	`18`
`Math.cos(p)`	The cosine of `p`	`Math.cos(100)`	`0.86231…`
`Math.exp(p)`	The exponent of `p`	`Math.exp(3)`	`20.08553…`
`Math.floor(p)`	`p` rounded down to the nearest integer	`Math.floor(98.4)`	`98`
`Math.log(p)`	The log of `p` base e	`Math.log(100)`	`4.60517…`
`Math.max(p,q)`	The greatest value out of `p` and `q`	`Math.max(33,87)`	`87`
`Math.min(p,q)`	The least value out of `p` and `q`	`Math.min(33,87)`	`33`
`Math.pow(p,q)`	`p` raised to the power `q`	`Math.pow(8,3)`	`512`
`Math.random()`	A pseudo-random floating-point number between 0 and 1	`Math.random()`	`0.?????…`
`Math.round(p)`	The integer closest to `p`; rounds up or down as necessary	`Math.round(32.501)`	`33`
`Math.sin(p)`	The sine of `p`	`Math.sin(100)`	`-0.50636…`
`Math.sqrt(p)`	The square root of `p`	`Math.sqrt(144)`	`12`
`Math.tan(p)`	The tangent of `p`	`Math.tan(100)`	`-0.58721…`

Table 5-2 The 18 Math Functions Supported by JavaScript

The math functions can be used in any statements in the same way you use standard operators, like this (which calculates the hypotenuse of a right-angled triangle where the shorter sides have lengths 12 and 7):

```
side1 = 12
side2 = 7
alert(Math.sqrt(side1 * side1 + side2 * side2))
```

Because of precedence (see the section "Operator Precedence" later in this chapter), the multiplication expressions are performed first in the third statement, and only then are the two results added together, with the result displayed being `13.89244 . . . .`

TIP

Remember to leave in the `Math.` portion of the arithmetic function names, as in `Math.sin(100)` (rather than `sin(100)`, which will not work).

Assignment Operators

In addition to the standard = operator, there are another five operators you can use for assigning values, as detailed in Table 5-3, which also shows examples of them in use, and the results of applying the examples.

The only unusual thing to note here is the third row, in which the string `'lbs'` is concatenated with the value 100 to create a new string, because `'lbs'` is a string and not a numeric value. This happens whenever a + operator is used and one of the operands is a string, even if the string is a number comprising one or more digits.

Comparison Operators

To enable programs to compare values, JavaScript has eight comparison operators, as detailed in Table 5-4, in which a couple of examples are provided for each operator, along with the result of trying each example.

I expect that most of this table will look straightforward to you, with the possible exception of the final two operators, === and !==. Because JavaScript supports numbers, strings, and other different types of objects that are able to hold the same or similar values, you can use these operators to ensure that you are comparing apples with apples (and not with pears, for example).

To illustrate this, here's a legal statement that may surprise you:

```
result = 23 * '1024'
```

Here, an attempt is being made to multiply a numeric value by a string. Curiously, JavaScript allows this and assigns the numeric value `23522` to `result`. This is because the

Operator	Description	Example	Value of p
=	Assignment	p = 100	100
+=	Assignment with addition	p = 100; p += 10	110
+=	Assignment with concatenation	p = 100; p += 'lbs'	100lbs
-=	Assignment with subtraction	p = 100; p -= 10	90
*=	Assignment with multiplication	p = 100; p *= 10	1000
/=	Assignment with division	p = 100; p /= 10	10
%=	Assignment with modulus	p = 100; p %= 10	0

Table 5-3   The Six JavaScript Assignment Operators

Operator	Description	Examples	Results
==	Is equal to	`100 == 10` `100 == '100'`	false true
!=	Is not equal to	`100 != 10` `100 != '100'`	true false
>	Is greater than	`100 > 10` `10 > 100`	true false
<	Is less than	`100 < 10` `10 < 100`	false true
>=	Is greater than or equal to	`100 >= 10` `100 >= 100`	true true
<=	Is less than or equal to	`100 <= 10` `100 <= 100`	false true
===	Is equal to and of the same type	`100 === '100'` `'100' === '100'`	false true
!==	Is not equal to or not of the same type	`100 !== '100'` `100 !== 100`	true false

Table 5-4 The Eight Comparison Operators in JavaScript

language is *weakly typed*, which means that it tries to be helpful and, if it can make sense of an unusual statement, it will return a result.

In the preceding example, JavaScript recognizes that `'1024'` is a number within a string and that, although it cannot multiply a string by a number, it can multiply two numbers. So, it first creates a copy of the string (which it converts to a number), and then performs the multiplication.

Therefore, in cases where you don't want this automatic variable type conversion, first check for a variable's type before applying an expression to it. For example, if `'1024'` happens to be the model name of a product, rather than a number, it will never make sense to multiply it by another number. There is more on this in the "Automatic Variable Typing" section, a little later in the chapter.

NOTE
The words `true` and `false` in JavaScript are actual keywords that represent the values they stand for. Therefore, the statement `(100 > 10) == true` is a valid statement, which itself evaluates to `true`.

Logical Operators
JavaScript provides three different logical operators that provide *and*, *or*, and *not* functionality to expressions. These are detailed in Table 5-5, along with a couple of examples for each, and the results of evaluating the examples.

Operator	Description	Examples	Results
&&	And	`a = 10; if (a > 5 && a < 15)` `a = 10; if (a == 10 && (a / 2) == 4)`	true false
||	Or	`a = 10; b = 12; if (a > 5 || b == 10)` `a = 10; if (a == 10 || (a / 2) == 4)`	true true
!	Not	`a = 10; if (!(a / 5) > 1)` `a = 10; if (!a > 5)`	true false

Table 5-5   The Three Logical Operators in JavaScript

Some languages allow the use of the words and, or, and not as operator names, but JavaScript supports only the &&, ||, and ! operator names. Using them, you can string expressions together to ask things like "if (this is true and that is not true)" or "if (this is false or that is true)" and so on.

The only operator you may have a little difficulty with is the ! operator, which simply turns a comparison on its head. For example, the following line will display an alert box with the string 'Hello':

```
a = 5; if (a == 5) alert('Hello')
```

However, the next line will not call up the alert at all:

```
a = 5; if !(a == 5) alert('Hello')
```

This is because the statement is equivalent to entering this:

```
a = 5; if (a != 5) alert('Hello')
```

Only by changing the initial assignment of the variable a to a value other than 5 can the alert box be displayed.

The Ternary Operator

There is a pair of JavaScript operators that takes three operands and is called (as a pair) the *ternary operator*. The primary ternary operator is the ? symbol, and the secondary ternary operator is the : symbol. Between them they are most useful for shortening pairs of comparison statements into single statements.

For example, the following pair of statements might comprise part of a stock reordering module:

```
if (apples > 24) alert('There are over two dozen apples')
else alert('It is time to restock on apples')
```

Using ternary syntax, this can be shortened to

```
apples > 24 ? alert('There are over two dozen apples') :
    alert('It is time to restock on apples')
```

In English (replacing the ? symbol with the word *then*, and the : with the word *otherwise*), what the code says to the JavaScript interpreter is "evaluate this expression *then* return this if the result is true *otherwise* return this."

In fact, using the power of the ternary operators, you can make an even simpler form of the statement that uses only one call to the `alert()` function, like this:

```
alert(apples > 24 ? 'There are over two dozen apples' :
    'It is time to restock on apples')
```

Automatic Variable Typing

Earlier in the chapter, I touched on the subject of variable typing when we looked at how a number can be multiplied with a string (as long as the string contains a number). The way this automatic typing works is that the type of a variable that is being assigned a value is determined only after JavaScript has decided what that type ought to be.

Knowing this, you can take control over the automatic typing when you need to. For example, you can ensure that a number, whether currently stored as either a number or a string, will be a string when assigned to a new variable, like this:

```
newvariable = oldvariable + ''
```

Likewise, you can ensure that a new variable will be a number with the following statement:

```
newvariable = oldvariable * 1
```

In the former case, all numbers will become strings (and all strings will stay strings) because of the forced string concatenation. In the latter case, all numbers will remain as numbers and all strings will be turned into numbers, by multiplying them by the value 1.

However, this will not work in the case of a string that doesn't contain a numeric value, in which case the new variable will be given the type NaN, which stands for Not a Number.

To help you write code that can decide what to do with particular variable types, you can always find out the type of a variable using the `typeof` operator, like this:

```
vartype = typeof varname
```

Here the variable `vartype` is assigned a string value containing the type of the variable `varname`. You can also use the keyword in conditional statements, like the following, which is a very useful test you can conduct to see if a variable has actually been defined yet:

```
if (typeof varname == 'undefined') alert('the variable is undefined')
```

NOTE

The types of variables supported by JavaScript are `boolean`, `number`, `string`, `function`, and `object`. Additionally, there are the pseudo types of NaN, which is returned when an arithmetic operation is attempted where one operand is not (and cannot be converted to) a number, and `undefined`, where a variable has not yet been assigned a value and therefore doesn't exist.

Operator Precedence

When evaluating an expression, JavaScript uses operator precedence to give higher priority to some operators over others. For example, the following expression, if evaluated without precedence, results in the value 10: (6 - 5 equals 1, then 1 * 7 equals 7, and finally 7 + 3 equals 10):

```
6 - 5 * 7 + 3
```

However, by convention, the multiplication symbol has a higher precedence than subtraction, and therefore in JavaScript the expression is calculated in this order: 5 * 7 equals 35, then 6 - 35 equals -29, then -29 + 3 equals -26—a quite different result.

If you actually want the first form of evaluation (from left to right only), then you need to use an operator with an even higher precedence (namely brackets), like this:

```
(6 - 5) * 7 + 3
```

In this case the brackets have the highest precedence, followed by the multiplication operator, and then the addition operator. Therefore, evaluation of this expression will take place from left to right.

Table 5-6 lists the operators available, in order of precedence from highest to lowest, and the type of operator.

For the sake of completeness, Table 5-6 lists some other operators that I haven't discussed, such as bitwise and shift operators. These are beyond the scope of this book, but they are included in the table for programmers who know other languages (where the precedence may be different) but are new to JavaScript.

Ask the Expert

Q: **Is there a better way to edit JavaScript source code than with a simple text editor?**

A: Software for writing program code has progressed in leaps and bounds in recent years. Text editors have been supplanted by powerful program editors that highlight your syntax using different colors, and that can quickly locate for you things like matching (and missing) brackets and braces, and so on.

My favorite is Notepad++ (Windows only: *notepad-plus.sourceforge.net*), but there are others worth looking at, including jEdit (Windows, Mac, and Linux: *jedit.org*) and Editra (Windows, Mac, and Linux: *editra.org*).

JavaScript Functions

JavaScript functions provide two main benefits. First, they make it easy for you to split a large program into smaller chunks, each with a specific task to accomplish. Second, they offer the ability to give variables local scope, which limits their application to just the current function.

Operator(s)	Types
`[] . new`	Member
`()`	Parentheses or function call
`++ --`	Increment / decrement
`+ - ~ ! typeof void delete`	Unary + / unary negation / bitwise not / logical not / `typeof` / `void` / `delete`
`* / %`	Multiplication / division / modulus
`+ -`	Addition / subtraction
`<< >> >>>`	Bitwise shift
`< > <= >=`	Relational
`== != === !==`	Equality
`&`	Bitwise and
`^`	Bitwise exclusive or
`|`	Bitwise or
`&&`	Logical and
`||`	Logical or
`? :`	Ternary conditional
`= += -= *= /= %= <<= >>= >>>= &= ^= |=`	Assignment
`,`	Separator

Table 5-6 The Precedence of JavaScript Operators from Highest to Lowest

The syntax of a function starts with the keyword `function`, which is followed by the name of the function and then a pair of brackets. Any arguments the function accepts are then listed within these brackets (separated by commas), as shown in the following function to convert Celsius temperatures to Fahrenheit:

```
function convertCtoF(temp)
{
   return temp * (9 / 5) + 32
}
```

The body of a function is enclosed within a pair of curly braces, and usually (but not always) the function will include one or more `return` keywords for returning values to the calling statement. The preceding example function works by taking the value passed to it and placing it into a new local variable called `temp`. Then this variable is multiplied by the fraction 9/5 and the value 32 is added—the equation for converting temperatures—and the result of this expression is then returned.

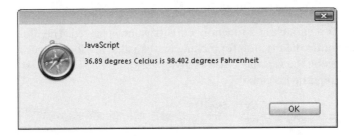

Figure 5-4 The result of converting 36.89 degrees Celsius to Fahrenheit

To use this function, you call it by passing a temperature to it to convert from Fahrenheit to Celsius, using code such as the following, which converts the Celsius value in the variable c to Fahrenheit, and places that value in the variable f—with the result of the conversion then displayed using an alert box, as shown in Figure 5-4:

```
c = 36.89
f = convertCtoF(c)
alert(c + ' degrees Celsius is ' + f + ' degrees Fahrenheit')
```

Global Variables

Variables that you create in the main body of your code (as opposed to those created within functions) have what is known as *global scope*. This means that their values can be accessed from any part of a program.

There is a problem with using global variables, though, in that (especially in larger programs) you can soon start to run out of short, self-explanatory variable names. The solution to this is to use local variables where you can.

Local Variables

Local variables are declared inside functions and their value is retained only during the current call to that function. To declare a variable as local, you precede it with the var keyword, like this:

```
var myLocalVariable
```

Or you can assign a value at the same time if you wish, like this:

```
var myLocalVariable = 42
```

If you leave out the var keyword inside a function, then it is assumed that the variable has been predefined (or is yet to be, but that's bad programming) and therefore that it has global scope—and that the function is simply being allowed to access it. Alternatively, if you use the var keyword outside of a function, then the keyword is ignored and the variable specified will be given global scope.

Function Arguments

When you pass a variable to a function, only its value is passed. Therefore, the variable name you provide within the function for picking up the value has local scope only. For example, in the following code the variable `fred` is given the value 17 and, because this happens outside of a function, its scope is global:

```
fred = 17;           alert(fred)
dosomething(fred);   alert(fred)

function dosomething(fred)
{
    fred += 24
}
```

To show the current value of `fred`, it is then passed to an `alert()` call, which dutifully displays its value of 17. Then the function `dosomething()` is called, passing `fred` as a value.

Within the function, the same variable name, `fred`, is then used for picking up the passed value. However, it is actually a totally different variable (even though it has the same name) because it has only local scope.

Therefore, when the local variable `fred` is incremented by a value of 24 and the function returns, the second call to `alert()` (again passing the global variable `fred`) still displays 17 for its value (and not 41), since the addition within the function happened only to a local variable with the name `fred`.

This illustrates one of the biggest benefits of local variables; you can reuse the same variable names over and over.

An Exception to Passing Variables to Functions by Value There is one exception to the rule that variables passed to functions have only their values passed, and that is that arrays are passed in their entirety. Even if you use a different name for an array argument within a function, any changes you make inside the function are made to the original array.

CAUTION

The fact that arrays are passed in their entirety (rather than by value) is an important point to remember because it catches out many programmers who are new to JavaScript and may (wrongly) believe they can manipulate the contents of the passed array without it affecting the contents of the original one.

Choosing a Naming Convention

In JavaScript, a common convention for the naming of variables and functions is to start the name with a lowercase letter and to then place the first letter of any following words in uppercase, so that `mylocalvariable` would be called `myLocalVariable`. The idea is to allow for faster visual recognition when viewing code.

Therefore, to enable global variables to be easily distinguished from local ones, I generally use only capital letters for global variables; so, using this naming style, the preceding example would look like the following, which is much clearer:

```
FRED = 17;              alert(FRED)
dosomething(FRED);  alert(FRED)

function dosomething(fred)
{
    fred += 24
}
```

Conditional Expressions

Using conditional expressions, you can control the flow of a program so that certain statements are executed only under certain conditions. There are a number of conditional expression statement types, including `if()`, `else`, and `switch()`.

The if() Statement

The `if()` statement asks a question and only executes the matching statement if the answer to the question is `true`. For example, the following code checks whether the variable `age` has a value between 13 and 19 inclusive and, if so, displays a message in an alert box:

```
if (age > 12 && age < 20)
{
    alert('You are a teenager.')
}
```

The question (or expression) part of the statement must be placed within brackets, but the curly braces are only required where there is more than one statement to execute, like this:

```
if (age > 12 && age < 20)
{
    message = 'You are a teenager.'
    alert(message)
}
```

Otherwise, for single statements, the braces can be omitted, as follows:

```
if (age > 12 && age < 20) alert('You are a teenager.')
```

The else Statement

The `else` statement allows you to provide an action for JavaScript to perform if the expression doesn't evaluate to `true`, like this:

```
if (age > 12 && age < 20) alert('You are a teenager.')
else alert('You are either a child or an adult.')
```

The else if() statement

If you wish you can continue to add `else` and `if()` statements together, like this:

```
if       (age < 13)             alert('You are a child.')
else if (age > 12 && age < 20) alert('You are a teenager.')
else if (age > 19 && age < 40) alert('You are a young adult.')
else if (age > 39 && age < 65) alert('You are middle aged.')
else                            alert('You are a senior citizen.')
```

Incidentally, there is a way you can use the structure of `if()` ... `else` statements to rewrite this code more efficiently, by checking for eldest age first and working backwards—avoiding the need to check the age twice in most statements, like this:

```
if       (age > 64) alert('You are a senior citizen.')
else if (age > 39) alert('You are a mature adult.')
else if (age > 19) alert('You are a young adult.')
else if (age > 12) alert('You are a teenager.')
else                alert('You are a child.')
```

The switch() Statement

Because chaining lots of `if()` and `else` statements together sometimes makes for cumbersome coding, the `switch()` statement has been provided as an easier alternative. Using it you can eliminate the need for `if()` and `else` statements when a group of discrete values requires testing.

For example, assume you have asked a user to enter one out of five possible values denoting their approximate age, out of `c` for child, `t` for teenager, `y` for young adult, `m` for mature adult, and `s` for senior citizen, and this value is now in the variable `key`.

You can then use code such as the following to decide what to display:

```
switch(key)
{
   case 's': alert('You are a senior citizen.'); break
   case 'm': alert('You are a mature adult.');   break
   case 'y': alert('You are a young adult.');    break
   case 't': alert('You are a teenager.');       break
   default:  alert('You are a child.')
}
```

Notice how the `if()` and `else` statements are replaced with `case` keywords, and that a `default` option is also available, which in this case always selects the child message.

Notice also how each statement (other than the last) has the keyword `break` following it. This tells the JavaScript interpreter to exit from the `switch()` statement and continue execution on the next line following it. Without it, each of the `alert()` calls following the first matching statement would also be made. However, the `default` case doesn't require a `break` statement in this case because there are no more lines of code below it within the `switch()` statement.

By the way, this example code can be further improved by reducing the five calls to alert() to a single instance, by introducing a new variable m, like this:

```
switch(key)
{
    case 's': m = 'You are a senior citizen.'; break
    case 'm': m = 'You are a mature adult.';   break
    case 'y': m = 'You are a young adult.';    break
    case 't': m = 'You are a teenager.';       break
    default:  m = 'You are a child.'
}
alert(m)
```

If you were going to use this code within a function, the only other change you might wish to make is to preface it with the following line, so that the variable name m can also be reused if required:

```
var m
```

Looping Sections of Code

Something computers are very good at is tirelessly repeating tasks over and over, and JavaScript supports this via while(), do ... while(), and for() loops, each of which offers a different way of managing looping program flow.

while() Loops

Using a while() statement, you can keep a loop going round and round until a chosen condition is no longer met. In fact, the loop will also begin looping only if the condition is already met, as in the following example, which sums all the numbers between 1 and 10:

```
p = 0
a = 1
while (a < 11) p += a++
alert(p)
```

I've made the contents of the while() expression a little more interesting to show the use of both the += and ++ operators. What is happening is that each time around the loop, the current value of the variable a is looked up and added to the variable p using the += operator. Then the ++ operator following the a variable increments it, ready for the next time around the loop.

When a reaches a value of 11, it no longer satisfies the condition that it should have a value less than 11, and so the loop is not reentered and execution flows straight to the following line, which displays the result 55 in an alert box.

If you need more than a single statement within a while() loop, then you must enclose the statements within curly brackets, as with this less concise version of the example:

```
p = 0
a = 1
while (a < 11)
```

```
{
    p += a
    ++a
}
alert(p)
```

do ... while() Loops

Sometimes you'll want a loop to execute at least once before testing for any conditions, and you can do this with a do ... while() statement. The following example reworks the preceding one to use this version of the while() loop:

```
p = 0
a = 1
do
{
    p += a
    ++a
} while (a < 11)
alert(p)
```

for() Loops

With a for() statement, you get a lot more control over your loops and don't have to set up so many variables in advance. For example, the following code replicates the functionality of the preceding examples using only a for() loop:

```
for (p = 0, a = 1 ; a < 11 ; ++a)
{
    p += a
}

alert(p)
```

Since this particular example contains only a single statement, you can omit the braces to really reduce the code's size, like this:

```
for (p = 0, a = 1 ; a < 11 ; ++a) p += a

alert(p)
```

Constructing a for() Loop

As you can see in the preceding example, for() loops comprise three parts separated with semicolons, as follows:

1. Initialization of variables—executed once only at the start

2. A condition test—tested before each loop

3. Code to execute after each loop

Within the first and last parts you may include as many statements as you like, separated by commas.

Here's how you would construct a typical `for()` loop:

1. Set up all the variables used within a loop with their required values in the first part.

2. Supply a condition that evaluates to `true` in order for the loop to occur.

3. Provide one or more statements to update variables before the next loop iteration—one of which generally will update one or more variables tested in the conditional part; otherwise the loop may never stop repeating.

Breaking Out of a for() Loop

Sometimes you will have several statements within a loop and may achieve the computation required by the loop early. In such cases, you can use the `break` keyword (the same one as used by the `switch()` statement) to stop looping and send program flow to the next line of code following the loop.

In the following example, an array called `haystack` is created and its 18th element (at offset 17) is assigned the string `"Needle"`. The loop then repeats until the needle is discovered, at which point an alert is displayed to note the discovery, and the `break` keyword is used to stop looping and send program flow to the line following the loop.

```
haystack      = []
haystack[17]  = "Needle"

for (j = 0 ; j < 20 ; ++j)
{
    document.write(j + ' ')

    if (haystack[j] == "Needle")
    {
        alert("Found at location " + j)
        break
    }
}
```

In this example, you see a new function call, `document.write()`. This is a built-in function that causes JavaScript to output the value passed into the portion of the web page where the JavaScript resides. The result of running this code is shown in Figure 5-5.

The continue Statement

Sometimes you won't want to break out of an entire loop, but instead skip further execution of the current iteration and move on to the next iteration. You do this by using the `continue` keyword, as in the following example, which picks a number at random between 0 and 99, and then lists any divisors the number has (as shown in Figure 5-6):

```
n = Math.floor(Math.random() * 100)
document.write(n + '<br /><br />')
```

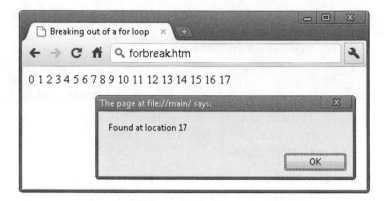

Figure 5-5 Breaking out of a for loop using the break keyword

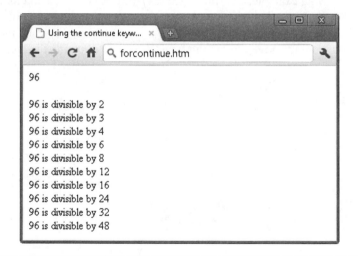

Figure 5-6 Using a continue statement to discover divisors of a number

```
for (j = 2 ; j < n / 2 + 1 ; ++j)
{
   if (n % j > 0) continue
   document.write(n + ' is divisible by ' + j + '<br />')
}
```

This code starts by assigning a random number between 0 and 99 to the variable n, which is then displayed. Then a for() loop begins, comprising the first part in which the variable j is given the value 2, the second part in which a conditional expression checks for j being less than n / 2 + 1 (the highest possible divisor of n), and the third part in which j is set to increment by 1 after each loop iteration.

Within the loop, whenever the value of n divided by j is not an integer (in other words, the modulus value is greater than 0), the continue statement is issued to quickly skip this loop iteration and move on to the next. This is because n is not exactly divisible by j, and since we don't want to waste any valuable processing time, the current iteration is skipped.

On the other hand, if n *is* exactly divisible by j, then the continue statement is not issued and, instead, a phrase is displayed detailing the discovered divisor.

Trapping and Displaying JavaScript Errors

When debugging JavaScript code on Internet Explorer and Firefox, you can make your life a little easier if you add the following code to the start of your programs:

```
window.onerror = function(message, file, line)
{
    alert('Error: ' + message + ', in\n' + file + ', at line: ' + line)
}
```

This catches all errors and then pops up an alert box that describes the error and tells you the file and line number where the error occurred, as shown in Figure 5-7, in which an error was caused by a mistake in the following statement (the final e has been left off the word write):

```
document.writ('Hello World')
```

Unfortunately, only Firefox and Internet Explorer support this feature. However, although iOS, Android, Safari, Chrome, and Opera make it a little harder than IE and Firefox do for you to be instantly informed of any errors, you can still be notified when an error occurs by using the following code (even if the filename and line number are not provided by it):

```
try
{
    // Place all your code
    // within this try section
}
catch(err) { alert(err) }
```

Just place all of your code inside the try section and any errors will be trapped and reported, as shown in the iPhone screen grab in Figure 5-8. Usually, you'll be able to locate the error quite quickly with a simple search on the string provided in the message.

CAUTION

Make sure you remove any debugging code from your web pages before you move them to a live, or production, web server.

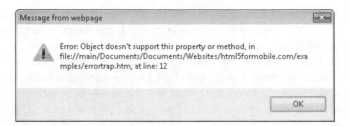

Figure 5-7 Catching an error using the `onerror` event

Figure 5-8 Catching an error on an iPhone using the `try` and `catch` statements

Summary

This chapter contains possibly the shortest introduction to JavaScript there can be, while still giving you a good grounding in the language. Don't worry if any aspects of it still seem unclear, because in the next chapter I'll start showing you how this all works in the real world, by manipulating HTML elements and utilizing CSS directly from JavaScript.

Chapter 6

Using JavaScript
with HTML5

Key Skills & Concepts

- Accessing the DOM from JavaScript

- Accessing CSS styles from JavaScript

- Accessing all instances of a class

- Drawing on the canvas

- Determining a user's location

- Managing local storage

The great thing about JavaScript is that it could have been designed purely as a stand-alone scripting language and it would still have been very useful. But the developers did something that would help form the future of the Web, which was to link it to the HTML Document Object Model (DOM).

Whenever you see something dynamic happening on a web page, such as an image popping up when you pass the mouse over a link, graphic images zooming out when you click them, or menus altering according to your selections, it is usually accomplished using JavaScript.

With JavaScript, you can do almost anything you like with a web page, such as easily add new paragraphs; change focus and select text; replace images; play sound effects, music, and videos; and much more. And when you add CSS to the mix, you can dynamically apply style changes to a page, completely changing the way it looks without altering the HTML.

Accessing the DOM from JavaScript

Consider the following example HTML web page, which has a `<head>` area with meta information and a title, and a `<body>` area with a link, a form, and an embedded image:

```html
<html>
   <head>
      <meta name='robots' content='index, follow' />
      <title>Hello</title>
   </head>
   <body>
      <a href='http://google.com'>Visit Google</a>
      <form id='login' method='post' action='program.php'>
         <input id='name' type='text' name='username' value='jane' />
         <input type='submit' />
      </form>
   <img src='/photos/family/auntmary.jpg' />
   </body>
</html>
```

Each of these elements can be accessed from JavaScript. For example, the document title can be read in the following way (which assigns the title contained in the HTML to the JavaScript variable `title`):

```
title = document.title
```

Or you can write to the property like this:

```
document.title = 'An example web page'
```

But in order to access most other object properties, you need to assign a name (referred to as an ID) to an object. For example, in the preceding form, once you have the `name` property of the `<input>` tag, you can find its current value (if any) in the following manner, which assigns the value to the variable `username`:

```
username = document.forms.login.name.value
```

The reason that `.value` is added after `.name` (but not after `.title` in the preceding example) is that `.title` is already a property, whereas `.name` is a form input object that itself has properties, including its value in `.value`.

Let's now add the following four lines of code before the closing `</body>` tag, and then load the preceding example into a browser:

```
<script>
    document.write(document.title)
    alert(document.forms.login.name.value)
</script>
```

The browser displays the word `Hello` (the value of `document.title`) underneath the input field, and then it displays the word `jane` (the current value of the input with the ID of name) in an alert box, as shown in Figure 6-1, which was created using the *javascriptexample .htm* file in the *examples.zip* file at *html5formobile.com.*

Accessing CSS Styles from JavaScript

Using JavaScript, you can also change on-the-fly many of the same styles you can define using CSS. This is possible because the CSS attributes are also DOM object properties. For example, as explained in Chapter 3, here's how you would use CSS to set an attribute for a particular ID (in this case called `under`):

```
#under { text-decoration:underline; }
```

Any text within the element that has an ID of `under` will now be underlined, and this element can also be accessed from JavaScript. So let's change it to another decoration type using this JavaScript statement:

```
document.getElementById('under').style.textDecoration = 'line-through'
```

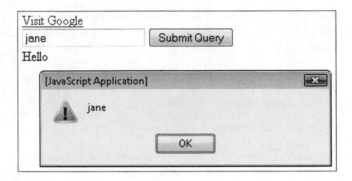

Figure 6-1   The result of loading the example HTML page into a browser

All text items within the object that has the ID of under will now be changed from underlined to line-through. To help make this clearer, the following example combines these two statements into a working HTML page, and the result of loading it into a browser is shown in Figure 6-2 (created with *javascriptcssexample.htm* from the *examples.zip* file):

```
<html>
    <head>
        <style>
            #under { text-decoration:underline; }
        </style>
    </head>
    <title>Hello World</title>
    <body>
        <div id='under'><h1>How are you?</h1></div>
        <div id='under'>A second line</div>
        <div id='under'>And a third</div>
        <script>
            document.getElementById('under').style.textDecoration =
                'line-through'
        </script>
    </body>
</html>
```

Straight away you can see from Figure 6-2 that the "How are you?" text has been changed to line-through, but take a look at the two lines underneath; they are both still underlined. The reason for this is that the same ID name was used multiple times, but JavaScript only acted on the first instance.

Although CSS may have allowed the use of an ID as if it were a class (which applies to a group of elements, rather than just one), JavaScript certainly doesn't; as soon as it finishes modifying the first instance it stops because it assumes that the job is now done. Therefore, the second and third lines are not changed by the script.

Figure 6-2 Using JavaScript to change an attribute from underline to line-through

Accessing Multiple Elements by Class

If you wish to modify all the elements in a class, you can do so from JavaScript, but it's a little more involved since it's necessary to walk through the DOM and search for all instances of the class. For example, assume we have replaced all the id assignments in the preceding example with class, as follows:

```
<div class='under'><h1>How are you?</h1></div>
<div class='under'>A second line</div>
<div class='under'>And a third</div>
```

It is now possible to modify the properties of all these elements from JavaScript using a simple loop, like this:

```
tags = document.getElementsByClassName('under')
for (j = 0 ; j < tags.length ; ++j)
   tags[j].style.textDecoration = 'line-through'
```

Here an array called tags is created and populated with all the elements that access the class under. Then a for() loop is used to iterate through the array and apply the line-through style to the text-decoration style property of each element (as shown in Figure 6-3, which was created with *javascriptcssexample2.htm* from the *examples.zip* file).

By the way, because there is only a single statement within the for() loop, I have not applied curly braces around the statement—but if there were two or more statements, then curly braces *would* be required around them.

CAUTION

When referring to a CSS property such as text-decoration from JavaScript, you must replace all instances of the - character followed by a lowercase letter with an uppercase letter, like this: textDecoration. Otherwise, JavaScript would interpret the - character as a subtraction operator.

How are you?

~~A second line~~

~~And a third~~

Figure 6-3 Using JavaScript to access all instances of a class

Canvas

The <canvas> element is a huge leap forward for HTML because it provides a standard drawing area that JavaScript can access, meaning you no longer have to rely on server-side programs to generate images. In fact, it's powerful enough to be used as an alternative to the popular Adobe Flash plug-in, and becomes essential for creating decent animation of platforms that don't support Flash, such as iOS and early versions of Android.

The <canvas> tag supports only two attributes: width and height. By default, these are 300 by 150 pixels, but you can choose any other dimensions; for example, the following defines a 320×240-pixel canvas:

```
<canvas id='example' width='320' height='240'></canvas>
```

It is important that you provide a unique ID for each canvas so that JavaScript will have a means to easily reference them. In the preceding example I chose the ID example.

On browsers that don't support a canvas, you can place alternate HTML to be displayed within the opening and closing tags, like this:

```
<canvas id='example' width='320' height='240'>
   <h1>HTML5 Canvas</h1>
   This web page uses the HTML5 canvas element, which is available
   on most modern browsers. If you wish to view this page at its
   best please upgrade your browser to the most recent version.
</canvas>
```

Accessing a Canvas from JavaScript

In order to write to and read from a canvas, you must first use the getContext() function (or *method*, as functions in JavaScript are also known). This context is used by all methods that access the canvas.

For now only the 2d rendering context is available, but in the future a number of other contexts may also be supported (most likely starting with 3d). Anyway, to create a 2d context, you must first create an object to access the canvas, in the following way, which uses the ID example from the preceding example HTML:

```
canvas = document.getElementById('example')
```

Once you have the canvas object, you can then create a context from it, like this:

```
context = canvas.getContext('2d')
```

You can now use all the methods detailed in the remainder of the section on the <canvas> tag by preceding them with this context object, like the following, which creates a filled rectangle with its top-left corner at location 10,10, and with both a width and height of 100 pixels (as shown in Figure 6-4, created with *canvas.htm* from the *examples.zip* file):

```
canvas.style.background = '#ddd'
context.fillRect(10, 10, 100, 100)
```

The first line sets the background of the canvas to light gray, and the second draws the rectangle on it. Since no color has been specified, the rectangle is black (the default).

Converting a Canvas to an Image

It is not possible for users to right-click and copy or drag-and-drop a canvas in the same way as an image, but you can create a copy of the canvas as an image using the toDataURL()

Figure 6-4   Drawing a filled-in rectangle on a canvas

method. To show how this works, assume that, in addition to the preceding example code, you have created an image in the HTML, like this:

```
<img id='image' />
```

Notice that no `src` attribute has been applied because the source is going to be supplied from the canvas, like this:

```
image     = document.getElementById('image')
image.src = canvas.toDataURL()
```

The first statement creates the object `image` for manipulating the attributes of the image, and the second extracts the canvas data and places it into the `src` attribute of `image`.

Because quite a number of different lines of HTML and JavaScript have been covered already in this section, it makes sense at this point to place them all into a single web page and see them working together, like this (available as *todaturl.htm* in the *examples.zip* file at *html5formobile.com*):

```
<!-- todataurl.htm -->
<html>
    <head>
        <title>toDataURL() Example</title>
    </head>
    <body>
        <canvas id='example' width='320' height='240'>
            <h1>HTML5 Canvas</h1>
            This web page uses the HTML5 canvas element, which is available
            on most modern browsers. If you wish to view this page at its
            best please upgrade your browser to the most recent version.
        </canvas>

        <img id='image' />

        <script>
            canvas = document.getElementById('example')
            canvas.style.background = '#ddd'

            context = canvas.getContext('2d')
            context.fillRect(10, 10, 100, 100)

            image     = document.getElementById('image')
            image.src = canvas.toDataURL()
        </script>
    </body>
</html>
```

Quickly scanning through this, the code begins with placing a title in the `<head>` section, and then the first item in the `<body>` is a `<canvas>` tag, along with some alternate HTML for browsers that don't recognize it. Following this is an empty `<img>` tag with the ID `image`.

Next comes the JavaScript, within which the object `canvas` is created for accessing the canvas, and the background of the canvas is set to the color `#ddd`. Then the object `context` is created for accessing the canvas using `2d` rendering, after which a 100×100-pixel rectangle is drawn, with its top-left corner at location 10,10. Finally, the object `image` is created for accessing the `<img>` tag, and its `src` attribute is assigned an image constructed from the contents of the canvas, which is immediately displayed.

The result of loading the example into a browser looks like Figure 6-5, and it is now possible to drag-and-drop the right-hand image to the desktop, or right-click and copy it.

NOTE

Although the background color of the canvas is set to `#ddd` in the preceding example (as is clearly seen in Figure 6-4), it is *not* part of the canvas, as shown by the rightmost image in Figure 6-5, where the background color does not appear. Rather, the background color is simply a style of the `<canvas>` element—which will also be applied to the alternative HTML if the canvas element is not recognized by a browser. The background color is simply a style applied *under* the canvas, and not as a part of the canvas.

Choosing the Image Type to Create

If an optional `imagetype` argument is supplied to the `toDataURL()` method, it defines the type of image to return, which can be either `image/png` (the default) or `image/jpeg`. Possibly other image formats will also be available in the future.

NOTE

Using image types other than the default (such as `image/jpeg`) currently appears to work only with WebKit browsers such as Safari, Chrome, and iOS. Android doesn't appear to support the `toDataURL()` function at all.

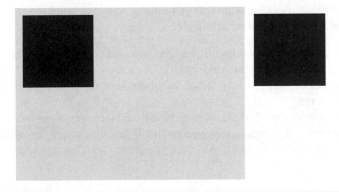

Figure 6-5 Copying the contents of a canvas to an image

Where the `imagetype` argument is supplied, subsequent arguments may also be passed. For example, if `imagetype` has a value of `image/jpeg`, an optional second argument can be a floating-point value between 0.0 and 1.0, representing the required quality level between lowest quality/most compression, and highest quality/least compression.

Following are two example statements that use this method for returning the canvas as a PNG, and then as a JPEG image:

```
dataurl = canvas.toDataURL()                  // Default PNG image
dataurl = canvas.toDataURL('image/jpeg', 1) // Highest quality JPEG
image
```

CAUTION

Remember that the `canvas` object is used by the `toDataURL()` method, *not* the `context` object. This is because the latter is for applying changes to the canvas using the context rendering assigned, while the former refers to the canvas object itself.

The string value returned by `toDataURL()` can be assigned to the `src` attribute of an image (as you've already seen), or given to the `innerHTML` property of an object (which contains all the HTML that appears within the tags of an element), so that the string data can be viewed as text, as shown here (and used in the file *todataurl2.html* in the *examples.zip* file):

```
<div id='mydiv'></div>

<script>
    element          = document.getElementById('mydiv')
    element.innerHTML = canvas.toDataURL()
</script>
```

Ask the Expert

Q: How does this supplying of an image to the `<img>` tag work—I thought you could only use a URL for the `src` attribute?

A: The `toDataURL()` method returns a long string of alphanumeric characters containing an image created from the canvas, prefaced with the URL type of `data:`. Your browser understands to display the data embedded in this kind of URL, rather than attempt to load in an image.

If you were to view the URL generated, it would look something like the following truncated string, only much longer, and varying in length according to the image size:
`data:image/png;base64,iVBORw0KGgoAAAANSUhEUgAAAUAAAADwCAYA...`

Managing Rectangles

You've already seen the `fillRect()` method used to create a black square, but there are also two other methods you can use to manage rectangles: `clearRect()`, which creates a clear rectangle, and `strokeRect()`, which creates a bordered rectangle.

clearRect(x, y, width, height)

This method creates a rectangular area on the canvas of width `width` and height `height`, with its top-left corner located at the position x,y, using transparent black. This means that all the RGBA (red, green, blue, and alpha transparency) values of a pixel are set to 0.

You use the method like this:

```
context.clearRect(10, 10, 100, 100)
```

The cleared area will be stripped of all color, leaving only any underlying background color that may have been applied to the `<canvas>` tag.

fillRect(x, y, width, height)

This method creates a filled rectangle of width `width` and height `height`, with its top-left corner located at the position x,y. The default color is black but can be changed using the `fillStyle` attribute to another solid color or gradient (see the upcoming section "Colors, Gradients, and Patterns").

Here's an example of a statement using this method:

```
context.fillRect(10, 10, 100, 100)
```

strokeRect(x, y, width, height)

With this method, you can draw the outline of a rectangle of width `width` and height `height`, with its top-left corner located at the position x,y, without modifying anything within it. The outline uses the current `strokeStyle`, `lineWidth`, `lineJoin`, and `miterLimit` properties, which are detailed later in the chapter, starting with `strokeStyle` in the "Colors, Gradients, and Patterns" section.

Here's an example of a statement using this method:

```
context.strokeRect(10, 10, 100, 100)
```

Combining the Three Rectangle Methods

To illustrate how these methods can be used, the following example combines one call to each, the result of which can be seen in Figure 6-6 (created with *rectangles.htm* in the *examples.zip* file):

```
context.fillRect(10,    10, 150, 220)
context.clearRect(20,    20, 130, 130)
context.strokeRect(170, 10, 140, 140)
```

Figure 6-6 Applying the three different types of rectangles to a canvas

The first statement creates a tall, black, filled rectangle in the left half of the canvas. Then the second statement draws a clear square in the top two-thirds or so of the dark rectangle. The third statement then draws another square on the right side of the canvas, but this time with only an outline.

Colors, Gradients, and Patterns

There are a few different ways you can add color to a canvas using the `fillStyle` and `strokeStyle` properties. For example, to change the color of fill operations, you need to specify the fill style to use, which can be any of the following:

- A color specified either by name (such as `'red'`) or by using a color string (such as `'#ff0000'`)

- A gradient created with either the `createLinearGradient()` or `createRadialGradiant()` method

- A repeating pattern created using the `createPattern()` method

- A nonrepeating pattern created using the `createPattern()` method

Creating a Fill Color

To specify a solid fill color, you can use statements such as the following:

```
context.fillStyle = 'blue'
context.fillStyle = '#0000ff'
```

The short versions of color numbers are also supported, like this:

```
context.fillStyle = '#00f'
```

Whichever means you use to specify it, the color selected will then be applied to any method that uses a fill operation, such as `fillRect()` and `fillText()`.

Creating Linear Gradients

To create a linear gradient, you need to specify the colors to use and the positions at which they should change. For example, in the following statement the gradient is set to start at the location 0,0 and end at 0,100:

```
gradient = context.createLinearGradient(0, 0, 0, 100)
```

Because the x position doesn't change (it stays at 0), this gradient will flow vertically from the top of the canvas to 100 pixels down. Only the shape to be filled will display the gradient; this statement simply sets up its bounds.

You can make a gradient flow from any location to any other in a canvas, which means that the direction of flow can be at any angle you choose. For example, this statement will flow the gradient diagonally down and to the right:

```
gradient = context.createLinearGradient(0, 0, 100, 100)
```

Having specified where in the canvas the gradient should be applied (and in which direction), the next task is to assign the colors to be used. At the minimum you should enter a start and an end color, as follows—in which the first argument is the percentage position through the gradient that the color should appear (which should be a floating-point value between 0.0 and 1.0), and the second argument is the color for that position in the gradient:

```
gradient.addColorStop(0, '#fff')
gradient.addColorStop(1, '#000')
```

The first line sets up the initial color at the 0 percent position to `#fff` (white), and the final color at the 100 percent position to `#000` (black). This will cause a linear gradient of white through to black, from the gradient start to its end. However, you can use as many colors and shades as you like in a gradient, so, for example, the following statements will create a rainbow effect, smoothly changing from color to color, as shown in the bottom-right box of Figure 6-7 (created with *lineargradient.htm* in the *examples.zip* file):

```
gradient.addColorStop(0.00, '#f00')
gradient.addColorStop(0.16, '#fa0')
gradient.addColorStop(0.33, '#ff0')
gradient.addColorStop(0.50, '#080')
gradient.addColorStop(0.66, '#00f')
gradient.addColorStop(0.83, '#508')
gradient.addColorStop(1.00, '#e8e')
```

Figure 6-7 A variety of different linear gradient effects

All that's now left to do is to apply the gradient to the `fillStyle` property and perform the fill using code such as the following, which creates a 100×100-pixel rectangle containing the gradient, putting it in the top-left corner of the canvas:

```
context.fillStyle = gradient
context.fillRect(0, 0, 100, 100)
```

To show different types of linear gradients in action, here is the code used to create Figure 6-7, on the same 320×240 canvas used by the preceding examples:

```
canvas = document.getElementById('example')
canvas.style.background = '#ddd'
context = canvas.getContext('2d')

gradient = context.createLinearGradient(70, 10, 70, 115)
gradient.addColorStop(0, '#fff')
gradient.addColorStop(1, '#000')
context.fillStyle = gradient
context.fillRect(10, 10, 145, 105)

gradient = context.createLinearGradient(10, 125, 145, 230)
gradient.addColorStop(0, '#fff')
gradient.addColorStop(1, '#000')
context.fillStyle = gradient
context.fillRect(10, 125, 145, 105)

gradient = context.createLinearGradient(165, 70, 310, 70)
```

```
gradient.addColorStop(0, '#fff')
gradient.addColorStop(1, '#000')
context.fillStyle = gradient
context.fillRect(165, 10, 145, 105)

gradient = context.createLinearGradient(165, 230, 310, 125)
gradient.addColorStop(0.00, 'red')
gradient.addColorStop(0.16, 'orange')
gradient.addColorStop(0.33, 'yellow')
gradient.addColorStop(0.50, 'green')
gradient.addColorStop(0.66, 'blue')
gradient.addColorStop(0.83, 'indigo')
gradient.addColorStop(1.00, 'violet')
context.fillStyle = gradient
context.fillRect(165, 125, 145, 105)
```

The first three lines set up the canvas and context objects. Make a note of this first section of code because it is used by all the remaining examples, and therefore will not be shown again. Following these are four sections of code for creating the four gradients shown in Figure 6-7.

The first section creates a vertical gradient flowing down the box. The coordinates used by the `createLinearGradient()` method ensure that the gradient starts at the center of the top edge of the first box and flows to the center of its bottom edge. If I had used the left of the top edge and right of the bottom edge, for example, then the gradient would flow from top left to bottom right, as has happened in the box just below it, at the bottom left of Figure 6-7.

The third box (at the top right of the figure) shows a horizontal gradient flowing from the center of its left edge to the center of its right edge, and the final box (at the bottom right of the figure) shows a gradient flowing from the bottom of its left edge to the top of its right edge. The gradient in this box uses rainbow colors, rather than the simple white to black employed for the other boxes.

Creating a Radial Gradient

Radial gradients can be created in a similar manner, but two additional arguments are required for specifying the start and end radius of the circle. In other words, you must supply the initial center location of the circle and its radius, followed by the final center location and its radius. For example, by swapping this line (from the preceding example),

```
gradient = context.createLinearGradient(70, 10, 70, 115)
```

with the following line,

```
gradient = context.createRadialGradient(82, 62, 0, 82, 62, 70)
```

the top-left box in Figure 6-7 becomes the top-left box in Figure 6-8 (created with *radialgradient.htm* in the *examples.zip* file).

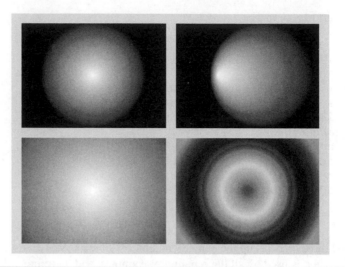

Figure 6-8 A variety of different radial gradient effects

The only differences are that the createRadialGradient() method has been used instead of createLinearGradient(), the x and y coordinates chosen are those of the center of the box, and the two radii are 0 pixels wide for the initial radius and 70 pixels wide for the final radius.

Similarly, the bottom-left box in Figure 6-8 uses the same code as the preceding example, except that the createRadialGradient() is used, like this:

```
gradient = context.createRadialGradient(82, 177, 0, 82, 177, 150)
```

Here the circle is also centered in the middle of the box, and the initial radius is also 0 pixels. However, the final radius is now 150 pixels and, because it is much further out, the box shows only the inner portion of the gradient.

The top-right box in Figure 6-8 is almost the same as the top-left one, but it uses different start and end positions for the center of the circle so that the original location is shifted to the left, and the final one is shifted to the right, achieving a sort of spotlight effect. The code used to create it is

```
gradient = context.createLinearGradient(165, 70, 310, 70)
```

The final box (at the bottom right) is similar to the first one (at the top left), except that a rainbow gradient has been applied instead of simple white to black. It was created using this statement:

```
gradient = context.createRadialGradient(237, 177, 0, 237, 177, 80)
```

All the other lines in the example file in the preceding linear gradient section remain the same.

Creating a Pattern

In addition to employing solid and gradient fills, you can also use patterns, which can either repeat or be displayed only once (in a similar fashion to background images). To do this, you supply an image and the type of repetition required to the `createPattern()` method, like this:

```
<p>Image: pattern.gif (100 x 59 pixels)</p>
<img src='pattern.gif' />

<p>Canvas (150 x 150 pixels)</p>
<canvas id='example' width='150' height='150'></canvas>

<script>
   image          = new Image()
   image.src      = 'pattern.gif'
   image.onload   = function()
   {
      pattern = context.createPattern(image, 'repeat')
      context.fillStyle = pattern
      context.fillRect(0, 0, 150, 150)
   }
</script>
```

In this example, a 100×59-pixel image is displayed at the top of the page, then a canvas of 150×150 pixels is created, within which a filled rectangle is placed with the same dimensions as the canvas, and with its fill style set to the pattern created by the following line:

```
pattern = context.createPattern(image, 'repeat')
```

The image is used only after it has been loaded in; otherwise, it might not always display on all browsers due to the code potentially running before the image is available to be accessed. To achieve this timing, the `onload` event of the image object has an anonymous, inline function attached to it, in which the code to use the image has been placed.

The `onload` event of any object is triggered as soon as that object is fully loaded and ready to be accessed. This code could equally have attached to the `window.onload` event (instead of `image.onload`), since this event is triggered only when all objects have been loaded.

As you can see in Figure 6-9 (created with *patterns.htm* in the *examples.zip* file), by passing the argument `repeat` to the function, the image on the left has repeated in both the horizontal and vertical directions in the canvas on the right.

You can also choose how (or whether) the image should repeat, by using the argument `repeat-x` to repeat only horizontally, `repeat-y` to repeat only vertically, or `no-repeat` to prevent any repetition.

Figure 6-9   The pattern image and how it appears when repeated in a fill function

Once you have created a pattern, you can also use it as the fill pattern for any functions that support fills, such as `fillText()` (see the next section), as shown in Figure 6-10 (created with *patterns2.htm* in the *examples.zip* file).

Writing Text

Before you write any text to a canvas, you need to choose the font to use and its size, like this:

```
context.font = '12px, Times'
```

You can also decide the type of alignment required, `start`, `end`, `left`, `right`, or `center`, like this:

```
context.textAlign = 'center'
```

When you are ready to write your text, you can use the `fillText()` function to place it on the canvas using whichever fill style has been assigned, out of a solid color, gradient, or pattern. The default is always a solid-black fill. To write the text, you use a statement such as the following, which places the text at the top left of the canvas, and allows it a maximum width of 200 pixels:

```
fillText('Text string', 0, 0, 200)
```

The text will then be displayed according to the text alignment used.

You can also write text to a canvas using the `strokeText()` method, which displays it in outline form. This function uses the value in the `strokeStyle` property to decide how to display the text, and the value may be a solid color, a gradient, or a pattern. Figure 6-11 (created with *stroketext.htm* in the *examples.zip* file) shows some text displayed in a 5-pixel, solid-red stroke.

Figure 6-10   Using the pattern fill on text

Figure 6-11   Writing text to a canvas using the `strokeText()` method

The following statements were used to draw this text:

```
context.lineWidth    = 5
context.textBaseline = 'top'
context.strokeStyle  = 'red'
context.font         = '150px Arial'
context.strokeText('Hello!', 0, 0)
```

The first line sets the width of the stroke by changing the `lineWidth` property, the second line tells the browser to use the top of the text for vertical alignment using the `textBaseline` property, the third line selects a color of `red` for the stroke using the `strokeStyle` property, the fourth line assigns a font and size using the `font` property, and the final line displays the text at the top left of the canvas using the `strokeText()` method.

The `lineWidth` property can be used by any function that draws lines (see the following section). It can be any positive floating-point value and has a default of 1 pixel.

The `textBaseline` property tells the browser where to align the text relative to the coordinates supplied to it, out of the following:

- **top**   Aligns to the top of the text
- **middle**   Aligns to the middle of the text

- **alphabetic**   Aligns to the alphabetic baseline of the text
- **bottom**   Aligns to the bottom of the font

Determining the Text Width

Sometimes you need to know how wide some text will be in order to best position it. To find out this value, set all the properties as you would before writing the text, and then issue statements such as the following:

```
metrics = context.measureText('Hello!')
alert('Text width: ' + metrics.width + ' pixels')
```

The `measureText()` function is a method that returns information (or *metrics*) about the text, which it places in the object it returns. In the case of the preceding code, this is assigned to the `metrics` object. It has only one value (currently), which is the `width` property, and this is what is displayed by the call to `alert()`, as shown in Figure 6-12—of course, you will probably use this value constructively rather than simply display it in an alert box.

Lines and Paths

When drawing lines, there are four styles you can apply: `lineWidth`, `lineCap`, `lineJoin`, and `miterLimit`. Between them you can create almost any kind of line and line join you need. You've already seen the `lineWidth` property in the preceding example. It takes a positive floating-point value and has a default width of 1 pixel.

With the `lineCap` property, you can choose how the ends of lines should appear, out of the values `butt` (the default), `round`, and `square`, while the `lineJoin` property can be any of `round`, `bevel`, or `miter` (the default).

In Figure 6-13 (created with *lines.htm* in the *examples.zip* file) the three horizontal lines on the left were drawn in order from top to bottom using `lineCap` properties of `butt`, `round`, and `square`, respectively, while the three chevrons to the right were each drawn in order from top to bottom using `lineJoin` properties of `round`, `bevel`, and `miter`.

In the left half of Figure 6-13, thin vertical lines are placed behind the thick horizontal ones to show where the default start and end of each line would be without modifying the

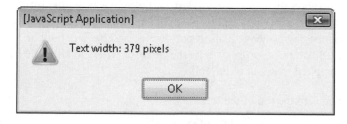

Figure 6-12   Displaying the width of some text using an alert box

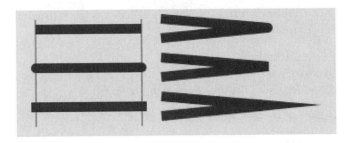

Figure 6-13   An assortment of line and corner styles

lineCap property. On the right of the figure, for the bottom chevron it was necessary to also apply a miterLimit property value sufficiently large to allow the miter to extend all the way to its natural point. Without this setting, the bottom chevron would look like the middle one. The miter length is the distance from the point at which two lines meet to the point at which two lines drawn along the outer edges of each line would meet. If this value is greater than miterLimit, then the miter is not drawn. The default value of miterLimit is 10 pixels.

By applying different values for the lineCap, lineJoin, lineWidth, and miterLimit properties, you can achieve a wide variety of line and corner styles.

Drawing Lines

To draw the lines shown in Figure 6-13, a number of properties and methods have been brought together. For example, the top horizontal line uses this code:

```
context.lineCap = 'butt'
context.beginPath()
context.moveTo(20, 20)
context.lineTo(130, 20)
context.stroke()
context.closePath()
```

In the first line, the lineCap property is given the value butt. If this is the first line being drawn, setting the property is not necessary because butt is the default value for the property. However, it's a good idea to get into the habit of explicitly setting the property value so that any prior values are overridden. It also means you can copy and/or move the code elsewhere in a program and it will still draw correctly.

The remaining lines start with a call to beginPath() and end with a call to closePath(). These methods tell the browser where the start and end of a path are. Between them, there are three statements. The first, moveTo(), sets the drawing position to the location 20,20. Imagine this call as moving an imaginary pen to that point on the canvas. Then the lineTo() method is called, which causes the imaginary pen to draw a line all the way to the location 130,20. However, at the moment the line is only notional, and will be drawn only when the `stroke()` method is called—its job is to actually apply all the `moveTo()` and `lineTo()` calls.

Connecting Lines Together

To join lines together you simply issue consecutive `lineTo()` statements, as with the following code, which draws the top chevron in Figure 6-13:

```
context.lineJoin = 'round'
context.beginPath()
context.moveTo(150, 10)
context.lineTo(260, 20)
context.lineTo(150, 30)
context.stroke()
context.closePath()
```

In this example, the `lineJoin` property is set to `round`, and instead of a single call to the `lineTo()` method, there are two calls. Between them they draw a diagonal line down and to the right, and then another down and to the left, and where they connect the corner has been rounded.

Using Paths to Draw

In addition to the lines and corners covered in the preceding section, you can use paths to draw many different shapes using a number of additional methods such as `fill()`, `stroke()` (see the preceding section), and `clip()`, plus several others.

Filling in a Shape

You can fill even the most complex shape by first using the `moveTo()` and `lineTo()` methods to "draw" the outline. As you'll recall, the result of calling these functions is displayed only after an action function such as `stroke()` is called. In the case of filling in a shape, the action command to use is `fill()`.

In Figure 6-14 (created with *pathfill.htm* in the *examples.zip* file) an irregular shape has been outlined and then filled using a radial gradient. The code that does this is as follows (and the gradient used is the one from the "Creating Linear Gradients" section earlier in this chapter):

```
context.beginPath()
context.moveTo(10,  10)
context.lineTo(70, 140)
context.lineTo(90,  70)
context.lineTo(30, 140)
context.lineTo(70, 110)
context.lineTo(140, 70)
context.lineTo(90,  30)
context.lineTo(10,  10)
context.fill()
context.closePath()
```

Figure 6-14   Filling an irregular shape using a radial gradient

The code is quite straightforward. Within the `beginPath()` and `closePath()` methods there is a single call to `moveTo()`, followed by seven calls to `lineTo()` to draw the outline, followed by a single call to `fill()` to fill in the shape using whatever value has been assigned to the `fillStyle` property, out of a color, gradient, or pattern.

The `fill()` method is smart enough that you can even go back on yourself and cross over previously defined lines when issuing `lineTo()` calls, and `fill()` will fill in only those sections that are contained within the outer perimeter of the shape.

NOTE
If you create a screen grab of a canvas on which you have drawn and then zoom the image in using a graphics program, you'll notice that everything is neatly anti-aliased; edges and diagonal lines are smoothed by placing colors of varying lightness and shades along them to match the underlying color. Using this technique, the drawings you create look cleaner, without the appearance of jagged edges.

Determining Whether a Point Is in the Path
If you need to know whether or not a particular location is in the current path, you can query the `isPointInPath()` method as shown in the following example, which tests the path for location 23,65 and assigns either `true` or `false` to the variable `pointisin`, depending on the result returned:

```
pointisin = isPointInPath(23, 65)
```

Constraining the Drawing Area
Just as with any good graphics program, you can create an area in a canvas outside of which all drawing commands are ignored. For example, on the left side of Figure 6-15 (created with *clip.htm* in the *examples.zip* file), a zigzag line has been drawn from the top to the bottom

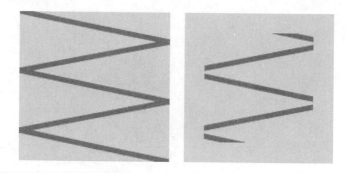

Figure 6-15 A zigzag line drawn without and then with a clipped canvas area

of the canvas, but on the right, a clipped area has been created within the canvas, outside of which the zigzag lines are not drawn.

Here's the code that was used to create the right half of Figure 6-15:

```
context.rect(20,  20, 110, 110)
context.clip()

context.lineWidth   = 5
context.strokeStyle = 'green'

context.beginPath()
context.moveTo(0,      0)
context.lineTo(150,   30)
context.lineTo(0,     60)
context.lineTo(150,   90)
context.lineTo(0,    120)
context.lineTo(150, 150)
context.stroke()
context.closePath()
```

The second pair of lines sets a line width of 5 pixels and the color green, and then the third group of lines draws a zigzag line from the top to the bottom of the screen. But because the first two lines define a rectangle and then issue a call to the `clip()` method, only the area within the clipped area is drawn on.

The `rect()` method is the quick way to define a rectangular area of the canvas, and the two lines used at the start of this example are equivalent to the following, longer-winded section of code:

```
context.beginPath()
context.moveTo(20,   20)
context.lineTo(130,  20)
```

```
context.lineTo(130, 130)
context.lineTo(20,   20)
context.clip()
context.closePath()
```

Drawing Curves

HTML5 supplies some quite-complex curve-drawing functions, such as `quadraticCurveTo()`, which draws a Bézier curve that looks like the center of it has been pulled by some unseen force. For example, in Figure 6-16 (created with *quadcurve.htm* in the *examples.zip* file) a line has been drawn starting at halfway down the left side of the canvas and moving all the way to the bottom right. However, an "attractor" (known as a Bézier control point) has been placed at the top right of the canvas, which pulls the line into a curve.

Here's the code that created Figure 6-16:

```
context.moveTo(0, 75)
context.quadraticCurveTo(150, 0, 150, 150)
context.stroke()
```

The first line moves the drawing start position to halfway down the left of a 150×150-pixel canvas. The next line draws a curve from there to the bottom right (the last two arguments of the method), using a control point located at the top right of the canvas (the method's first two arguments).

You can have even more fun with curves by using the `bezierCurveTo()` function, which uses an additional control point, as shown in Figure 6-17 (drawn on another 150×150-pixel canvas, and created with *beziercurve.htm* in the *examples.zip* file).

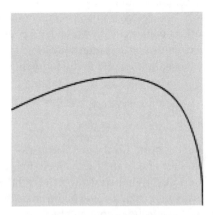

Figure 6-16 A quadratic curve created using a start point, an "attractor," and an end point

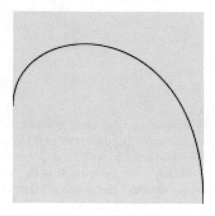

Figure 6-17 A Bézier curve created using a start point, two "attractors," and an end point

This is the code that was used to create Figure 6-17:

```
context.moveTo(0, 75)
context.bezierCurveTo(0, 0, 150, 0, 150, 150)
context.stroke()
```

The difference here is that the first *two* pairs of arguments to the `bezierCurveTo()` method are "attractors" (or Bézier control points), so the curve is pulled both to the top left and to the top right of the canvas.

Drawing Arcs

You can draw an arc (a section from the circumference of a circle) by supplying two locations representing tangents on the circle's circumference that intersect with the current path point.

For example, in Figure 6-18 (created with *arcto.htm* in the *examples.zip* file) two tangents are shown with straight lines, and an arc is drawn under the tangents using a thicker line, showing the portion of the circumference it represents.

To do this, the `arcTo()` method is used in the following way:

```
context.moveTo(0, 75)
context.arcTo(75, 30, 150, 75, 150)
context.stroke()
```

The first line moves the start point for the arc to halfway down the left edge of the canvas. Then the second line declares the end of the first tangent line at location 75,30, and the second tangent line ends at location 150,75—halfway down the right canvas edge.

Using these two imaginary tangents, a curve is drawn such that if it were turned into a complete circle, and the two tangent lines continued for an equal length in the other directions, then the two lines would rest on the circle in such a way that a line drawn from where each tangent touches the circle to the circle's center would be at right angles to the tangent line.

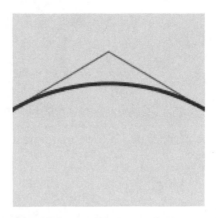

Figure 6-18   An arc created using a pair of tangents

Drawing Circles

Another way you can create an arc, or even a circle (which is an arc of 360 degrees), is with the `arc()` method, as shown in Figure 6-19 (created with *arc.htm* in the *examples.zip* file), in which a semicircle has been drawn on the left and in the middle and a circle has been drawn on the right.

The following statement was used to create the first semicircle in Figure 6-19:

```
context.arc(75, 75, 74, 0, Math.PI, false)
```

This tells the browser to locate the center of a circle at position 75,75 with a radius of 74 pixels, starting at the 3 o'clock position (as defined by the start angle value in radians of 0). The value for the end angle in radians of π (`Math.PI`) is then used to define a half circle. If the value were `Math.PI / 2`, then a quarter circle would be drawn instead, or if it were `Math.PI / 180`, then an arc of only a single degree would be drawn.

The final argument of `false` causes the arc to be drawn in a clockwise direction. If this value were `true`, then the arc would be drawn in a counterclockwise direction. Therefore, to create the second semicircle in Figure 6-19, only the value `false` in the preceding statement is changed (to `true`), like this:

```
context.arc(75, 75, 74, 0, Math.PI, true)
```

And to obtain the completed circle, it is simply a matter of supplying a value of `Math.PI * 2` for the ending angle, instead of simply `Math.PI`, like this:

```
context.arc(75, 75, 74, 0, Math.PI * 2, true)
```

Figure 6-19 Drawing two semicircles and a circle using the `arc()` method

Ask the Expert

Q: Why are you using the value of π here, and what are radians anyway?

A: The π (Pi) symbol has a value of approximately 3.1416. It represents the number of times the length of a circle's diameter fits into its circumference.

The `arc()` method requires the start and end angles to be supplied to it in radians (rather than the more commonly known degrees), and the value of a radian is `180 / π`. Therefore, since a semicircle is a 180-degree arc, you can simply supply π as the end angle value to create a semicircle, or π * 2 to create a circle.

If you wish to convert degrees directly to radians, the formula is `radians = degrees * π / 180`. In other words, a radian is equal to approximately 57.2958 degrees, and a degree is equal to approximately 0.01745 radians.

The value of 360 degrees for a circle was presumably chosen due to its high number of factors—1, 2, 3, 4, 5, 6, 8, 9, 10, 12, 15, 18, 20, 24, 30, 36, 40, 45, 60, 72, 90, 120, 180, and 360—providing almost two dozen different ways of dividing a circle into equal slices. So when you consider that the diameter of a circle in proportion to its circumference is π (and therefore the radius of a circle in proportion to the circumference is 2π), and that the area of a circle is $πr^2$, then using radians and π (rather than degrees) probably makes more sense when drawing arcs.

Drawing Images

With HTML5 you can draw an image directly onto a canvas, which may be either an image object or another (or the same) canvas. For example, in Figure 6-20 (created with *drawimage .htm* in the *examples.zip* file) an image of a star has been drawn in multiple positions on the canvas. Because the image is a PNG and uses transparency, only the visible parts of the image are drawn onto the canvas.

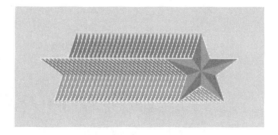

Figure 6-20   Drawing an image to a canvas in multiple places

The code to create Figure 6-20 is as follows:

```
image     = new Image()
image.src = 'star.png'

image.onload = function()
{
   for (j = 25 ; j < 150 ; j += 4)
      context.drawImage(image, j, 25)
}
```

In the first two lines the star image is loaded in and saved in the `image` object. Then the `onload` event of `image` is attached to via an inline, anonymous function that runs only after the image has been fully loaded.

Within the function a `for()` loop is used to draw the image several times at different positions along a horizontal line. The `j += 4` expression ensures that the images are 4 pixels apart from each other.

Modifying the Image Width and Height

You can also choose the width and height to use for drawing the image by adding additional arguments, as in the following statement, which increases the original dimensions of the image from 75×71 pixels, to 130×120 pixels. When added to the preceding example, the result is as shown in Figure 6-21.

```
context.drawImage(image, 60, 0, 130, 120)
```

Using Only Part of an Image

You can also choose to use just a part of an image for drawing, with code such as the following:

```
context.drawImage(image, 30, 32, 14, 14, 0, 0, 56, 28)
```

What this does is take a rectangular section from the image whose top-left location is at 30,32 and whose width and height are each 14 pixels. This section of the image is then drawn

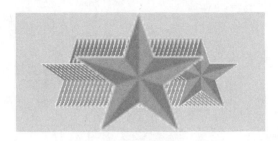

Figure 6-21   Adding an enlarged star to Figure 6-20

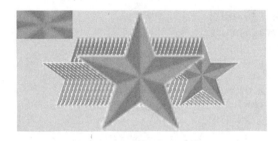

Figure 6-22   Adding an enlarged section of the source image to Figure 6-21

to the canvas at location 0,0 but is stretched horizontally from 14 to 56 pixels and vertically to 28 pixels. The result of this statement is shown in Figure 6-22.

Using a Canvas as an Image for Drawing

As well as using external images, you can grab one from the same (or another) canvas like this:

```
context.drawImage(canvas, 0, 0, 250, 120, 0, 90, 62.5, 30)
```

Here the same canvas that is being drawn on is used as a source image. The entire canvas is used starting at location 0,0 with dimensions of 250×120 pixels, and the destination location is 0,90, with the image drawn at a reduced width and height of 62.5×30 pixels, as shown in Figure 6-23.

The argument `canvas` in the statement is the object previously returned by a call to `getElementById()` on the canvas ID (as used by all these examples), but you can equally use the `canvas` property of `context` in its place, like this (with the change shown in bold):

```
context.drawImage(context.canvas, 0, 0, 250, 120, 0, 90, 62.5, 30)
```

Figure 6-23   Drawing a reduced copy of the canvas itself into the bottom-left corner

NOTE

It is also possible to draw HTML5 video onto a canvas but doing so is a little more complicated, requiring the setting up of interrupts and copying the video frame by frame. If you are interested in how to do this the web page at *html5doctor.com/ video-canvas-magic* has a good example of the technique.

Adding Shadows

You can add shadows to any element that you draw onto a canvas by first assigning values to set up a shadow offset, blur, and color, like this example:

```
context.shadowOffsetY = 6
context.shadowOffsetX = 6
context.shadowBlur    = 5
context.shadowColor   = '#888'
```

This will create a shadow with a blur that uses a radius of 5 pixels, in a mid-gray color, and that is offset down and to the right by 6 pixels. Figure 6-24 shows these shadow settings applied to four different elements: a filled square, an outlined circle, some text, and an image.

NOTE

The HTML for Figure 6-24 is available as *shadows.htm* in the *examples.zip* file at *html5formobile.com*.

Direct Pixel Manipulation

If all these advanced drawing tools aren't enough for you, then you can go right down to the level of direct pixel manipulation to achieve even more effects. The way you do this is by loading a portion of the canvas into an array using the getImageData() method, like this:

```
imagedata = context.getImageData(0, 0, 138, 130)
```

Figure 6-24 Four different elements sharing the same shadow properties

This loads into the `imagedata` object the pixel data for a 138×130-pixel square section at the top-left corner of the canvas. The canvas element supports millions of colors as well as transparency for each pixel, which is managed by allocating four locations per pixel for its red, green, blue, and alpha (transparency) components, each accepting a value of between 0 and 255.

These locations are stored contiguously so that the pixel at the top left of the canvas (at 0,0) can be accessed as follows:

```
imagedata.data[0] // The red portion of 0,0
imagedata.data[1] // The green portion of 0,0
imagedata.data[2] // The blue portion of 0,0
imagedata.data[3] // The alpha portion of 0,0
```

Then, the pixel one to the right of this (at 1,0) can be accessed like this:

```
imagedata.data[4] // The red portion of 1,0
imagedata.data[5] // The green portion of 1,0
imagedata.data[6] // The blue portion of 1,0
imagedata.data[7] // The alpha portion of 1,0
```

Once the end of the first row of pixels is reached, the array continues with the next line. So, for a 138-pixel-wide section, there are 4×138 (552) locations on each row. Therefore, the pixels at locations 137,0 and 0,1 are accessed as follows:

```
imagedata.data[548] // The red portion of 137,0
imagedata.data[549] // The green portion of 137,0
imagedata.data[550] // The blue portion of 137,0
imagedata.data[551] // The alpha portion of 137,0
```

```
imagedata.data[552] // The red portion of 0,1
imagedata.data[553] // The green portion of 0,1
imagedata.data[554] // The blue portion of 0,1
imagedata.data[555] // The alpha portion of 0,1
```

Or, to make these numbers a little easier to handle, you can address the array using expressions like the following, where the variables x and y contain the pixel to reference, and w is the width of the area:

```
imagedata.data[x * 4 + y * w     ] // Red
imagedata.data[x * 4 + y * w + 1] // Green
imagedata.data[x * 4 + y * w + 2] // Blue
imagedata.data[x * 4 + y * w + 3] // Alpha
```

Changing Pixels in an imagedata Array

Using the information in the preceding section, it's possible to access pixels directly to, for example, copy a section of canvas, change it from color to monochrome, and then save it back to a new location. And here's some code to do just that using a 138×130-pixel image and a 276×130-pixel canvas:

```
// See pixeldata.htm in examples.zip
image      = new Image()
image.src = 'leaf.png'

image.onload = function()
{
   context.drawImage(image, 0, 0)
   imagedata = context.getImageData(0, 0, 138, 130)

   for (y = 0 ; y < 130 ; ++y)
   {
      pos = y * 138 * 4

      for (x = 0 ; x < 138 ; ++x)
      {
         average = (imagedata.data[pos     ] +
                    imagedata.data[pos + 1] +
                    imagedata.data[pos + 2]) / 3

         for (j = 0 ; j < 3 ; ++j)
            imagedata.data[pos + j] = average

         pos += 4
      }
   }

   context.putImageData(imagedata, 138, 0)
}
```

The first two lines load in an image of a maple leaf, and then the image's `onload` event is attached to with an anonymous inline function that runs only after the image is fully loaded.

Within the function, the leaf is first drawn onto the left side of the canvas, and immediately afterward that half of the canvas is grabbed to the `imagedata` object using the `getImageData()` method.

NOTE

The value returned by the `getImageData()` method is an object with three properties, the first two of which are `width` and `height` so that, for example, if the object is called `imagedata`, then `imagedata.width` will contain the width of the data and `imagedata.height` will contain the height. Therefore, the pixel data is stored in the array `imagedata.data`. You can also look up the length of the data array by examining the property `imagedata.data.length`.

With this pixel data now in an array, two `for()` loops iterate through it, one for the rows (using the variable `y`), and the other for the columns (using the variable `x`). The `y` loop looks like this:

```
for (y = 0 ; y < 130 ; ++y)
```

Each time around the `y` loop, the variable `pos` is assigned a value representing the array location for the first pixel of that row, like this:

```
pos = y * 138 * 4
```

This value is used to index into the array.

Then the `x` loop for the current row `y` is entered, in which each set of three color values (red, green, and blue) is read and added together. The total is then divided by 3 to obtain the average value. The lines of code that read the color data are the following (the alpha component in the fourth location for each pixel is not used by this example and is ignored):

```
average = (imagedata.data[pos    ] +
           imagedata.data[pos + 1] +
           imagedata.data[pos + 2]) / 3
```

Next, the average value of the three components of the color, which has been stored in the variable `average`, is written back to the array using a simple loop, like this:

```
for (j = 0 ; j < 3 ; ++j)
   imagedata.data[pos + j] = average
```

With the data now updated, the pointer into the array, `pos`, is then incremented by 4, ready to manage the next pixel in the row the next time around the loop, like this:

```
pos += 4
```

Figure 6-25 Directly manipulating pixel data to convert an image to monochrome

Once the data is fully processed, it is then written back to the canvas, but into the right side so that you can compare the two images, like this:

```
context.putImageData(imagedata, 138, 0)
```

The result of all this is the image shown in Figure 6-25 (created with *pixeldata.htm* in the *examples.zip* file). Of course, this being a black and white book, both leaves appear identical, but in a web browser the left is in color, while the right is in grayscale.

TIP
By directly manipulating the pixel data of a canvas, you can perform many advanced effects such as posterizing, smoothing, sharpening, and so on, although the logic for doing these things is beyond the scope of this book. But at least you now have the tools to write your own filters and manipulations—in fact, there's enough power in the HTML5 canvas feature to create an editing program like Adobe Photoshop, entirely in JavaScript!

Creating New Pixel Data Objects
You can also create a blank pixel data object (in which all color and alpha values are zero) as follows, by simply providing the required *width* and *height* to the createImageData() method:

```
imagedata = createImageData(width, height)
```

Or you can create a new pixel data object from an existing one using the following statement, which also populates the new object with the copied object's pixel data:

```
newimagedataobject = createImageData(imagedata)
```

Compositing and Transparency
With compositing you can specify the way an element is to be drawn onto the canvas in the latest versions of all major browsers.

Figure 6-26 (created with *compositing.htm* in the *examples.zip* file) shows a dozen instances of a PNG image of a leaf (with a transparent background) that has been drawn over a filled rectangle, using each of the following compositing types:

- **source-over** The default. The source image is copied over the destination image.

- **source-in** Only parts of the source image that will appear within the destination are shown, and the destination image is removed. On Chrome and Safari, any alpha transparency in the source image causes the destination under it to be removed. On Firefox, IE0, and Opera, the entire destination is removed.

- **source-out** Only parts of the source image that do not appear within the destination are shown, and the destination image is removed. On Chrome and Safari, any alpha

Figure 6-26 All the variations of compositing as displayed by the Chrome and Safari browsers

transparency in the source image causes the destination under it to be removed. On Firefox, IE9, and Opera, the entire destination is removed.

- **source-atop**   The source image is displayed where it overlays the destination. The destination image is displayed where the destination image is opaque and the source image is transparent. Other regions are transparent.

- **destination-over**   The source image is drawn under the destination image.

- **destination-in**   On Chrome and Safari, the destination image displays where the source image is not displayed, and also within the source image shape, but not in any areas of source image transparency. On Firefox, IE9, and Opera, any transparency of the source image is ignored, and the destination image appears only within the source image shape.

- **destination-out**   Only those parts of the destination outside of the source image's nontransparent sections are shown.

- **destination-atop**   The source image displays where the destination is not displayed. Where the destination and source overlap, the destination image is displayed. On all browsers except Chrome and Safari, any transparency in the source image prevents that area of the destination image from being shown. On Firefox, IE9, and Opera, any part of the destination outside of the nontransparent part of the source is not displayed.

- **lighter**   The sum of the source and destination is applied such that where they do not overlap they display as normal, but where they overlap the sum of both images is shown, but lightened.

- **darker**   The sum of the source and destination is applied such that where they do not overlap they display as normal, but where they overlap the sum of both images is shown, but darkened. This property value is ignored by Firefox, IE9, and Opera, which will simply use the default of source-over instead.

- **copy**   The source image is copied over the destination. On Chrome and Safari, any transparent area of the source causes any destination that it overlaps to not display. On Firefox, IE9, and Opera, the entire destination image is ignored and does not display.

- **xor**   Where the source and destination images do not overlap they display as normal. Where they overlap their color values are exclusive ored. This is a logic process in which only one pixel in both the source and destination images may be set in order for the resulting pixel to be set. If both the source and destination pixels are set (or they are both unset) then the resulting pixel is unset.

The Opera, Firefox 4, and IE9 browsers interpret these styles differently from how Chrome and Safari interpret them, as shown in Figure 6-27, in which the differences can be seen to amount mainly to how transparency is handled by removing the square entirely when it should not be displayed, rather than only the area underneath the leaf.

Figure 6-27 How the Firefox 4, IE9, and Opera browsers interpret the compositing styles

Global Alpha Transparency

At any time, you can set the `globalApha` property to a value between 0.0 and 1.0 to change the default transparency of future drawing commands, like this:

```
context.globalAlpha = 0.5
```

A value of 0.0 means no transparency, while 1.0 means fully transparent. Therefore, the preceding statement will cause the future drawing of all elements to the canvas to be half transparent—or half opaque, whichever way you want to look at it.

Transformations

To further enhance the drawing abilities of HTML's canvas feature, there are four types of transformations you can apply: scaling, rotation, translation, and transformation.

Scaling an Element

There are a number of different ways you can change the dimensions of an object, but most of these require calculating the new dimension required. With scaling, however, you can simply apply two scaling factors for the horizontal and vertical dimensions and the browser does the rest for you.

For example, in Figure 6-28 (created with *scaling.htm* in the *examples.zip* file) the following statement is issued four times:

```
context.fillRect(10, 10, 100, 100)
```

However, before each of the second, third, and fourth instances, the following statement is also issued:

```
context.scale(1.5, 1.5)
```

To help you to see what's going on, the fill color is also changed each time. Here's the complete code used:

```
context.fillStyle = 'green'
context.fillRect(10, 10, 100, 100)
```

Figure 6-28 Applying the same rectangle four times while also using the `scale()` method

```
context.scale(1.5, 1.5)
context.fillStyle = 'red'
context.fillRect(10, 10, 100, 100)

context.scale(1.5, 1.5)
context.fillStyle = 'blue'
context.fillRect(10, 10, 100, 100)

context.scale(1.5, 1.5)
context.fillStyle = 'orange'
context.fillRect(10, 10, 100, 100)
```

What is happening is that each time the `scale()` method is called, all future drawing commands are scaled by the amounts specified. Therefore, the preceding code is equivalent to this:

```
context.fillStyle = 'green'
context.fillRect(10, 10, 100, 100)

context.fillStyle = 'red'
context.fillRect(15, 15, 150, 150)

context.fillStyle = 'blue'
context.fillRect(22.5, 22.5, 225, 225)

context.fillStyle = 'orange'
context.fillRect(33.75, 33.75, 337.5, 337.5)
```

You can scale in both positive and negative directions, and can use different values for the vertical and horizontal axes, such as in these example statements:

```
context.scale(2.2,   -0.5)
context.scale(-0.3, -1.7)
context.scale(3,      1.6)
```

Rotating an Element

To rotate elements, simply supply a rotation value in radians to the `rotate()` method, as in following statement, which applies a 90-degree rotation clockwise:

```
context.rotate(Math.PI / 2)
```

For example, Figure 6-29 (created with *rotating.htm* in the *examples.zip* file) shows a square that has been drawn at the location 100,0 several times, but before each drawing, the following statement has been issued:

```
context.rotate(Math.PI / 20)
```

Figure 6-29 Several squares rotated around the canvas origin at 0,0

If you were to draw a line from the top-right corner of each square through its top-left corner, and continue on to the left edge of the canvas, all the lines would meet at the top-left corner. This is because the origin used for the rotation is at 0,0.

If you want to change the point of origin (for example, to rotate the square in place), you first need to use the `translate()` method, explained next.

Translating an Element

Translating an element is the process of moving its origin to a different location. For example, to rotate the square in the preceding section around its own center, you would first move the point of rotation to that position. So, for example, in a 200×200-pixel canvas, the center is at location 100,100. Therefore, the following will move the origin to that position:

```
context.translate(100, 100)
```

From now onward, all coordinates must be issued relative to that new location. Therefore, to center a 140×140-pixel square within the canvas, you need to issue the following statement, with the top-left corner moved both left and up from the new origin by 70 pixels (half the width and height of the square):

```
context.fillRect(-70, -70, 140, 140)
```

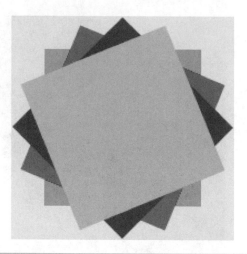

Figure 6-30 Rotating squares around themselves and the center of a canvas

Now you can issue all the rotations you like, and draw more squares using the same coordinates, and they will all be rotated around the center. For example, the following code creates the image shown in Figure 6-30 (created with *translation.htm* in the *examples.zip* file):

```
context.translate(100, 100)

context.fillStyle = 'green'
context.fillRect(-70, -70, 140, 140)

context.rotate(Math.PI / 8)
context.fillStyle = 'red'
context.fillRect(-70, -70, 140, 140)

context.rotate(Math.PI / 8)
context.fillStyle = 'blue'
context.fillRect(-70, -70, 140, 140)

context.rotate(Math.PI / 8)
context.fillStyle = 'orange'
context.fillRect(-70, -70, 140, 140)
```

Transforming an Element

The preceding `scale()`, `rotate()`, and `translate()` methods all apply a transformation matrix to the canvas, which you can also do by supplying your own matrix to the `transform()` method. You could simulate the `scale()` and other methods, or create new transformations such as a shear, using the following statement, which results in the image shown in Figure 6-31 (created with *transform.htm* in the *examples.zip* file) when applied to a

Figure 6-31   Using the `transform()` method to apply a shear to a square

square (the third argument is the one that causes the shear):

```
context.transform(1, 0, -0.5, 1, 0, 0)
```

Varying the value from –0.5 to smaller or greater values will modify the amount and/or direction of shear.

Resetting the Transformation Matrix

You can also use the following transform to reset the current matrix to its defaults:

```
context.transform(1, 0, 0, 1, 0, 0)
```

This command restores the matrix to where it was before any `scale()` or other similar methods were used. It is very useful because each `scale()` call (or `rotate()` and so on) is cumulative, and so this particular transform provides a quick method to start again from scratch for other elements you might want to transform differently.

However, if you will be using another `transform()` call after performing a matrix state reset, there's another method you can use that automatically does the reset for you before applying the new transform. Instead of using the `transform()` method, you use the `setTransform()` method, like this:

```
context.setTransform(1, 0, -0.5, 1, 0, 0)
```

This single statement is the equivalent of the following two statements:

```
context.transform(1, 0,  0,   1, 0, 0)
context.transform(1, 0, -0.5, 1, 0, 0)
```

TIP

Try modifying the arguments to the `transform()` method yourself by different (small) amounts and see what effect you can achieve. You should find you can get very creative. For more information about transformation matrixes, there's a comprehensive article at the following URL: *wikipedia.org/wiki/Transformation_matrix*.

Saving and Restoring the Current Context

When you plan to issue several sets of complex drawing commands, along with writing text, applying transformations, and so on, you can save yourself a lot of annoyance by using the `save()` and `restore()` methods before and after each group of statements, because each group can start again with a default set of properties.

With the `save()` method, the current transformation matrix and clipping region, along with all the properties in Table 6-1, will be saved. These can all then be restored at a later point using the `restore()` method.

Geolocation

By obtaining the location of a mobile user you can offer many helpful services such as mapping and providing local information, but, of course, since this information can be sensitive, it's up to the user to choose whether or not they want you to supply it. Therefore, you need to write JavaScript code that will support two eventualities: access granted and access denied.

If you are going to make your code portable across browsers other than iOS and Android, you need to start it with something like the following:

```
if (typeof navigator.geolocation == 'undefined')
{
    // Code for browsers without geolocation
    alert("Sorry, your browser doesn't support geolocation..)
}
else
{
    // Geolocation code goes here
}
```

This causes an alert box to be displayed if the browser doesn't support geolocation, but you don't need to issue an alert and could instead place any other code (such as a routine to

`fillStyle`	`miterLimit`
`font`	`shadowBlur`
`globalAlpha`	`shadowColor`
`globalCompositeOperation`	`shadowOffsetX` and `shadowOffsetY`
`lineCap`	`strokeStyle`
`lineJoin`	`textAlign`
`lineWidth`	`textBaseline`

Table 6-1 The Properties Accessed with the `save()` and `restore()` Methods

display a map) within the `if()` section. Within the `else` you then place the JavaScript that performs the Geolocation. If you don't intend your code to run anywhere other than on iOS and Android, then you can ignore the preceding code.

To call up the geolocation routines, you need to issue the following statement:

```
navigator.geolocation.getCurrentPosition(granted, denied)
```

This calls up the browser's geolocation feature, which either prompts the user to grant or deny access or remembers a previous saved grant or deny the user may have created and uses that—when some browsers ask if they can pass on your location, they also ask whether to remember your decision in the future.

The two arguments passed to the function `getCurrentPosition()` are the names of two functions you must also write to handle both the granted and denied cases. Here's what the granted code might look like (where `position.coords` is assigned `latitude` and `longitude` properties containing the user's coordinates):

```
function granted(position)
{
    alert("You are at location: " +
        position.coords.latitude + "," +
        position.coords.longitude)
}
```

And the denied code might look like this (where `error.code` contains one of four error values):

```
function denied(error)
{
    var message

    switch(error.code)
    {
        case 1: message = 'Permission Denied'; break
        case 2: message = 'Position Unavailable'; break
        case 3: message = 'Operation Timed Out'; break
        case 4: message = 'Unknown Error'
    }

    alert("Error with Geolocation: " + message)
}
```

Following is a real-world example you can use to display a Google map of a user's location, as shown in Figure 6-32 (created with a modified version of *geolocation.htm*—to emulate the Eiffel Tower location—in the *examples.zip* file). It commences with some explanatory text and then creates a `<div>` into which the result of the geolocation lookup is placed.

Figure 6-32 Using geolocation to return a map for a user standing by the Eiffel Tower

After that an `<iframe>` is created, into which a Google map will be inserted if the geolocation is successful. The `<script>` section is the same as in the preceding example, but with a few tweaks to produce the status message and map:

```
This example will ask your browser for its location if it
supports this feature.<br /><br />



<div id='status'></div><br />
<iframe id='map' width='640' height='320'></iframe>

<script>
   if (typeof navigator.geolocation == 'undefined')
   {
      alert("Sorry, your browser doesn't support geolocation.")
   }
   else
```

```
{
    navigator.geolocation.getCurrentPosition(granted, denied)

    function granted(position)
    {
        document.getElementById('status').innerHTML =
            'Permission Granted'
        var gmap = 'http://maps.google.com/maps?q=' +
            position.coords.latitude + ',' +
            position.coords.longitude
        document.getElementById('map').src = gmap
    }

    function denied(error)
    {
        var message

        switch(error.code)
        {
            case 1: message = 'Permission Denied'; break;
            case 2: message = 'Position Unavailable'; break;
            case 3: message = 'Operation Timed Out'; break;
            case 4: message = 'Unknown Error'; break;
        }

        document.getElementById('status').innerHTML = message
    }
}
</script>
```

TIP

Managing browsers that don't support the W3C Geolocation API is beyond the scope of this book, but if you need to do this you can always use the JavaScript Geolocation framework on the Google Code website, at the following URL: *code.google.com/p/ geo-location-javascript.*

Local Storage

In the past, the only way you could store data on a user's computer was with cookies, which hold only 4Kb of data each and can be used only in limited quantities. They also have to be passed back and forth on every page reload, and, unless your server uses SSL (Secure Sockets Layer) encryption, each time a cookie is transmitted, it travels in the clear (unencrypted).

But with HTML5 you have access to a much larger local storage space (typically between 5MB and 10MB per domain depending on the browser) that remains intact between page reloads and between website visits (and even after powering a computer down and back up again), and which is not sent to the server on each page load.

You handle the data in pairs comprising a key and its value. The key is the name assigned for referencing the data, and the value can hold any type of data, but it is saved as a string.

All data is unique to the current domain. Any local storage created by websites with different domains is separate from the current local storage, for security reasons, and is not accessible by any domain other than the one that stored the data.

Storing and Retrieving Local Data

To access local storage you use methods of the localStorage object such as setItem(), getItem(), removeItem(), and clear(). For example, to locally store a user's username and password you might use code such as this:

```
localStorage.setItem('username', 'Muhammad-Ali')
localStorage.setItem('password', 'IAmTheGreatest')
```

If the size of the value is larger than the disk quota remaining for the storage area, an "Out of memory" exception is thrown. Otherwise, when another page loads or when the user returns to the website, these details can be retrieved to save the user from having to enter them again, like this:

```
username = localStorage.getItem('username')
password = localStorage.getItem('password')
```

If the key doesn't exist, then the getItem() function returns null.

You don't have to use these function names if you don't want to, and can access the localStorage object directly because the two following statements are equivalent to each other:

```
localStorage.setItem('key', 'value')
localStorage['key'] = 'value'
```

And the two following statements are therefore also equivalent to each other:

```
value = localStorage.getItem('key')
value = localStorage['key']
```

Figure 6-33 (created with *localstorage.htm* in the *examples.zip* file) shows an alert box displaying values retrieved from local storage.

Removing and Clearing Local Data

To remove an item of data from the local storage, all you need to do is issue a command such as this:

```
username = localStorage.removeItem('username')
```

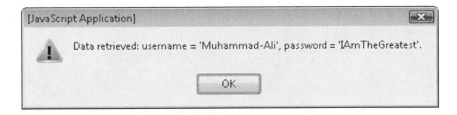

Figure 6-33 Retrieving data from local storage and displaying it in an alert box

This retrieves the item of data and places it into a variable (in this case `username`), and then deletes the data from local storage. If you don't need to first read the data you are removing, you can simply call the function on its own, like this:

```
localStorage.removeItem('username')
```

You can also completely clear the local storage for the current domain by issuing this command:

```
localStorage.clear()
```

Summary

You now have all the HTML5 and CSS3 tools you need to create great web pages, but before you look at how to turn those web pages into web apps or online store apps, it's important to show you how to program the server end of the equation to serve up your fancy new HTML5 pages. To do this, the following two chapters (the final two in this part of the book) show you how to use PHP and MySQL, and how to perform Ajax communication in the background between a web browser and web server.

Chapter 7

Introduction to PHP

Key Skills & Concepts

- Getting started with PHP

- Numeric, string, and superglobal variables

- Single and multidimensional arrays

- Constants and predefined constants

- Operators and precedence

- Functions and local and global variable scope

- Conditional expressions and loops

- Form processing and Ajax requests

If your primary interest in HTML5 is to create marketplace apps for iOS and Android, you may wish to skip this chapter (and the following one on MySQL), since such apps use only client-side scripting with JavaScript. However, if you intend to create web applications or websites with dynamic user interaction and Ajax support, then you'll need to use a scripting language such as PHP, which is the most popular, and is also available on most web servers.

PHP also has remarkably similar structure to JavaScript, so, with just a few tweaks here and there, what you learned in the introduction to JavaScript in Chapter 5 can also be used with PHP. This means that, having learned JavaScript, you should find this chapter a breeze, and after finishing it you'll have the basics of another programming language under your belt.

Checking for PHP on Your Web Server

Before you delve into the PHP language, you first need to ensure that your web server supports it. Most do, but it's necessary to make the check to be sure. To do this, create a simple text file with the following contents, save it using the filename *phptest.php*, and upload the file to your web server:

```php
<?php
   phpinfo();
?>
```

With the program uploaded to your web server, enter its URL into a web browser (for example, *myserver.com/phptest.php*). If PHP is installed, you will be presented with a screen similar to Figure 7-1, although the version number of PHP and other details may vary.

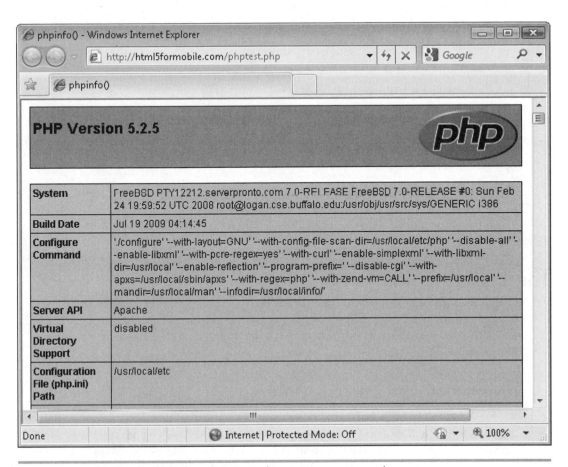

Figure 7-1 The result of loading the example HTML page into a browser

If you do see the screen in Figure 7-1, then you're all set to go. If you see a blank page or an error, then you probably don't have PHP installed on the server and should ask your server administrator to add it for you.

Using a Local Web Development Server

For quick and easy web development, you may want to create a local installation of PHP on your computer. Doing so is free and relatively straightforward using the Zend Server Community Edition (CE) installer, which is from the people who created the PHP engine.

Having a local web development server means you can instantly test your code without having to upload it first to your web server. It's not necessary to have this server to develop with PHP, but it can save you a lot of time. You can get more information and download the Zend Server CE installer for any of the PC, Mac, or Linux operating systems at the following URL:

zend.com/en/products/server-ce/

As long as you read the prompts, provide sensible answers to the questions asked, and use common sense, you should be able to install Zend Server CE without too much difficulty. If you will be using the MySQL database program (covered in the following chapter), be sure to check the box next to its name if it is unchecked in any of the installation screens.

TIP

In my book *Plug-in PHP: 100 Power Solutions* (McGraw-Hill/Professional, 2010), Chapter 1 takes you through the process of installing Zend Server CE on a PC, Mac, or Linux operating system, along with helpful advice and screenshots to show you what you should see.

The Basics of PHP

In much the same way that you activate the JavaScript engine in a web browser using `<script>` and `</script>` tags, you activate the web server's PHP engine using `<?php` and `?>` tags, as in this simple code, which checks for the presence of PHP using the function `phpinfo()`:

```
<?php
    phpinfo();
?>
```

Because PHP was designed to augment HTML web pages, how you use these tags is very flexible indeed. For example, the following HTML code, which places the call to `phpinfo()` inside an HTML table, is completely valid:

```
<table><tr><td><?php phpinfo(); ?></td></tr></table>
```

You will quite often see examples of PHP tags dropped into HTML, particularly in content management systems (CMSs) such as WordPress.

The echo Keyword

I have a personal aversion to continually dropping in and out of PHP, as I find that pages that do this are usually very hard to follow and maintain. Instead, on pages that use any PHP, I prefer, if possible, to have just one section of PHP, which sometimes may comprise the whole page, like this:

```
<?php
echo <<< ECHOEND
<html>
    <head>
```

```
    <title>A web page displayed using PHP</title>
  </head>
  <body>
    <p>This page was created with PHP</p>
  </body>
</html>
ECHOEND;
?>
```

In this example the PHP section of the page is shown in bold. It uses a single command, which is the `echo` statement followed by the `<<<` operator and the label `ECHOEND;`. What this command does is tell the PHP engine to output everything from just after `<<<` `ECHOEND` up to the line preceding the `ECHOEND;` label.

This kind of text output is known as a *heredoc*, and you can use any label name you like as long as the start label matches the end one. You can also use a heredoc during string variable assignments, like this:

```
$variable = <<< EOS
This is a multi-line string.
It includes a line feed.
EOS;
```

There are two major benefits of the heredoc syntax:

- Since no quotation marks are used to encapsulate a string, you can use all the quotation marks you like within it, without having to escape any by preceding them with a \ symbol (see the section "Escaping Characters," a little further on).

- All heredoc strings allow you to place variables directly inside them, and the variable names will be substituted for their current value when output.

The Difference Between Single and Double Quotes

In just the same way that heredoc strings allow the direct embedding of variables, so do double-quoted strings. For example, the following embeds two strings within another:

```
$forename = "Simon";
$surname  = "Cowell";
$fullname = "$forename $surname";
```

In this case the resulting string in `$fullname` is `"Simon Cowell"`. You can also prevent this behavior by using single quotes, like this:

```
$forename = "Simon";
$surname  = "Cowell";
$fullname = '$forename $surname';
```

In this case the resulting string in `$fullname` is `"$forename $surname"`.

NOTE

Because double quotes support variable embedding, these string assignments are slower than using single-quoted strings. Therefore, I generally use single-quoted strings whenever no embedding is required. In small programs the difference is minimal, but in large web apps with a lot of string handling, you could slow down page displays by a second or even more without this optimization.

Using Comments

PHP supports both the comment types of JavaScript. These are /* and */ for multiline comments, and // for comments that automatically close at the next line feed.

Here are two examples:

```
/* This is a
   multi-line
   comment */

// This is a single line comment
```

Semicolons

Unlike JavaScript, where semicolons are mostly optional, all PHP statements must end with a semicolon, even where there is only a single statement on a line. Forgetting to use a semicolon is a common error, particularly for new PHP programmers.

However, there is one place in PHP where you may omit the semicolon, and that's directly before the closing ?> tag. This allows you to write the shortest possible PHP insertions into HTML, like this:

```
Info about this web server follows: <?php phpinfo() ?>
```

CAUTION

It is not a good idea to reveal your PHP server setup to your users with phpinfo() because it may provide information a hacker could leverage. Instead I recommend you use the function only for your own purposes.

PHP Variables

As you may have noticed from the preceding examples, all PHP variables must begin with a $ symbol—the main reason for this is to allow for embedding of strings in heredocs and double-quoted strings.

As well as the initial $ symbol, PHP variable names may contain only the letters a–z and A–Z, the digits 0–9, and the _ character. PHP variables names are case sensitive, so that, for example, $HighScore is a different variable from $highscore. These naming rules apply to all types of PHP variables, including arrays and objects.

PHP variables have a lot in common with JavaScript variables in that they are loosely typed, which means they can be converted to a string, integer, floating point, or any other type according to the context in which they are used. This makes the language powerful and flexible, but does mean that when you want a variable to be of a particular type, you must explicitly cast the variable to the type needed, as you'll see later.

Numeric Variables

Numeric variables in PHP are pretty much the same as in JavaScript, and the spice jar analogy from Chapter 5 also applies to PHP, in that you can consider a numeric variable to be a container or jar into which you can insert a value by writing it on a piece of paper and placing it inside.

Assigning a Value to a Variable

To assign a numeric value to a variable, you use the following syntax, which assigns the value 17 to the variable $age:

```
$age = 17;
```

You can also assign the value in one variable to another, like this:

```
$apples = 12;
$fruit  = $apples;
```

Adding Numeric Values

Adding together the values stored in variables is also a simple matter using the + operator, like this:

```
$fruit = $apples + $pears;
```

Later in this chapter, in the section "PHP Operators," you'll learn about the other mathematical operators that are available.

Using Floating Point Numbers

You can treat floating point numbers (that is, numbers with a fractional value after the period) in a similar manner to integers, like the following example, which totals the number of hours worked in a week (arriving at a total of 40 hours, which is displayed by the echo statement):

```
$mon   = 7.75;
$tue   = 7.50;
$wed   = 8.25;
$thu   = 8;
$fri   = 8.50;
$hours = $mon + $tue + $wed + $thu + $fri;
echo "You worked for $hours hours";
```

Notice that, unlike the other days of the week, the variable $thu is assigned an integer, not a floating point value, but that it makes no difference to the addition expression—as far as PHP is concerned, a number is a number unless you use code to specifically deal with numbers as either integers or floating point numbers.

Also notice that the echo statement embedded the value in the $hours variable (rather than the "$hours" string of characters) because it is enclosed in double quotes.

String Variables

Again, like JavaScript, using PHP string variables is analogous to using a spice jar to hold a number written on a piece of paper, except that for string variables the paper contains text, not a number.

Assigning a value to a string variable uses this syntax:

```
$myname = 'James Bond';
```

In this case the string variable $myname is assigned the string's value. Note the use of single quotation marks for the string. This is because the string value to assign doesn't contain any PHP variables, and so it's faster to use a single-quoted (rather than double-quoted) string, because the PHP variable parser is not called up to preprocess the string.

You can also assign strings that are numbers, like this:

```
$pi = '3.1415927';
```

Although the variable $pi contains a string, if you try to access it as if it were a number, as you'll see later, PHP allows you to do so and performs the conversion automatically for you.

String Concatenation

To attach one string to another (concatenate them) you use the . operator (rather than the + operator, as used by JavaScript), like this:

```
$forename = 'Steve';
$surname  = 'Jobs';
$fullname = $forename . ' ' . $surname;
```

After the assignment, $fullname contains the string "Steve Jobs" (with a space added between the two names). You can also concatenate numbers and strings, like this:

```
$number  = 1600;
$street  = 'Pennsylvania Avenue';
$address = $number . ' ' . $street;
```

Escaping Characters

When using double or single quotes to enclose a string, you can use the other type of quote inside the string without any problem, like these examples:

```
$tvshow = "America's Got Talent";
$quote  = 'Piers said "You need to raise the bar."';
```

But when you want to include the same type of quotation mark within a string, then you need to escape it by prefacing it with a \ character, like this:

```
$quote  = 'Sharon said "I didn\'t like that performance."';
```

Escape characters are also used to insert special characters such as linefeeds (\n), carriage returns (\r), and tabs (\t) only into double-quoted (not single-quoted) strings. To insert a \ character itself into a string, you also escape it, like this:

```
$info = 'The escape character is the \\ symbol';
```

CAUTION

Escape characters are common to many languages, but, specific to PHP, when you wish to display a $ symbol in a double-quoted string, you should also escape it (\$), in case PHP confuses any characters following it with a variable name whose value (rather than name) it should place in the string.

Superglobal Variables

PHP supplies each instance of a script with a set of superglobal variables that the script may need. These include a lot of information about the current program, as detailed in Table 7-1.

Variable	Type	Contents
$GLOBALS	Array	All variables that are currently defined in the global scope of the script. The variable names are the keys of the array.
$_SERVER	Array	Information such as headers, paths, and script locations. The entries in this array are created by the web server and there is no guarantee that every web server will provide any or all of these.
$_GET	Array	Variables passed to the current script via the HTTP GET method.
$_POST	Array	Variables passed to the current script via the HTTP POST method.
$_FILES	Array	Items uploaded to the current script via the HTTP POST method.
$_COOKIE	String	Variables passed to the current script via HTTP cookies.
$_SESSION	Array	Session variables available to the current script.
$_REQUEST	String	Contents of information passed from the browser; by default $_GET, $_POST, and $_COOKIE.
$_ENV	Array	Variables passed to the current script via the environment method.

Table 7-1 The PHP Superglobal Variables

For example, the following statement displays the URL of any page that the current one was referred from:

```
echo $_SERVER['HTTP_REFERER'];
```

You'll see various examples of these superglobals in use later in this chapter (and in other chapters too), in the section "Processing Web Form Data."

Arrays

In PHP, arrays fulfill the same function as they do in JavaScript—they store a linked array of values, in a similar manner to taping a bunch of spice jars together to use as a related collection of containers.

To create an array, you can use the `array()` function, like this:

```
$operatingsystems = array('Windows', 'OS X', 'iOS', 'Android');
```

Here the array `$operatingsystems` has four elements, each of which contains a string value—the name of a popular operating system.

As with regular variables, you can also assign numbers to array elements, like the following array, which has ten elements, each of which contains a prime number:

```
$primes = array(2, 3, 5, 7, 11, 13, 17, 19, 23, 29);
```

Arrays do not have to contain only the same types of values; you can mix and match types as required, like this:

```
$randomthings = array(42, 'Sausages', '1961', 22.2, 'Jelly Beans');
```

Okay, I don't know what that particular array would be used for, but it's certainly legal PHP. To access any of the elements of the preceding example arrays, you enclose an index value within a pair of square brackets, like this:

```
echo $operatingsystems[2];  // Displays 'iOS'
echo $primes[7];            // Displays 19
echo $randomthings[3];      // Displays 22.2
```

NOTE

As you can see from these three examples, the thing to remember with both JavaScript and PHP arrays is that the first element is always accessed with an index value of 0. Therefore, for example, `$primes[7]` is actually the *eighth* element of the array.

Associative Arrays

Also like JavaScript, you can choose to access arrays using names rather than index numbers. When you do this you are using an associative array, which you can create like this:

```
$likes = array('Mary' => 'Pizza', 'Bill' => 'Chips', 'Ann' => 'Cake');
```

This array contains three elements containing the values `Pizza`, `Chips`, and `Cake`, in turn. The `=>` operator takes two values. On the left is the name to assign to the array element, and on the right is the value.

If you wish, you can access these values using a numeric index, like this:

```
echo $likes[1]; // Displays Chips
```

However, each of the elements has also been given a name you can use to refer to it, so you can access the same element more easily like this:

```
echo $likes['Bill']; // Displays Chips
```

With associative arrays you can ignore the numeric ordering of elements (which can lead to all sorts of problems with large arrays of data) and simply use names for each element instead. Imagine how easy this could make writing a program to keep track of a teacher's homework assignments. Instead of referencing each student's details by a number (which the teacher would have to either remember or look up each time), supplying a name (such as `'Joe Smith'`) to an array element makes it much easier to maintain the data.

As with standard arrays, you can store any data type in an array element and can use more than one data type in an array.

Multidimensional Arrays

You can even place an entire array within a single array element. As with JavaScript, this is how you can create arrays of more than one dimension. For example, to create an empty Tic-Tac-Toe board, you might create a structure like this, which is almost the same as the JavaScript version in Chapter 5:

```
$tictactoe = array(
    array('.', '.', '.'),
    array('.', '.', '.'),
    array('.', '.', '.')
)
```

The main differences between the PHP and JavaScript versions of this array are the `$` preceding its name and the use of the `array()` function in PHP as opposed to `Array()` (with an uppercase *A*) used in JavaScript.

For example, to fill the center position in this game with an X symbol, you would use the following statement (remembering that array elements start at 0):

```
$tictactoe[1][1] = 'X';
```

Or, to display the value in the bottom-left corner, you would use code such as this:

```
echo $tictactoe[0][2];
```

Multidimensional Associative Arrays   You can also add extra dimensions to associative arrays. For example, expanding on the concept of managing student homework assignments, take a look at the following structure, which assumes there is one assignment assigned each month:

```
$assignments = array(
   'Joe Smith' => array('Jan' => 'B+', 'Feb' => 'C', 'Mar' >= 'A-')
);
```

Here an array called $assignments is created. At the moment it has only one element, but this element contains another array that contains the assignment grades for the first three months of the year. Assuming there are no spring or summer breaks, and that a school year goes from January to December, a full year's results might look like this:

```
$assignments = array(
   'Joe Smith' => array('Jan' => 'B+', 'Feb' => 'C', 'Mar' >= 'A-',
                        'Apr' => 'B+', 'May' => 'B', 'Jun' >= 'B+',
                        'Jul' => 'B-', 'Aug' => 'C', 'Sep' >= 'B',
                        'Oct' => 'A-', 'Nov' => 'A', 'Dec' >= 'A+')
);
```

Thankfully, by the end of the year Joe Smith has attained an A+, but I wouldn't like to go to that establishment—it's all study and no play! However, for the teacher it's not too bad because there's an easy system in place to track the students' assignments. For example, to see how well Joe did for his August assignment, all that's necessary is to use the following:

```
echo $assignments['Joe Smith']['Aug']; // Displays 'C';
```

More students can be added to this array, as with the following code, in which I've kindly given the two additional students straight-A grades:

```
$assignments = array(
   'Joe Smith'     => array('Jan' => 'B+', 'Feb' => 'C', 'Mar' >= 'A-',
                            'Apr' => 'B+', 'May' => 'B', 'Jun' >= 'B+',
                            'Jul' => 'B-', 'Aug' => 'C', 'Sep' >= 'B',
                            'Oct' => 'A-', 'Nov' => 'A', 'Dec' >= 'A+'),
   'Claire Jones'  => array('Jan' => 'A',  'Feb' => 'A', 'Mar' >= 'A',
                            'Apr' => 'A',  'May' => 'A', 'Jun' >= 'A',
                            'Jul' => 'A',  'Aug' => 'A', 'Sep' >= 'A',
                            'Oct' => 'A',  'Nov' => 'A', 'Dec' >= 'A'),
   'David Johnson' => array('Jan' => 'A',  'Feb' => 'A', 'Mar' >= 'A',
                            'Apr' => 'A',  'May' => 'A', 'Jun' >= 'A',
                            'Jul' => 'A',  'Aug' => 'A', 'Sep' >= 'A',
                            'Oct' => 'A',  'Nov' => 'A', 'Dec' >= 'A'))
);
```

NOTE

Of course, you likely wouldn't hard-code such a data structure. Instead, you would use an HTML form as a front end, and use a database as a back end to store and read back the data (as discussed in the following chapter on MySQL), which would then be automatically assigned to the array.

Constants

A constant is a sort of variable that, once a value is assigned to it, retains that value no matter what, and cannot be changed. To create a constant you use the `define()` function, like the following example, which assigns the value `299792458` (the number of meters light travels in a second) to the constant `SPEED_OF_LIGHT`:

```
define("SPEED_OF_LIGHT", 299792458);
```

Constant names can use the letters a–z and A–Z and the underscore character _, but, by convention, generally only uppercase letters are used. Also, constant names are *not* preceded with a $ symbol.

NOTE

One major benefit of constants is that, due to their immutability, no part of a PHP script can change them, and the same goes for other scripts that are included by an initial script. This provides a very robust way of protecting important values from being overridden, either by yourself, accidentally, or by other programmers who maintain your code but don't fully understand how it works.

Predefined Constants

PHP maintains a number of predefined constants, known as magic constants, that contain useful information. For example, the constants `__LINE__` and `__FILE__` (each with two preceding and two following underscore characters) refer to the current line and file of a script, respectively. Therefore, when debugging, it can be very useful to use code such as this:

```
echo "Debugging point at line " . __LINE__ . " in file " . __FILE__;
```

The resulting output of the statement will be something like the following, depending on where your document root is, the file running, and the line number of the statement:

```
Debugging point at line 12 in file /www/mywebsite.com/myprogram.php
```

PHP Operators

PHP supports the same range of operators as JavaScript (and a couple more), which all work in the same way. Therefore, Table 5-1 in Chapter 5 also lists all the arithmetic operators available in PHP.

Arithmetic Functions

Unlike JavaScript, which requires you to preface its math functions with the word `Math.`, PHP uses no such prefix; so, for example, simply issuing the call `abs(-2)` returns the value 2 (the absolute value of `-2`), `sqrt(16)` returns 4 (the square root of `16`), and so on.

TIP

The full set of PHP math functions is mostly the same as the JavaScript set in Table 5-2 in Chapter 5 (but without the preceding `Math.`), although there are some differences and some additional ones, so you may wish to refer to the following URL for a complete breakdown: *php.net/manual/en/ref.math.php*.

Assignment Operators

Referring again to Chapter 5, Table 5-3 lists all the available assignment operators in JavaScript, which are identical to PHP with one difference—in PHP the assignment operator is a `.` symbol, not a + symbol, so assignment with concatenation in PHP is `. =` (not `+=`). Assignment with addition in PHP is the same as in JavaScript (`+=`).

Otherwise, all the other operators work in the same way in both JavaScript and PHP.

Comparison Operators

Yet again you can refer to Chapter 5 to see the comparison operators that PHP supports, because they are identical to those in JavaScript. They are detailed in Table 5-4.

Logical Operators

PHP beats JavaScript when it comes to logical operators because it also offers the keyword operators `and` and `or`, as well as the useful `xor` (exclusive or) operator. Table 7-2 lists them all.

The operators `and` and `or` are the same as `&&` and `||` except that they have a lower precedence, giving you the ability to create subtly more complex expressions. For example, in the following `if()` statement, the two outer expressions will be evaluated first:

```
if ($a == 1 && $b == 2 and $c == 3 || $d == 5)
{
    // Some code
}
```

Because and has a lower precedence than either of the `&&` and `||` operators, `$a == 1 && $b == 2` will be calculated and its result will be saved, and then `$c == 3 || $d == 5` will be calculated and its result saved. Only after this will the central `and` be processed using the two saved partial results.

The preceding expression is therefore equivalent to this:

```
if (($a == 1 && $b == 2) && ($c == 3 || $d == 5)) ...
```

Operator	Description	Examples	Results
&&	And	`$a = 10; if ($a > 5 && $a < 15)` `$a = 10; if ($a == 10 && ($a / 2) == 4)`	true false
and	And*	`$a = 10; if ($a > 5 and $a < 15)` `$a = 10; if ($a == 10 and ($a / 2) == 4)`	true false
||	Or	`$a = 10; $b = 12; if ($a > 5 || $b == 10)` `$a = 10; if ($a == 10 \|\| ($a / 2) == 4)`	true true
or	Or*	`$a = 10; b = 12; if ($a > 5 or $b == 10)` `$a = 10; if ($a == 10 or ($a / 2) == 4)`	true true
!	Not	`$a = 10; if (!($a / 5) > 1)` `$a = 10; if (!$a > 5)`	true false

xor	Exclusive or	`$a = 0; $b = 0; if ($a xor $b)`
		`$a = 0; $b = 1; if ($a xor $b)`
		`$a = 1; $b = 0; if ($a xor $b)`
		`$a = 1; $b = 1; if ($a xor $b)`
			false
			true
			true
			false

*and and or are lower precedence than && and ||.

Table 7-2   The Six PHP Logical Operators

The xor Operator

The xor operator isn't available in JavaScript, but it is very powerful. It returns true if either of two input values is true (but not both), otherwise it returns false.

Here are four statements using the xor operator and the results they return:

```
if (false xor false) ... // Returns false
if (false xor  true) ... // Returns true
if (true  xor false) ... // Returns true
if (true  xor  true) ... // Returns false
```

A great way to think about this is to take the example of needing to clean up a very stubborn stain. You have both an ammonia cleaner and a bleach cleaner ($a and $b) and you must use one or the other of them, but definitely not both together—as that generates a poisonous gas.

So here are the four possibilities:

```
$a = 0; $b = 0; // $a xor $b is false
$a = 1; $b = 0; // $a xor $b is true
$a = 0; $b = 1; // $a xor $b is true
$a = 1; $b = 1; // $a xor $b is false
```

Immediately you can see that using neither $a (ammonia) nor $b (bleach) results in a value of `false`. In other words, if using neither product, then the stain cannot be cleaned because no chemical is applied. Also, if both $a and $b are set, that returns `false` too, because the products should never be used together, for safety reasons.

On the other hand, if either $a is 1 or $b is 1 (but not neither or both), then the result is `true`—so it's okay to go ahead and use either the ammonia or the bleach, whichever is set to 1.

The Ternary Operator

The PHP ternary operator works in exactly the same way as it does in JavaScript. It provides a single-statement method for accomplishing what would otherwise take two statements. For example, take a look at the following pair of expressions embedded in an `if()` ... `else` construct:

```
if ($raining) echo 'Use umbrella';
else echo 'Umbrella not needed';
```

Using the ? ternary operator and its matching : operator, you can shorten this to:

```
echo ($raining) ? 'Use umbrella' : 'Umbrella not needed';
```

Automatic Variable Typing

As already mentioned, in PHP, variables can change their type according to the context in which they are used. This is very much the same behavior as JavaScript's and means that, for example, a string containing a number such as `'27.54'` will be treated as a string when used in string operations such as `echo '27.54'.' degrees'`, which displays the string `27.54 degrees`.

Or, if the same string is used in an arithmetic expression such as `'27.54' * 3`, it is converted to a floating point number (`82.62`).

However, when you want to force a variable to a particular type, you can *cast* it using the following bracketed operators: `(int)`, `(integer)`, `(bool)`, `(double)`, `(float)`, `(real)`, `(string)`, `(array)`, and `(object)`. The only ones of these that may require explaining are the `(int)` and `(integer)` operators, which cast to an integer and are the same as each other, as are the `(double)`, `(float)`, and `(real)` operators, which cast to a floating point number, and the `(bool)` operator, which casts to a Boolean value that can hold only the value `true` or `false`.

For example, the following statement converts the string `'3.1415927'` to an integer and displays the value 3—the part before the period (*significand*), without the floating point remainder (*mantissa*):

```
echo (int) '3.1415927';
```

Such casting does not round up or down, it simply strips out the mantissa. Therefore, the following also displays only the significand value of 3 (since 3.1415927 + 0.8 is less than 4):

```
echo (int) '3.1415927' + 0.8;
```

To convert the string to a floating point number, you would use the following:

```
echo (float) '3.1415927';
```

Likewise, for example, you can convert the exponential number 25.123e7 (25.123 with the period shifted seven places to the right) to a string using the following statement, which displays '251230000':

```
echo (string) 25e3;
```

Operator Precedence

PHP operators are applied using precedence rules that have, for example, been chosen to give operators such as * and / a greater precedence than + and -. In Table 5-6 of Chapter 5 you can see all the JavaScript operators and their precedences. These are almost all the same as PHP except that the `typeof`, `void`, `delete`, and `>>>` JavaScript operators are not used in PHP, and the JavaScript . operator is not used to denote membership in PHP.

PHP Functions

Functions in PHP are used in the same way as in JavaScript, but the defining and use of local and global variables is a little different. For example, the following calls the built-in function `round()` to return the nearest integer value to the number 6.56 (which is 7):

```
echo round(6.56);
```

You could also write your own function to do this, as follows:

```
function newround($value)
{
   $significand = (int) $value;
   $mantissa    = $value - $significand;
   if ($mantissa >= 0.5) return $significand + 1;
   else return $significand;
}
```

In this example the significand and mantissa are separated out into unique variables, then $mantissa (which will be a value between 0.0 and 0.9 recurring) is compared with the value 0.5. If it is greater than or equal to that value, then $significand + 1 is returned, otherwise just $significand is returned. The function can be called as follows (which also displays the result 7):

```
echo newround(6.56);
```

NOTE
PHP supports object-oriented programming (OOP), which is very powerful, but beyond the scope of this book—and, in any case, it is not needed for the simple uses to which this book puts PHP, such as interfacing web servers with mobile devices, generally using Ajax. If you are interested, my book *Learning PHP, MySQL & JavaScript* (O'Reilly, 2009) includes a comprehensive tutorial on using PHP for object oriented programming.

Local Variables

Unlike in JavaScript, in PHP all variables have the scope of the context in which they are defined. For example, in the newround() function in the preceding section, the variables $significand and $mantissa have local scope only to the newround() function. Outside of the function, any attempt to obtain a value from these variables will fail, unless these names have also been assigned externally to the function. And in that case they will retain a value separate from that within the function.

Global Variables

In PHP, global variables are those that are defined outside of any function. They can be automatically written to and read from by any code that is not within a function simply by referring to them. However, although they are global, they do not have global scope within functions unless a function declares them as global using the global keyword, like this:

```
$USERNAME = 'OptimusPrime';
greeting('Welcome');

function greeting($message)
{
    global $USERNAME;
    echo $message . ' ' . $USERNAME;
}
```

By using the statement global $USERNAME; the function is allowed access to the global variable and is able to display "Welcome OptimusPrime." If that statement were omitted, the variable and its value would be invisible to the function, which would display only "Welcome."

No error message is displayed when this happens because PHP assumes that, since you have referred to a local variable called $USERNAME, you will probably be using it later in the function, and thus PHP initializes the function with the value ' ' (an empty string).

By the way, $USERNAME is in all uppercase letters because that is the convention I use so that I always know when I am dealing with a global variable.

CAUTION

If you have programmed in C, you will be used to global variables automatically being accessible from all your code, including within functions. So remember that PHP requires you to explicitly declare global variables as such when used in functions.

Static Variables

In addition to local and global variables, PHP also supports the use of static variables. These are local variables that retain their value when a function exits, and the value is not accessible by any part of the program other than the function.

Although you are unlikely to use static variables as a beginner, when you start to write more advanced code (perhaps with functions that are called regularly in a time-sharing architecture), you'll find that having a variable restore its value each time a function is reentered can be very useful.

To declare a variable as static, you use the `static` keyword, like this:

```
static $highscore;
```

Conditional Expressions

Like JavaScript, PHP supports conditional expressions such as `if()`, `else`, `else if()`— or `elseif()`—and `switch()`. In fact, their use is so similar that I refer you to the section "Conditional Expressions" in Chapter 5 for full details, a brief summary of which follows.

The if() Statement

The syntax of the `if()` statement is like this:

```
if ($expression)
{
    // Statements
}
```

If there is only one statement, you may leave out the curly braces.

The else Statement

The `else` statement adds a second clause to an `if()` statement, like this:

```
if ($expression)
{
    // Statements
}
else
{
    // Alternative statements
}
```

As with `if()`, if there is only a single statement within the `else`, the curly braces can be omitted.

The elseif() Statement

In PHP you can use either `else if()` or `elseif()` (without the space) if you prefer. You use the statement like this:

```
if ($expression)
{
    // Statements
}
elseif($otherexpression)
{
    // Other statements
}
else
{
    // Alternative statements
}
```

You may include as many `elseif()` statements as you like in a chain. If you also use an `else` statement, it must appear last. If an `elseif()`—or `else if()`—has only a single statement in it, you may omit the curly braces.

The switch() Statement

Instead of typing many long-winded chains of `if ... elseif() ... else` statements, you can use a `switch()` statement in conjunction with the `case`, `default`, and `break` keywords, like this:

```
switch($value)
{
    case(value):
        // Statements
        break;
    case(othervalue):
        // Other statements
        break;
    default:
        // Default statements
}
```

The values *value* and *othervalue* (and so on) should be values to compare with that in `$value`: string values if `$value` is a string, otherwise numeric values. Once a test is satisfied, all statements from there on are executed. Therefore, if there are more `case` keywords in the `switch()` that you don't want program flow to drop into, you must place a `break` keyword as the final statement of a `case`. The `default` case (if used) is satisfied only if all other tests fail.

The final `case` or `default` in a `switch()` doesn't require a `break` keyword since there is no more code to fall through to. However, if you will be reordering your tests, it can be helpful to always use the `break` keyword for all cases, so that you can move them about without further changes.

Looping Sections of Code

As with JavaScript, PHP supports all three `while()`, `do ... while()`, and `for()` loops for causing sections of code to loop around and repeat. Again, the usage is identical to JavaScript, so I refer you to the "Looping Sections of Code" section in Chapter 5 for full details. The following sections are summaries of how to use each type of loop.

Using while() Loops

A `while()` loop makes one test before deciding whether to enter the loop, and then re-performs the test each time around. If the expression in the test evaluates to `true`, the loop will be entered (or reentered), like this:

```
while($expression)
{
    // Statements
}
```

When there is only a single statement in a `while()` loop, the curly braces can be omitted.

Using do ... while() Loops

In a `do ... while()` loop, the loop will always execute at least once because the test is made only after each time around the loop, like this:

```
do
{
    // Statements

} while ($expression);
```

As with `while()`, when there is only a single statement in a `do ... while()` loop, the curly braces can be omitted.

Using for() Loops

A `for()` loop allows you to initialize variables and make a test before a loop is entered, and also update variables after each loop iteration, like this:

```
for($variable = 1 ; $variable < $value ; ++$value)
{
    // Statements
}
```

You can also add additional variables for initialization before entering the loop, and for updating after each iteration, by separating them with commas, like this:

```
for($variable = 1, $var2 = 20 ; $variable < $value ; ++$value,
--$var2)
{
    // Statements
}
```

If there is only a single statement inside a `for()` loop, the curly braces can be omitted.

Breaking Out of and Continuing Loops

Also like JavaScript, within a `while()`, do ... `while()`, or `for()` loop you can use the `break` keyword to break right out of the loop, or the `continue` keyword to break out of just the current iteration and begin the next iteration (if any).

Processing Web Form Data

By far the biggest use you are likely to put PHP to is processing the data posted from web forms. For example, here's a PHP file that contains both a section of HTML and a PHP program:

```
<!-- processform.php -->
<html>
   <head>
     <title>Form Processing</title>
   </head>
   <body>
     <form method='post' action='processform.php'><pre>
             Name: <input type='text'    name='name'     />
            Email: <input type='text'    name='email'    />
         Username: <input type='text'    name='username' />
         Password: <input type='password' name='password' />
                   <input type='submit' value='Submit details' />
     </pre></form>
   </body>
</html>

<?php
if (isset($_POST['name']))
{
    $name     = $_POST['name'];
    $email    = $_POST['email'];
    $username = $_POST['username'];
    $password = $_POST['password'];

    echo "The data you entered was:<ul>" .
```

```
          "Name = $name<br />" .
          "Email = $email<br />" .
          "Username = $username<br />" .
          "Password = $password</ul>";
}
?>
```

The filename of this example is *processform.php* and the HTML section creates a simple form (using only the `<pre>` tag for formatting) that asks for four values (Name, Email, Username, and Password), which are then posted back to the same file, because of the `action='processform.php'` argument of the `<form>` tag.

The PHP section of the file checks whether the `$_POST` value of `'name'` has a value. If it does, that means some data was posted, so the PHP section extracts the data and displays it with a multiline `echo` statement using the `.` operator to concatenate the various parts. The result looks something like Figure 7-2.

The `<ul>` and `</ul>` (unordered list) tags are used to indent the contained HTML.

Figure 7-2   Posting data to PHP and processing it

POST Requests

The data in the preceding example was sent using a `post` request. This type of request sends the data as HTML headers, which are transmitted in the background and are not visible by the user.

The type of request is chosen using the `method='post'` argument of the `<form>` tag.

GET Requests

Other types of requests are also available, such as the `GET` request. Instead of passing the posted data in HTML headers, when you use the argument `action='get'` all the data is packed into a single string called a *query string*, which is then attached to the URL to which the data is being posted.

For example, the preceding data sent using a `GET` request results in the following query string, in which the + character replaces any spaces, the token `%40` replaces the @ symbol, and the data elements are separated from each other using & characters:

```
name=Clint+Eastwood&email=clint%40eastwood.com&username=DirtyHarry
&password=makemyday
```

When sent to a web server, the query string is prefaced with a ? character and attached to the URL of the file to which the data is being posted, resulting in a long URL such as this:

```
http://html5formobile.com/examples/processform.php?name=Clint+Eastwood
&email=clint%40eastwood.com&username=DirtyHarry&password=makemyday
```

The benefit of `GET` requests and query strings is that URLs can be shared that contain useful data. For example, a Google search for the term PHP can be shared like this: *google.com/search?q=PHP*. Also, data sent in a `GET` request can be easily read in and processed with an in-browser language such as JavaScript, which is a technique used later in this book for passing data to mobile apps created with JavaScript.

The downside of `GET` requests is that the entire complicated and unsightly URL is displayed in the browser's address bar.

Processing GET Requests in PHP

Although the only change required in the HTML to use the `GET` method instead of the `POST` method is to use the `method='get'` argument of a `<form>` tag, in PHP you need to change a few lines of code to access the `$_GET` array (instead of the `$_POST` array). Here's what the entire file (now called *processform2.php*) looks like, with the differences highlighted in bold:

```
<!-- processform2.php -->
<html>
    <head>
        <title>Form Processing</title>
    </head>
```

```
    <body>
        <form method='get' action='processform2.php'><pre>
                Name: <input type='text'      name='name'     />
               Email: <input type='text'      name='email'    />
            Username: <input type='text'      name='username' />
            Password: <input type='password' name='password' />
                      <input type='submit' value='Submit details' />
        </pre></form>
    </body>
</html>

<?php
if (isset($_GET['name']))
{
    $name     = $_GET['name'];
    $email    = $_GET['email'];
    $username = $_GET['username'];
    $password = $_GET['password'];

    echo "The data you entered was:<ul>" .
        "Name = $name<br />" .
        "Email = $email<br />" .
        "Username = $username<br />" .
        "Password = $password</ul>";
}
?>
```

NOTE
Both of these form processing examples are available in the *examples.zip* file at *html5formobile.com*, where they can also be run online by clicking the Chapter 7 link.

Combining JavaScript with PHP for Ajax Calls

Ajax technology is at the heart of all the modern web 2.0 websites that exchange information between the web browser and server in the background, without the user being aware.

To do this, a server-side programming language such as PHP is required. If you have been told that Ajax is complicated, don't worry, as I will demonstrate that it really is quite simple, particularly because I supply ready-made functions for you to call.

Ask the Expert

Q: What exactly is Ajax?

A: The term Ajax (or AJAX, as it used to be written) refers to Asynchronous JavaScript and XML. However, this is a misnomer, because the data transmitted to and from the server by an Ajax call can be in any format, not just XML.

An Ajax call exchanges data between a web browser and web server in the background, without the user being aware of it, and is commonly used for things such as checking whether a chosen username already exists, supplying suggested search terms, and so on.

Microsoft initially came up with the XMLHttpRequest object used by Ajax in Internet Explorer 5, and then decided to use an entirely different approach for IE6. Following Microsoft's lead, other browser developers chose yet another way of doing things, meaning that there are now three different ways of creating an Ajax object, depending on the browser in use.

The main benefit of Ajax is that using it in web pages no longer requires a reposting of information to a server to make an update, because any of the data in a page can be sent to the server at any time. For example, each form field can be separately sent to the server in the background for on-the-fly validation, and if it fails prompts can then be provided back to the user directly on the same web page they are filling in—all without ever submitting the form.

Google's Gmail service is a great example of Ajax, in that everything you type is saved for you so that if your browser crashes (for example), you can easily recover draft e-mails and replies with a mouse click. Gmail also uses Ajax to provide many other features, such as spell checking.

Creating an Ajax Object

Following is a simple JavaScript function that takes into account all the different types of construction methods used in different browsers for creating an Ajax object:

```
function CreateAjaxObject(callback)
{
    try       { var  ajax = new XMLHttpRequest()                      }
    catch(e1) { try { ajax = new ActiveXObject("Msxml2.XMLHTTP")      }
    catch(e2) { try { ajax = new ActiveXObject("Microsoft.XMLHTTP") }
    catch(e3) { ajax = false }}}
```

```
if (ajax) ajax.onreadystatechange = function()
{
   if (this.readyState == 4   &&
       this.status    == 200 &&
       this.responseText != null)
   callback.call(this.responseText)
}

return ajax
}
```

I won't explain in detail how this code works, because all you need to know is how to use it and what it does, which is to try all three methods for creating an Ajax object in turn. If they all fail, then no object is returned. But if one of them succeeds, then the object is returned, ready to use, and the *callback* function name passed to the function is set up to be called as soon as a response is received from the server.

The term "callback" refers to a function that is executed only after an initial function call has completed. In this instance a callback is required because you don't want your main web page to become unresponsive while waiting for an Ajax communication between the web page and server to complete. Instead, you assign a function to be called only after the server has returned new data to the browser.

Initiating a POST Request

The way I have written these JavaScript functions, you do not need to call the CreateAjaxObject() function yourself, because it is called for you by other functions as needed. For example, to send a POST request to a server via Ajax, you need only call the following JavaScript function:

```
function PostAjaxRequest(callback, url, args)
{
   var contenttype = 'application/x-www-form-urlencoded'
   var ajax        = new CreateAjaxObject(callback)
   if (!ajax) return false

   ajax.open('POST', url, true)
   ajax.setRequestHeader('Content-type',   contenttype)
   ajax.setRequestHeader('Content-length', args.length)
   ajax.setRequestHeader('Connection',     'close')
   ajax.send(args)
   return true
}
```

Again, there is no need to explain in detail how this works; you simply need to know that it takes a supplied callback function name, a program URL, and any arguments to supply to that program, and then performs in the same way as posting a form, only the posting happens automatically and in the background.

For example, for security reasons JavaScript is prevented from sharing its data with any website other than the calling one (or ones on the same domain). But by using Ajax to ask the server to exchange data with a different website on another domain, you can overcome this restriction.

To illustrate this, the code shown on the following page fetches the HTML of the index page from the *pluginphp.com* website and places it into a `<div>` tag, as shown in Figure 7-3.

Plug-in PHP: 100 Power Solutions
By Robin Nixon (McGraw Hill 2010, ISBN 978-0071666596)

Home | About | Reader Forum | Buy It | Download | Contact

Select Chapter: 1 2 3 4 5 6 7 8 9 10 11 12

PHP was originally developed in 1994 by Rasmus Lerdorf to replace a set of Perl scripts he had been using to maintain his personal website. Even in the early days Lerdof intended that PHP should be flexible and easily expandable, and through rewrites of the language parser, that has remained a key ethos of the project to this day, with numerous extension libraries available through the PEAR (PHP Extension and Application Repository) add-on. But simply having access to all these functions isn't very useful when you need to quickly put together a project to a tight deadline, because they typically provide very specific functionality. That's where this book comes into its own because it provides 100 ready-to-go plug-ins you can simply drop into your programs and use, normally with a simple, single call.

CONTENTS

1. Building a Development Server
2. PHP and Plug-ins ...
   ... Plus index of all plug-ins
3. Text Processing
4. Image Handling
5. Content Management
6. Forms and User Input
7. The Internet
8. Chat and Messaging
9. MySQL, Sessions and Cookies
10. APIs, RSS and XML
11. Incorporating JavaScript
12. Diverse Solutions

Figure 7-3 The HTML from another website loaded into a `div` element

```
<div id='mydiv'>The HTML will appear here</div>

<script>
   PostAjaxRequest(insert, 'fetchurl.php', 'u=pluginphp.com')

   function insert()
   {
      getElementById('mydiv').innerHTML = this
   }

   // function PostAjaxRequest etc...

   // function CreateAjaxObject etc...

</script>
```

Upon success, the string "The HTML will appear here" in the `<div>` tag is replaced with the HTML that is extracted from the URL supplied in the Ajax call—because no style sheets or other external files are also loaded by this example, the HTML displayed is unlikely to look as well formatted as the original, and on websites where images are referred to with relative URLs, the images will not display either.

To accomplish this HTML fetching, all that is required is to place the two functions `PostAjaxRequest()` and `CreateAjaxObject()` into a `<script>` section of a web page (which I have truncated in the preceding code for space reasons), then use one call to `PostAjaxRequest()` to initiate the Ajax call, and provide one callback function to deal with the information returned by the scrver.

In the preceding example the callback function is called `insert()`, the PHP program on the server is called `fetchurl.php`, and the argument passed to the PHP program is u=pluginphp.com, which places the string `'pluginphp.com'` into PHP's $_POST['u'] element.

The `insert()` function doesn't accept any named arguments. Instead it uses the pseudo variable `this`, which is passed to the function by the `CreateAjaxObject()` function once/if the Ajax call completes successfully. Therefore, all that is required in this function is to insert the value returned in `this` into the HTML of the `<div>` tag with the ID of `mydiv`, by accessing its `innerHTML` property.

NOTE
To differentiate functions I write from those built into JavaScript, I generally use a capital letter for the first character of my functions, while JavaScript functions start with a lowercase letter.

The PHP Side of the POST Ajax Request
On the PHP server the code for the program *fetchurl.php* is extremely simple and reads as follows:

```
<?php
   echo file_get_contents('http://' . $_POST['u']);
?>
```

This extracts the value passed to the program in the `$_POST['u']` element, prefaces it with the string `http://`, and then passes the concatenated string to the PHP function `file_get_contents()`, which fetches the contents of a file either from the local server or, if an Internet address is supplied, from the Web.

The `echo` command preceding the function call simply outputs the data received by the function, which is returned to the JavaScript Ajax function.

Initiating a GET Request

To handle a GET request (instead of a POST) via Ajax you can use another function I have written called `GetAjaxRequest()` (instead of the `PostAjaxRequest()` function). It looks like this:

```
function GetAjaxRequest(callback, url, args)
{
    var nocache = '&nocache=' + Math.random() * 1000000
    var ajax    = new CreateAjaxObject(callback)
    if (!ajax) return false

    ajax.open('GET', url + '?' + args + nocache, true)
    ajax.send(null)
    return true
}
```

Like the other Ajax functions, all you need to know about this one is that it handles a GET post with the web server via Ajax, and using it is identical to using `PostAjaxRequest()` in that it accepts the same arguments: a callback URL, a program URL to communicate with on the server, and any arguments to pass to that program.

NOTE

The `nocache` variable is appended to the query string in this function to prevent the browser from caching reload requests for the same URL. This ensures the data is always pulled directly from the server.

The PHP Side of a GET Ajax Request

In order to accept a GET request instead of a POST request, the *fetchurl.php* program should be slightly modified, as follows, to use the $_GET array (the change is highlighted in bold):

```
<?php
    echo file_get_contents('http://' . $_GET['u']);
?>
```

Summary

You now should have a good basic grasp of PHP as well as JavaScript. In the following chapter, the final one in this section, I'll introduce you to the MySQL database and show you how easy it is to use the application in conjunction with PHP to manage all your web data.

Chapter 8

Introduction to MySQL

Key Skills & Concepts

- Creating MySQL accounts
- Granting user privileges
- Accessing MySQL from PHP
- MySQL data types
- Creating tables and indexes
- Inserting and retrieving data
- Securing data and passwords

This chapter covers the basic information you need to begin operating MySQL. When you finish the chapter, you'll be able to manage simple databases with ease. You'll know how to perform actions such as adding and editing user accounts, creating databases and tables, and inserting data into and reading it back from tables.

This chapter assumes that you have MySQL installed and running and that you have command-line access to its web server via Telnet, SSH (Secure Shell), or even a keyboard, as in the case of a local development server. It also assumes you are using a Linux operating system or another one related to Unix (which also includes Mac OS X). If you are running Windows, installing MySQL and calling up the MySQL command line is different, and I recommend that you refer to the following URL if you need assistance with these tasks:

dev.mysql.com/doc/mysql-windows-excerpt/5.5/en/

Nowadays most popular hosting services (particularly for operating systems such as Linux or BSD) either provide MySQL preinstalled or are willing to add it upon request. If you request that it be added, make sure that they also install the PHP extensions that enable you to communicate with MySQL.

TIP

If you have no intention of using PHP to store data on a server, you can safely skip this chapter, although if you've never used MySQL before, you might wish to browse through it for future reference.

Creating a MySQL User Account

To use MySQL, you need a username and password with which to access it. Normally, MySQL has a `root` username and associated password with full privileges, so that it can be used to create other users and perform system maintenance.

To enter the MySQL command line, you enter the following at the operating system command line:

```
mysql
```

TIP

If the MySQL program is not mentioned in the system path, you should change to the program's folder first, or preface the program name with the path. Usually, you can determine where MySQL has been installed by entering `whereis mysql` at the command line.

On some systems, typing `mysql` will take you right into the program and you'll see the screen shown in Figure 8-1. This type of setup is not very secure because no password has been created for the user `root` and, if the server is hacked, it is very easy to access your MySQL databases. Therefore, on more secure servers you will normally be prompted for a username and password when you run the command.

When you first use the program, the username you need will probably be `root` and the password will be whatever password has been assigned to the `root` user (or, as mentioned, it may not have been created and you can just press ENTER). However, some system administrators disable the `root` username on MySQL and will provide you with a different username and password. So, if in doubt, ask your administrator.

Another way to log in to MySQL is to specify a username after the program name, like this (see Figure 8-2):

```
mysql -uusername -p
```

Here the username `root` has been supplied and the password has been prompted. This is not echoed to the screen when typed, for security reasons. You may also enter the password immediately following the `-p` argument, in which case you won't then be prompted for it, but it will show in clear text when you enter it.

```
html5formobile.com - PuTTY
PTY12212# mysql
Welcome to the MySQL monitor.  Commands end with ; or \g.
Your MySQL connection id is 10
Server version: 5.1.22-rc FreeBSD port: mysql-server-5.1.22

Type 'help;' or '\h' for help. Type '\c' to clear the buffer.

mysql>
```

Figure 8-1   Entering MySQL from the operating system command line

Figure 8-2 Entering MySQL and specifying the username to use

But, whichever way you log into MySQL, the first thing I recommend that you do is create a new username and password, with which you will grant permission to the PHP parser to access it. Without one, PHP will be unable to access MySQL.

To do this you use the CREATE USER command, as in the following, where *php* is the username and *password* is the password to use:

```
CREATE USER 'php'@'localhost' IDENTIFIED BY 'password';
```

TIP

In MySQL all commands should end with a semicolon, with the exception of multiline commands, for which you press ENTER at the end of each part and then use a semicolon after the final line.

When choosing a password, be sure to create one that you can remember (or keep a safe copy of it somewhere off the server), and make it too hard to guess or attempt to crack using brute force. A good password will consist of random upper- and lowercase letters, interspersed with digits and punctuation characters, such as g%Rf$hj*bC37+, which would be very hard to crack indeed (see Figure 8-3, in which previous input and output has been darkened to make the latest command stand out—as is also the case in the following two figures).

Granting Privileges to an Account

Once you have created the new php account (or whatever username you chose to give it), it is not yet useable because you also need to tell MySQL what it is allowed to do. You do that with the GRANT command, like this (see Figure 8-4):

```
GRANT ALL ON *.* TO 'php'@'localhost';
```

This gives the php account access to all of MySQL's features (ALL) on all databases and

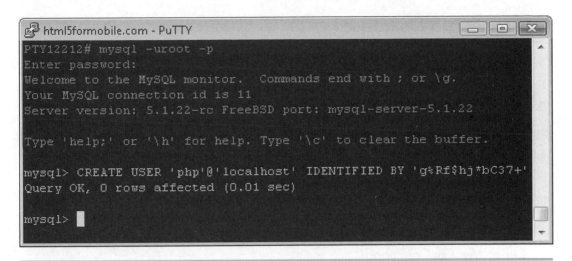

Figure 8-3 Creating the user `php` with the password `g%Rf$hj*bC37+`

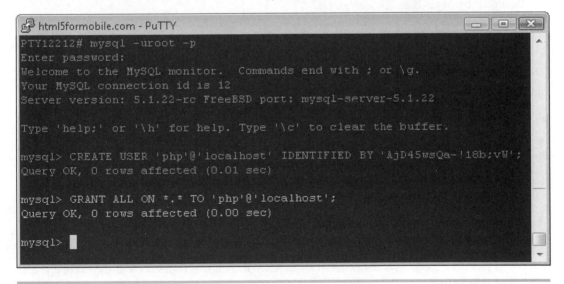

Figure 8-4 Granting access to all features on all databases and tables

tables (`*.*`). These are probably the settings you will normally need, but you can restrict the types of features an account can access, such as only allowing it to read data (and not insert any), and the database and/or tables an account can use. For details on how to do this, please refer to the following URL:

dev.mysql.com/doc/refman/5.1/en/grant.html

Creating a Database

With a user account created and granted privileges, you are now ready to create a database for use by your PHP programs. You can use any name for the database, but in the following example command I have chosen the name phpdb (see Figure 8-5):

```
CREATE DATABASE phpdb;
```

Unlike usernames, when accessing databases and tables, you do not place them within quotation marks—if you try to, an error will be returned.

With the new database created and ready for use, your work is finished at the MySQL command line because PHP can now take over, so you can enter quit to return to the operating system command line if you like, or you may want to stay connected to MySQL so that you can use its command line to ensure that commands that you issue to it from PHP are successful.

Other MySQL Commands

You can do many things in MySQL, but here are a few of the more common commands you will likely use from the command line (shown in uppercase, although lowercase is also accepted by MySQL):

- **DESCRIBE** *table*;   Shows all the field (or column) names in table *table*, and details the types of data they hold.

- **DROP DATABASE** *database*;   Deletes the database called *database*. Beware, the dropped database is virtually impossible to restore.

- **DROP TABLE** *table*;   Deletes the table called *table*. Beware, the dropped table is virtually impossible to restore.

- **QUIT;**   Exits from the MySQL command line.

- **RENAME** *oldname* **TO** *newname*;   Renames the table called *oldname* to *newname*.

- **SHOW DATABASES;**   Lists all the databases in this installation of MySQL.

- **SHOW TABLES;**   Lists all the tables in the current database.

- **STATUS;**   Displays information about MySQL's current status such as the username and database in use.

- **TRUNCATE** *table*;   Removes all data from the table called *table*, but keeps the table and its fields and field types.

- **USE** *database*;   Selects *database* as the currently active database.

For a complete list of MySQL commands, please refer to the following URL:

dev.mysql.com/doc/refman/5.0/en/mysql-commands.html

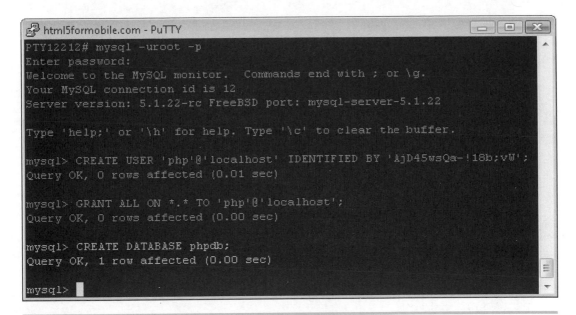

Figure 8-5 Granting access to all features on all databases

Accessing MySQL from PHP

Before you can use MySQL from PHP you will need to log into the database, and the safest way to do that is to create a short PHP program called *login.php*, as follows:

```php
<php // login.php
$db_hostname = 'localhost';
$db_database = 'phpdb';
$db_username = 'php';
$db_password = 'g%Rf$hj*bC37+';

$db_server = mysql_connect($db_hostname, $db_username, $db_password)
   or die('Cannot connect to MySQL: ' . mysql_error());
mysql_select_db($db_database)
   or die('Cannot select database: ' . mysql_error());
?>
```

This file can then be included in any other PHP program by using the `require_once` keyword, like this:

```
require_once 'login.php';
```

This loads in the `login.php` file once only, no matter how many times the command is included in a file or other included files. It is especially important that the opening `<?php` and closing `?>` tags surround the *login.php* code to ensure that nobody idly entering URLs at your website can view the username and password; these tags ensure that only PHP can see the raw code.

Another reason for using a single file for these details is that you can regularly change your password for security reasons, and you will only have to modify one line in one file when you do so.

And there you have it—assuming no errors are returned, the program will be logged in and set to go. However, on a production server you might wish to replace the terse and unfriendly `die()` calls with much better explanations for your users. Better still, make sure that these particular commands never fail.

The Basic MySQL Commands

The main commands you will use in MySQL are those for creating and deleting tables, and those for inserting, retrieving, and deleting data from those tables, as follows (with the terminating semicolons omitted since PHP doesn't use them):

```
CREATE TABLE table(column1, column2, etc...)
DROP TABLE table
INSERT INTO table VALUES('val1', 'val2', etc...)
SELECT * FROM table WHERE field='value'
DELETE FROM table WHERE fieldcontents='value'
```

There are many other qualifiers that extend this basic syntax, as you will see in the following examples, but on the whole these commands represent the majority of your MySQL accessing from PHP.

MySQL Data Types

MySQL tables contain rows and columns. Each row is an entry into the database containing data, and the columns represent the fields within each row. As you might imagine, there are many different types of data that can be placed into a table.

String and Binary Data Types

The string data types are referenced with the keyword CHAR, and binary data is referenced with the keyword BINARY. The CHAR data type supports textual data, while BINARY supports any data, such as images or other data. There are two types of each data type: variable length and fixed length.

Variable length fields are prefaced with the keyword VAR and take up only the size of data entered into a field (up to the maximum size you allocate), while fixed length fields always consume the same amount of data no matter what size of data you actually store in them.

Table 8-1 shows both types of data and the space they use (CHAR and BINARY), in both variable and fixed length forms (VARCHAR and VARBINARY), along with examples of usage.

Data Type	Bytes of Data Used	Examples
CHAR(n)	Exactly n (<= 256)	CHAR(5) "Hello" (uses 5 bytes) CHAR(32) "Pens" (uses 32 bytes)
VARCHAR(n)	Up to n (<= 65536)	VARCHAR(100) "Radio" (uses 5 bytes) VARCHAR(6) "TV" (uses 2 bytes)
BINARY(n)	Exactly n (<= 256)	Same as the CHAR examples but with binary data
VARBINARY(n)	Up to n (<= 65536)	Same as the VARCHAR examples but with binary data

Table 8-1 MySQL's String and Binary Data Types

Which data type to use is a choice you make depending on the data you will store. For example, if usernames may be up to 16 characters in size, you might choose a data type of VARCHAR(16), so that usernames of fewer than 16 letters will take up less room.

On the other hand, if you will be storing binary data that is always 300 bytes long, you would use the data type of BINARY(300).

NOTE

MySQL also supports TEXT and BLOB data types, which are similar to CHAR and BINARY but which may not have default values. They also have other attributes, as well as the ability to store even larger amounts of data. For more information on these data types, please refer to the following URL:
dev.mysql.com/doc/refman/5.0/en/blob.html

Numeric Data Types

MySQL supports numeric data types that take up anything from 1 to 8 bytes of storage and can accept signed or unsigned integer or floating point values. Signed numbers range from a negative value through to a positive value. For example, a TINYINT field can hold 256 different values, which are the values 0 through 255 when unsigned. But, if the data type is signed, values of -128 through 127 are stored.

Table 8-2 details each of the available numeric data types, their minimum and maximum signed values, and their minimum and maximum unsigned values (where applicable).

For example, to store a byte's worth of data with values of between 0 and 255 you would use the INT UNSIGNED data type. Or, to store standard floating point values you would use a data type of FLOAT.

However, unlike the string and binary types, if you follow any numeric data types with a number in brackets, the number doesn't specify the storage size of the data, but instead sets the display width for the data, and is commonly used with the ZEROFILL qualifier like this, INT(5) ZEROFILL, which will cause any numbers with a width of less than five characters to be padded with one or more zeros.

Data Type	Bytes	Minimum Value (Signed/Unsigned)	Maximum Value (Signed/Unsigned)
TINYINT	1	-128 0	127 255
SMALLINT	2	-32768 0	32767 65535
MEDIUMINT	3	-8388608 0	8388607 16777215
INT	4	-2147483648 0	2147483647 4294967295
BIGINT	8	-9223372036854775808 0	9223372036854775807 18446744073709551615
FLOAT	4	-3.402823466E+38 *(cannot be unsigned)*	3.402823466E+38 *(cannot be unsigned)*
DOUBLE	8	-1.7976931348623157E+308 *(cannot be unsigned)*	1.7976931348623157E+308 *(cannot be unsigned)*

Table 8-2   MySQL's Numeric Data Types

NOTE
MySQL also supports a number of different date and time data types, which are not used by any projects in this book. For more information on these data types, please refer to the following URL:
dev.mysql.com/doc/refman/5.1/en/date-and-time-functions.html

Auto-Incrementing
One very important data type qualifier is the keyword AUTO_INCREMENT, which is perfect for adding new records to a database that have no other unique field, because all auto-incremented fields are guaranteed to be unique—each time a record is inserted into a database that uses an auto-incrementing field, that field is incremented by one after the insertion.

Using Indexes
There's one final basic part of MySQL I need to introduce before we can start using it, and that's the concept of indexes. A good way to explain this concept is by way of an analogy.

Imagine that to find a particular book in a library, you have to walk up and down all the aisles until you locate it (if it is there). Further imagine that you want to find a book that has information on a particular subject, but you don't know the title of a suitable book. You could probably find the correct section in the library, but without knowing the title, you would have to browse through many books before locating the information you need.

Fortunately, you can use the Internet to quickly look up an ISBN number with which to locate the online seller with the cheapest price for a book. And the same goes for MySQL, but only if you set it up correctly with indexes.

To do this, you must decide which fields you plan to support searching for and then add indexes to them. For example, a database of registered website users could include some or all of the following details:

- Username

- Password

- Forename (first name)

- Surname (family name)

- E-mail address

- Short biography

Out of these details, you would never need to search for the password, as passwords should always be stored encrypted so that even your website doesn't know what they are, and you probably wouldn't need to search for the biography, but all the other fields are likely candidates for indexing.

Indexing Usernames

Before adding an index to a database, you need to ensure that it will be as small as possible while still providing a fast and efficient lookup. For example, if you allow usernames of up to 16 characters, it would be silly to have an index also of 16 characters because it would be as large as the table and wasteful of disk space.

Instead, you could probably estimate that the first five to seven characters (about a third of the total) would be enough to uniquely identify a single user or, if not, at least narrow down a list of tens of thousands (or maybe hundreds of thousands) of users to a handful, which, for the purposes of a database, is all MySQL needs to quickly look up an item of data.

Therefore, if the username field is to be called `username`, when you create it you might add `INDEX(username(6))` to the command used to create a table. What will then happen is that the first six characters of every username will be stored in a super-fast index so that, for example, all users with the string `jonath` as the first six letters of their username are stored together, and all those starting with `alison` are stored in their group, and so on.

Now, if you wish to quickly locate the record for user `jonathansmith32`, MySQL can quickly look up the `jonath` index, and then searching within it for that particular user will be extremely fast.

Indexing Other Types of Data

The same process used for the username field can be used for the forename and surname fields, and I have found that the e-mail address keys can be even shorter since many of them end with `hotmail.com`, `gmail.com`, or one of the other popular e-mail address domains.

If we estimate that an average e-mail address is 25 characters, and that up to half of those characters follow the @, we can narrow down the significant characters to a dozen or so. A third of that value gives a suggested key length of just four to six characters, or only about a fifth of the length of the average e-mail address.

Creating a Unique Index

Every table should have a field that uniquely identifies the data, such as *username* for a database of website users or *ISBN* for data about books. This ensures that attempts to insert the same data twice will fail.

Ask the Expert

Q: What happens if I don't create any indexes, and what is the best size for an index?

A: Without using an index, every single record has to be examined until the right one is found. In an unsorted database, that requires, on average, processing half the records for each search. Therefore, queries will take longer and longer to return as the database size increases.

I generally use a rule of thumb that the length of index keys should be about a third of the length of the whole string for short strings of under about 25 characters. But, as your strings grow longer, you can get by with smaller and smaller percentages such that, for example, index key widths for strings with an average length of 100 characters would probably only need to be 15–20 characters long to be efficient.

However, as the size of your database increases, you probably will find that increasing index key widths will also help reduce any slowdowns—but you only need to increase them by a little. For example, to go from hundreds of thousands of up to 16-character usernames to millions of such usernames, you might need to change the index key length from five to seven characters to perhaps six to eight characters. However, it's often a matter of trial and error to get the optimum speed with the minimum disk space usage. To do this, you would probably copy a database to another server, optimize it, and then copy it back to the original, rather than risk slowing down a database that's in use while you modify it. But exactly how to do that's beyond the scope of this book.

To do this you can use auto-incrementing on a numeric field, or simply preface an INDEX command with the keyword UNIQUE, like this: UNIQUE INDEX(username(6)).

Creating a Table

Armed with what data types MySQL accepts, we are now ready to write a simple PHP program that creates a table, populates it with some data, and then interrogates the database.

To do this, the following program, *mysqlcreate.php*, stores some test data in a PHP array, then creates the table users and inserts the data into the new table:

```php
<?php // mysqlcreate.php
require_once 'login.php';

$usernames = array(
   array('thepresident', 'iamprez',     'Barack',    'Obama'),
   array('elizabeth',    'oneisqueen', 'Elizabeth', 'Windsor'),
   array('superrich',    'windoz',      'Bill',      'Gates'),
   array('genius',       'e=mc2',       'Albert',    'Einstein'),
   array('onebutton',    'magical',     'Steve',     'Jobs'));

$query =
   "CREATE TABLE IF NOT EXISTS users(\n" .
   "   username VARCHAR(16),\n" .
   "   password CHAR(32),\n"    .
   "   forename VARCHAR(32),\n" .
   "   surname VARCHAR(32),\n"  .
   "   UNIQUE INDEX(username(6)),\n"   .
   "   INDEX(forename(8)),\n"   .
   "   INDEX(surname(8))\n)";

mysql_query($query);

for ($j = 0 ; $j < 5 ; ++$j)
{
   $u = $usernames[$j][0];
   $p = $usernames[$j][1];
   $f = $usernames[$j][2];
   $s = $usernames[$j][3];
   $query = "INSERT INTO users VALUES('$u', '$p', '$f', '$s')";

   mysql_query($query);
}
?>
```

Working through this program, the first line includes the *login.php* file (created earlier) with this call:

```
require_once 'login.php';
```

After that the $usernames two-dimensional array is populated with five rows of data, like this:

```
$usernames = array(
    array('thepresident', 'iamprez',    'Barack',    'Obama'),
    array('elizabeth',    'oneisqueen', 'Elizabeth', 'Windsor'),
    array('superrich',    'windoz',     'Bill',      'Gates'),
    array('genius',       'e=mc2',      'Albert',    'Einstein'),
    array('onebutton',    'magical',    'Steve',     'Jobs'));
```

Then the string variable $query is assembled to create the table using this code:

```
$query =
    "CREATE TABLE IF NOT EXISTS users(\n" .
    "    username VARCHAR(16),\n" .
    "    password CHAR(32),\n"    .
    "    forename VARCHAR(32),\n" .
    "    surname VARCHAR(32),\n"  .
    "    UNIQUE INDEX(username(6)),\n"   .
    "    INDEX(forename(8)),\n"   .
    "    INDEX(surname(8))\n)";
```

Notice that the index for the username is set to UNIQUE so that no two users can share the same username. The assembled string in $query looks like this:

```
CREATE TABLE IF NOT EXISTS users(
    username VARCHAR(16),
    password CHAR(32),
    forename VARCHAR(32),
    surname VARCHAR(32),
    UNIQUE INDEX(username(6)),
    INDEX(forename(8)),
    INDEX(surname(8))
)
```

The extra spaces and \n linefeed characters are for visual formatting only and are not essential to how the program works—in fact, the entire nine lines of code could be replaced with this single (but harder to read) line:

```
$query = "CREATE TABLE IF NOT EXISTS users(username VARCHAR(16),
password CHAR(32), forename VARCHAR(32), surname VARCHAR(32), UNIQUE
INDEX(username(6)), INDEX(forename(8)), INDEX(surname(8))";
```

After creating the string `$query`, the function `mysql_query()` is called, passing it the string as follows, which results in the table being created:

```
mysql_query($query);
```

You can verify this by entering the following two commands if you are still logged into the MySQL command line (see Figure 8-6):

```
USE phpdb;
DESCRIBE users;
```

Figure 8-6 shows that the table has been successfully created with four fields, with the names and types specified. It also shows that all of them, bar `password`, have indexes (indicated by either `UNI`, for unique, or `MUL`, for multiple, in the `Key` column).

Going back to the *mysqlcreate.php* code, the `for()` loop iterates through the `$usernames` array, each time around the loop assigning the username, password, forename, and surname to the variables `$u`, `$p`, `$f`, and `$s`, which are then placed in the variable `$query`, from where they are inserted into the table with another call to `mysql_query()`, like this:

```
for ($j = 0 ; $j < 5 ; ++$j)
{
    $u = $usernames[$j][0];
    $p = $usernames[$j][1];
    $f = $usernames[$j][2];
```

```
mysql> DESCRIBE users;
+----------+-------------+------+-----+---------+-------+
| Field    | Type        | Null | Key | Default | Extra |
+----------+-------------+------+-----+---------+-------+
| username | varchar(16) | YES  | UNI | NULL    |       |
| password | char(32)    | YES  |     | NULL    |       |
| forename | varchar(32) | YES  | MUL | NULL    |       |
| surname  | varchar(32) | YES  | MUL | NULL    |       |
+----------+-------------+------+-----+---------+-------+
4 rows in set (0.00 sec)

mysql>
```

Figure 8-6 Viewing a table's fields, data types, and indexes

```
    $s = $usernames[$j][3];
    $query = "INSERT INTO users VALUES('$u', '$p', '$f', '$s')";
    mysql_query();
}
```

Again, if you are still logged into the MySQL command line, you can check that the data was correctly inserted using this command (see Figure 8-7), which lists all rows in the table:

```
SELECT * FROM users;
```

Inserting More Data

Any additional data to add to the database (generally as a result of data posted from a form) is easily inserted with a pair of commands such as this (where $u, $p, $f, and $s contain the username, password, forename, and surname):

```
$query = "INSERT INTO users VALUES('$u', '$p', '$f', '$s')";
mysql_query($query);
```

Deleting Data

To remove a row of data, you use the DELETE FROM command, like this:

```
$query = "DELETE FROM users WHERE username='genius'";
mysql_query($query);
```

Figure 8-7 Viewing the data in a table

Or simply

```
mysql_query("DELETE FROM users WHERE username='genius'");
```

This will delete all records whose username is `genius`.

Or you can delete all users whose forename is `Bill`, like this:

```
mysql_query("REMOVE FROM users WHERE forename='Bill'");
```

Or you can, for example, issue a compound command to delete all users whose forename is `Bill` and surname is `Gates`, like this:

```
mysql_query(
    "REMOVE FROM users WHERE forename='Bill' AND surname='Gates'");
```

Or you can use the `OR` keyword to delete all users whose forename is `Steve` or whose surname is `Jobs`, like this:

```
mysql_query(
    "REMOVE FROM users WHERE forename='Steve' OR surname='Jobs'");
```

Retrieving Data

In a similar manner to deleting data, you can look it up using the `SELECT` keyword, like the following, which returns all users whose forename is `Steve`:

```
$result = mysql_query("SELECT * FROM users WHERE forename='Steve'");
```

To then find out just how many users were returned by the query, you can use the following command:

```
$rows = mysql_num_rows($result);
```

What this does is use the value in `$result` that was returned by the `SELECT` query to place the number of rows selected into the variable `$rows`. Using this value, you can then iterate through all the rows, like this:

```
for ($j = 0 ; $j < $rows ; ++$j)
{
    $u = mysql_result($result, $j, 'username');
    $p = mysql_result($result, $j, 'password');
    $f = mysql_result($result, $j, 'forename');
    $s = mysql_result($result, $j, 'surname');

    echo "$u: $f $s - Password='$p'<br />";
}
```

This displays all the rows in the following format:

```
elizabeth: Elizabeth Windsor - Password='oneisqueen'
```

Or you can use the more powerful `mysql_fetch_row()` function to return all the items in a row at once, like this much shorter code:

```
for ($j = 0 ; $j < $rows ; ++$j)
{
    $row = mysql_fetch_row($result);
    echo "$row[0]: $row[2] $row[3] - Password='$row[1]'<br />";
}
```

Each time `mysql_fetch_row()` is called, it returns the next row of data.

Returning Specific Fields

If you need to retrieve fewer fields than are stored in a row, you can speed things up and save memory by replacing the * following the `SELECT` command with a list of comma-separated field (or column) names, as with the following code, which returns only the forename and surname, since the username is already known (it is used to perform the query):

```
$result = mysql_query(
    "SELECT forename,surname FROM users WHERE username='thepresident'");
```

The code to retrieve the returned data is different since fewer fields are returned and, because the usernames are unique, only one row is returned, so it might look as simple as this:

```
$row = mysql_fetch_row($result);
echo "Name: $row[2] $row[3]";
```

Returning a Specific Number of Rows

To return only a set number of rows (and, consequently, run a query as fast as possible), you can use the `LIMIT` keyword, as in the following example, which will return a maximum of ten records:

```
$result = mysql_query(
    "SELECT * FROM users WHERE forename='Steve' LIMIT 10");
```

If you are writing a system that pages search results, for example, ten at a time, you could then perform a second query on the database to return the next (up to) ten rows, as in the following example, which starts the search at the tenth result:

```
$result = mysql_query(
    "SELECT * FROM users WHERE forename='Steve' LIMIT 10 10");
```

And to get the third group of ten (if any), you would use the following (and so on):

```
$result = mysql_query(
   "SELECT * FROM users WHERE forename='Steve' LIMIT 20 10");
```

Ordering Returned Results

To change the order of returned results, you can order them by any field in either ascending or descending order using the ORDER BY or DESC keyword, respectively. For example, the following will sort the returned results by forename in ascending alphabetical order:

```
$result = mysql_query(
   "SELECT * FROM users WHERE forename='Steve' ORDER BY forename");
```

Or, to order the results by surname in descending order, you could use this:

```
$result = mysql_query(
   "SELECT * FROM users ORDER BY surname DESC");
```

Putting This All Together into a Program

Having created the users table and populated it with some data, let's use the information from the preceding few sections to create a program to return results from the database, such as the following *mysqllookup.php*:

```
<html><!-- mysqllookup.php -->
   <head>
      <title>Looking up MySQL data</title>
   </head>
   <body>
      <form method='post' action='mysqllookup.php'>
         Enter Username <input type='text' name='username'/>
         <input type='submit' />
      </form>

<?php
if (isset($_POST['username']))
{
   require_once 'login.php';
   $u      = $_POST['username'];

   $query  = "SELECT forename,surname FROM users WHERE username='$u'";
   $result = mysql_query($query);
   $rows   = mysql_num_rows($result);

   if (!$rows) $display = "Not found";
   else
```

```
    {
        $row      = mysql_fetch_row($result);
        $display = "$row[0] $row[1]";
    }

    echo "Username: $u - $display";
}
?>
    </body>
</html>
```

This program comprises two parts: a beginning section of HTML (with a matching pair of closing HTML tags at the end of the listing), and within these a segment of PHP code, which I have highlighted in bold. The HTML creates a simple form with which a username can be entered for querying the MySQL database. The variable name `username` is used for posting to the PHP. In Figure 8-8 the username `genius` has been entered and the name of its owner has been displayed.

The PHP code first checks whether the `$_POST` array contains an entry with the name `username`, like this:

```
if (isset($_POST['username']))
```

If it does not, then nothing has been posted, so none of the PHP code is entered and program flow drops back to the closing HTML tags. But if `username` does exist, then a search term has been posted, so the *login.php* file is loaded in to make a connection with the database and the variable $u is assigned the search term that was posted, like this:

```
require_once 'login.php';
$u       = $_POST['username'];
```

Next, a query is assembled in the variable $query and is passed to the mysql_query() function, with the result of the call then saved in the variable $result, which is then tested using the mysql_num_rows() function to see whether any rows were returned, like this:

```
$query  = "SELECT forename,surname FROM users WHERE username='$u'";
$result = mysql_query($query);
$rows   = mysql_num_rows($result);
```

Figure 8-8 Querying MySQL from PHP

If `$rows` is not equal to at least 1, then nothing was returned and so the string `$display` is assigned the value `Not found`. But if `$rows` has a value, then at least one row was returned (in fact, only one can be returned due to `username` being a unique field), so the data is fetched from the row and placed in the `$display` variable, like this:

```
$row     = mysql_fetch_row($result);
$display = "$row[0] $row[1]";
```

Finally, the result of the query is displayed, like this:

```
echo "Username: $u - $display";
```

If a lookup is unsuccessful, the result is as shown in Figure 8-9, in which the username `anyusername` has not been found.

NOTE
If you need more information on using PHP and MySQL (and also JavaScript), you may be interested in my book *Learning PHP, MySQL, and JavaScript* (O'Reilly, 2009), which goes into a great deal of detail, from a beginner's point of view, on all three topics.

Security and Anti-hacking Measures
Beginners to MySQL often don't recognize the dangers posed by providing direct access from form inputs to MySQL, but there are many. It is dangerous because usually the `mysql_query()` function is called to create a query and, because it uses SQL (Structured Query Language), it is possible for users to pass malicious commands via a web form that, when sent to the function, can provide access to the database, or even corrupt or destroy the data.

Additionally, if a user posts HTML or JavaScript code via a web form that gets inserted into a database unchecked, when the data is returned from MySQL and displayed, so too is the HTML or JavaScript, which could corrupt the display, redirect users to malware sites, and more.

To completely prevent these types of hacks, you must sanitize all posted data before it gets anywhere near MySQL. In fact, you should always sanitize such data when used for any

Figure 8-9 The username has not been found in the database.

purpose. I'll give you two functions you can use to do this, one for general sanitizing of form data, and the other for further processing before using it in MySQL. The first function, called `htmlentities()`, is built into PHP and you use it like this:

```
$variable = htmlentities($_POST['name']);
```

This changes any HTML or JavaScript keywords into entities that can be stored and displayed but which will not be acted on as commands. The resulting string is then placed in the variable `$variable`.

For example, the string `<b>some text</b>` results in the string `&lt;b gt;some text&lt;/b&gt;` when passed through the `htmlentities()` function—the `<` character is replaced with `&lt;` and the `>` character is replaced with `&gt;`, which HTML will still display as the left and right angle brackets, but they will have no ability to create HTML tags.

Following is another function you can use to prevent malicious attempts at hacking MySQL:

```
function mysql_sanitize($string)
{
    if (get_magic_quotes_gpc())
        $string = stripslashes($string);
    return mysql_real_escape_string($string);
}
```

The `if()` statement deals with a simple form of hacking prevention called Magic Quotes that was used in older versions of MySQL and is now deprecated. The idea behind this tool was to automatically escape all incoming data sent via forms, but it causes more headaches than anything, so the `if()` statement turns off the use of Magic Quotes if they are enabled. Instead, the `mysql_real_escape_string()` function below it properly escapes all posted data, such that no known hacking strategies will get through (and almost certainly none ever will).

Therefore, as long as the `mysql_sanitize()` function is placed somewhere in a program, the following code will secure any posted data, making it safe to use in MySQL queries:

```
$variable = mysql_sanitize(htmlentities($_POST['name']));
```

This is the same as the earlier code recommended for converting HTML characters to entities, but with the addition of a call to the `mysql_sanitize()` function.

Modifying the mysqllookup.php Code

Taking these security measures into account, the preceding *mysqllookup.php* program should change this line

```
$u = $_POST['username'];
```

to the following:

```
$u = mysql_sanitize(htmlentities($_POST['username']));
```

And the following function definition should be added:

```
function mysql_sanitize($string)
{
    if (get_magic_quotes_gpc())
        $string = stripslashes($string);
    return mysql_real_escape_string($string);
}
```

Security and Passwords

I mentioned earlier that raw passwords should never be stored in a database because this poses a huge risk should the server ever be compromised. Instead, the best value to store for a password is one derived from it via a one-way function that cannot be reversed, such as a process known as MD5 (Message-Digest algorithm 5).

Using PHP's md5() function, you can pass it a string of any length and it will return a 32-character string of seemingly random gibberish. For example, the string mypassword results in the new string 34819d7beeabb9260a5c854bc85b3e44. So far, so good, but, unfortunately, there are hackers who have spent years building up so-called rainbow tables of every password or possible password they can think of. These rainbow tables contain millions of these hash strings, and you can bet that the preceding one is in there. For example, using Google, you can enter the preceding 32-byte hash and you will see over 400 pages that reference it!

So you can't store such direct hashes, but there is a way to prevent any rainbow table or Google search from looking up a hash, and that's called *salting*, which is the process of adding some secret characters to it that only you know.

For example, say you choose two sets of characters as follows for a pair of salts (you can use one salt or as many as you like): fT5$! and -:&;qK. You can now add these to the password string anywhere you like, such as in the following code, which places them at the start and end:

```
$hash = md5('fT5$!' . $password . '-:&;qK');
```

Using the same value of mypassword for $password gives a totally different hash of 43a3c94ed32cb41d1a964bc87c891605 and, as you'd expect, returns no results at Google (at least not until any online copies of this book get indexed).

So, remember, instead of storing raw passwords in your database, pass them through a salting process using one or more salts that you never reveal, and store only the result of this process, which in the preceding example would be the value in $hash. Then, when a user is logging into a site, for example, to verify whether the correct password has been entered, you simply run the newly submitted password through your salting process and compare the

32-character hash that results with the one stored in the database. If they are the same, then the passwords match.

At no point have you saved a copy of the user's password, yet you can still verify it whenever required. Your site is secure, and even if hackers break into your database, the passwords will never be revealed, which is a great service to those of your users who employ the same usernames and passwords on all sites they visit.

Summary

Of necessity, since this is a book about HTML5, not MySQL (or even PHP, for that matter), only the very bare bones of the database engine are presented here. However, there's sufficient information in this chapter to get you started with managing simple user data, as will be required in Chapter 10, which discusses how to build web applications.

Part II

Developing for Mobile Devices

This part of the book explains the things you need to do to give mobile visitors to your website the best experience possible. Chapter 9 includes tips on image and font scaling to make the best use of mobile screen resolutions and sizes, along with JavaScript code to manage this for you automatically, and a number of other tips for presenting your websites in the best possible way and making them highly interactive on touch devices.

Chapter 10 introduces a free eBook publishing platform you can use to create great-looking eBooks for display on desktop PCs and Macs, as well as iOS and Android devices. This application, called eML, supports audio, video, maps, sidebars, colors, lists, and everything else you could want to include in an eBook. It's also powerful enough to use as a content management system (CMS) for creating general websites, not just eBooks.

Then, Chapter 11 explains what you need to do when preparing to take an online website offline and turn it into a stand-alone application. Using this information, you'll be ready to move on to Part III of the book, in which you'll learn how to embed these applications within the simple frameworks provided on the companion website, to create fully functioning iOS and Android apps, without having to program in either Apple's Objective C or Android's Java.

Chapter 9

Developing Mobile Friendly Websites

Key Skills & Concepts

- Working with smaller screens

- Automatically resizing text and images

- Setting a constant width viewport

- Making your web pages flow

- Tips for easy touch input

- Making SMS (Short Message Service) and phone numbers accessible to smartphones

- Creating home screen icons

By following the guidelines in this chapter, you'll find it much easier to offer a great experience to those of your website visitors who use mobile browsers. You can either use the tips for your whole website, or use JavaScript to detect the current browser and reformat your current website as necessary.

Screen Dimensions

The most important thing to consider when creating mobile friendly websites is the screen size of the user. No matter how well iOS or Android manages zooming into and out of standard web pages, those web pages are not as easy to use on mobile devices as ones designed specifically for smaller screens. For example, Figure 9-1 shows a screen grab from a Dell Streak displaying the CNN home page.

It's a well-constructed home page, but it's formatted for desktop computers and, on a mobile device, you must zoom in to clearly view sections of interest. Of course, like many other top websites, CNN has an alternative website for mobile devices (see Figure 9-2), but why should a smartphone have to restrict itself to viewing a page intended for a simple "dumb" phone?

Now, I'm not criticizing CNN's mobile home page. It's good and does the job well for simple phones, but it looks very basic when viewed on a smartphone.

On the other hand, the 1024-pixel width of the standard page has been formatted for displays of at least that width, and when viewed in portrait mode on a browser that has only 480 pixels at its disposal, it cannot be read without zooming.

Figure 9-1   The CNN home page viewed on a Dell Streak

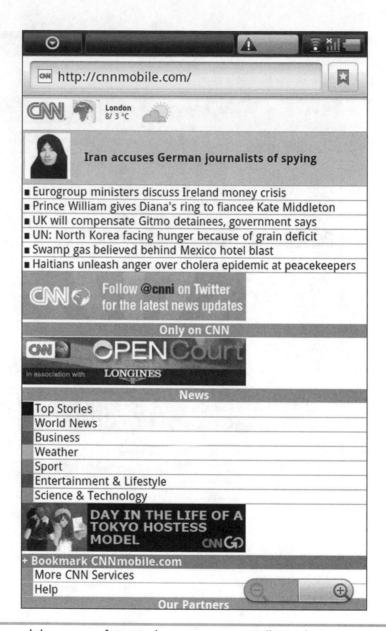

Figure 9-2 The mobile version of CNN's home page on a Dell Streak

Smartphone Format

Sites that wish to target iOS and Android (or other smartphone operating systems) need to offer a third category of web page format (other than desktop and simple mobile): smartphone format. This type of web page automatically takes into account the width of the browser being used, so that it becomes readable without having to use an un-pinch gesture to zoom in, and then scroll the screen to select other areas to view.

The great thing is that you don't actually have to build a website to be viewable at a width of 480 pixels; by using a width of double that (960 pixels), as long as you double your font and image sizes and use a liquid layout, the page will reformat well to a width of 480 pixels.

Ask the Expert

Q: **What is so good about the width of 960 pixels? Why not standardize on 1024 pixels?**

A: 960 pixels is a good width because it's the width in pixels of the iPhone 4 in landscape mode, and twice its width in portrait mode. Therefore, your pages are guaranteed to look as good as possible on that phone when you use a width of 960 pixels.

If a value of 1024 were used, this would scale best to resolutions of 512 or 768 pixels, which are uncommon widths on phones—although the iPad does have a resolution of 1024×768 pixels, and it does scale 960-pixel-wide pages to these dimensions very well.

In answer to the second part of the question, I suppose that a 1024-pixel standard width might also work well, but I have thoroughly tested all the code in this book at a 960-pixel width on a variety of iOS and Android devices, so I know that it does work well.

For example, to accompany this book I have developed a free eBook development and viewing language called eML (for eBook Markup Language). It comprises a simple JavaScript program that you include along with a page of HTML and any images or other media, and it reformats everything for you.

There's more information on this system in Chapter 10, but if you look at Figure 9-3 you'll see an eBook using the system being displayed on a PC running Microsoft Internet Explorer. Then, in Figure 9-4, a different section of the same web page is displayed on an iPhone, where the graphics have been enlarged and the fonts resized (all automatically) to make maximum use of the screen, and to provide decently sized buttons.

As you can see in the iPhone screen grab, the reformatted display is extremely easy to view. You may also have noticed that, whereas the menu text and reading window of Figure 9-3 are in scrollable frames, because scroll bars are very fiddly to use on touch devices, frames are not used on the iPhone version; instead you only have to swipe to scroll the screen. Similar account is also taken of iPad screen sizes and rotations, and Android

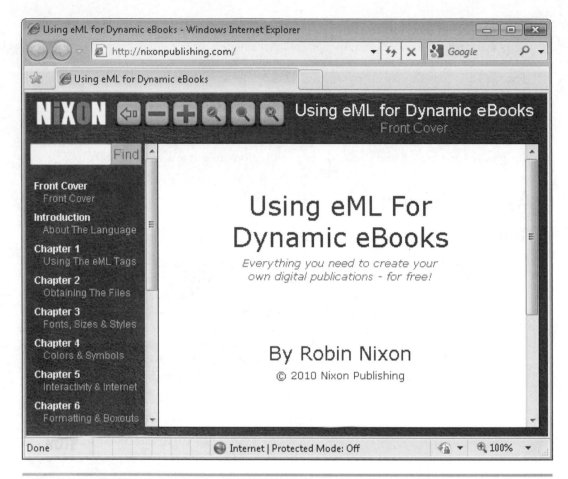

Figure 9-3 The eML eBook being displayed on a PC

phones and tablets such as the Galaxy Tab—as well as halfway houses such as the Dell Streak. On these devices eML will adjust display to make the best use of their resolution, dimensions, and other attributes.

The way to ensure you have a 960-pixel display to work on with iOS and Android applications is to include the following `<meta>` tag at the start of your HTML documents (or in the `<head>` section if you prefer):

```
<meta name="viewport" content="width=980" />
```

This tells both types of devices to format the screen to accommodate a 960-pixel-wide web page. Then, having done this, you can build your smartphone website with a fixed width of 960 pixels, but make sure you take into account the following sections.

Figure 9-4 The same eBook displayed on an iPhone

Font Sizes

Due to the different sizes and dimensions of mobile device displays, you should use conditional JavaScript and/or CSS to scale the font size up to a readable size in relation to a 960-pixel-wide page. For example, I have found by trial and error that the relative font sizes listed in Table 9-1 work quite well.

If you are using a base font size other than 12 pt, simply multiply the value of that font size by the value in the third column to calculate the new font size (middle column) for the device you are targeting. For example, if you are using a base font size of 10 pt and want to calculate the font size to use for the iPad, you would calculate 10×1.5 to get a font size of 15 pt.

Of course, these font sizes are my personal preference, but you should find that they are in the right ballpark, so you may only need to tweak them slightly for your own taste.

Device	Font Size	Relative to Desktop
Desktop computer	12 pt	1.00
Android	24 pt	2.00
iPhone/iPod Touch	21 pt	1.75
iPad	18 pt	1.50

Table 9-1 Suggested Font Sizes to Use on a 960-Pixel-Wide Web Page

NOTE

Android mobile devices tend to require slightly larger fonts than Apple mobile devices because their screen resolutions are generally of lower definition, and therefore seem to require that extra increase in size.

You can use code similar to the following web page to set up the font size for a `<div>` tag that encloses all the page's contents:

```
<meta name='viewport' content='width=980' />
<html><!-- dynamicfonts.htm -->
   <head>
      <title>Dynamic font sizing</title>
   </head>
<body>
   <div id='without'>
      <h3>Without dynamic resizing</h3>
       <ul>
         Standard Text<br />
         <h3>Heading 3</h3>
         <h2>Heading 2</h2>
         <h1>Heading 1</h1>
      </ul>
   </div>
   <div id='content'>
      <h3>With dynamic resizing</h3>
      <ul>
         Standard Text<br />
         <h3>Heading 3</h3>
         <h2>Heading 2</h2>
         <h1>Heading 1</h1>
      </ul>
   </div>
```

```
<script>
   e = document.getElementById('content').style
   e.background = '#ddd'
   e.width      = '960px'

   switch(GetBrowser())
   {
      case('Android')   : f = '24pt'; break
      case('iPhone')    : f = '21pt'; break
      case('iPad')      : f = '18pt'; break
      default           : f = '12pt'; break
   }

   e.fontSize = f

   function GetBrowser()
   {
      if (NavCheck('iPhone') || NavCheck('iPod'))
         return 'iPhone'
      else if (NavCheck('iPad'))
         return 'iPad'
      else if (NavCheck('Android'))
         return 'Android'
   }

   function NavCheck(check)
   {
      return navigator.userAgent.indexOf(check) != -1
   }
</script>
```

This web page begins by setting the viewport to a width of 960 pixels. Then, in the <body> section, a pair of identical <div> sections are displayed, the second of which has the base font size increased by the JavaScript following the HTML.

This script sets the background of the second <div> to light gray and widens it to exactly 960 pixels so that it occupies the full screen width. The switch() statement then applies different point sizes to the variable f, which is then used to change the font size of the <div> according to the type of browser being used, as determined by the NavCheck() function.

If the device is not an Android, iPhone/iPod, or iPad device, then a suitable font size for a desktop PC is selected. The result of displaying this page on an Android device (this time, on a Google Nexus One) is shown in Figure 9-5, which shows just the relevant portion of the screen.

Image Sizes

Resizing your images isn't quite as easy because they don't scale up as well as fonts do. However, they do tend to scale down better than up, so if you create all your images at the largest size you intend to display, they can be scaled down from there by the browser without too much loss of quality.

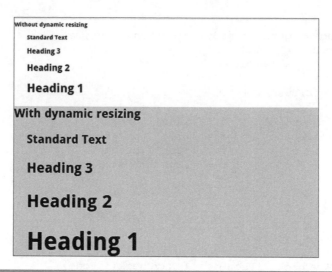

Figure 9-5 The results of displaying the *dynamicfonts.htm* file on an Android device

For example, Figure 9-6 shows a 480×480-pixel image of Earth that has been automatically reduced by 75 percent (to 240×240 pixels) for display on a desktop monitor (in this instance, using the Chrome browser).

But the same web page on the iPhone looks like Figure 9-7, in which the image is reduced by only 25 percent, since it needs to appear larger on such a small screen.

Also, in Figure 9-6, the text is displayed at the desktop size of 12 pt, but in Figure 9-7 it has been enlarged to 22 pt. Both the text and image resizing is accomplished with the following program, with the differences between it and the previous program shown in bold text:

```
<meta name='viewport' content='width=980' />
<html><!-- dynamicimages.htm -->
   <head>
      <title>Dynamic image sizing</title>
   </head>
   <body>
      <div id='content'>
         <img id='image' src='earth.gif' width='480' height='480'
            align='left' />
         <h3>The Earth</h3>
         Earth (or the Earth) is the third planet from the Sun, and the
         densest and fifth-largest of the eight planets in the Solar
         System.<br />
              It is also the largest of the
         Solar System's four terrestrial planets. It is sometimes
         #referred to as the World, the Blue Planet, or by its Latin
         name, Terra.<br />
              Home to millions of species
```

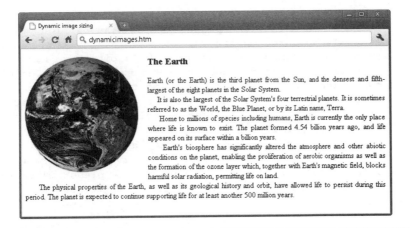

Figure 9-6 Although reduced to 25 percent of its original size, the image still looks sharp

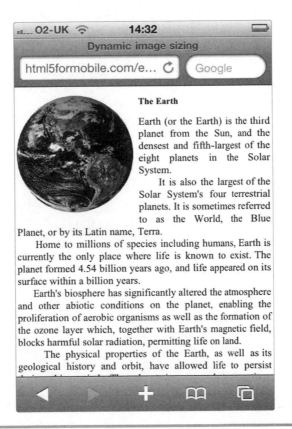

Figure 9-7 This image has been reduced from its original size by 25 percent

including humans, Earth is currently the only place where life
is known to exist. The planet formed 4.54 billion years ago,
and life appeared on its surface within a billion years.
     Earth's biosphere has
significantly altered the atmosphere and other abiotic
conditions on the planet, enabling the proliferation of aerobic
organisms as well as the formation of the ozone layer which,
together with Earth's magnetic field, blocks harmful solar
radiation, permitting life on land.
     The physical properties of the
Earth, as well as its geological history and orbit, have allowed
life to persist during this period. The planet is expected to
continue supporting life for at least another 500 million years.
</div>

```
<script>
   document.getElementById('image').style.margin = '0px 20px 20px 0px'
   e            = document.getElementById('content').style
   e.textAlign = 'justify'
   t            = document.getElementsByTagName('img')

   switch(GetBrowser())
   {
      case('Android')   : f = '24pt'; m = 1.00; break
      case('iPhone')    : f = '22pt'; m = 0.92; break
      case('iPad')      : f = '18pt'; m = 0.75; break
      default           : f = '12pt'; m = 0.50; break
   }

   for (j = 0 ; j < t.length ; ++j)
   {
      t[j].width  *= m
      t[j].height *= m
   }

   e.fontSize  = f

   function GetBrowser()
   {
      if (NavCheck('iPhone') || NavCheck('iPod')) return 'iPhone'
      else if (NavCheck('iPad'))                  return 'iPad'
      else if (NavCheck('Android'))               return 'Android'
   }

   function NavCheck(check)
   {
      return navigator.userAgent.indexOf(check) != -1
   }
</script>
```

Following are the most interesting lines from this program, in which the array t is assigned all the HTML <img> elements in the document, which are then processed in turn using the following for() loop, with their image widths and heights being reduced by between 0 percent for Android (by multiplying both dimensions by 1.00) and 75 percent for desktop browsers (by multiplying both dimensions by 0.50), with a 25 percent reduction on iPhones (by multiplying both dimensions by 0.87) and 50 percent on iPads (by multiplying both dimensions by 0.71):

```
t = document.getElementsByTagName('img')

    switch(GetBrowser())
    {
        case('Android')   : f = '24pt'; m = 1.00; break
        case('iPhone')    : f = '22pt'; m = 0.92; break
        case('iPad')      : f = '18pt'; m = 0.75; break
        default           : f = '12pt'; m = 0.50; break
    }

    for (j = 0 ; j < t.length ; ++j)
    {
        t[j].width  *= m
        t[j].height *= m
    }
```

Liquid Flow

The two preceding examples illustrate the use of liquid flow, in which elements are not forced into predefined locations. Instead, images are placed on the left or right and text flows around them.

If you wish, you can include more columns than just one, but if you do so, I recommend that you create them as left floated or aligned <div> tags, so that any that don't fit alongside the others will gracefully fall down below, rather than extend the page to the right—thus requiring horizontal scrolling to view them.

For example, you could use HTML such as the following, in which I have used the align='left' attribute of the <div> element, but could equally have used a style rule of float:left:

```
<div align='left'>
   Some contents
</div>
<div align='left'>
   More contents
</div>
<div align='left'>
   Even more contents
</div>
```

Depending on how wide you set these elements or how wide they become due to the elements within them, browsers with insufficient width available to place them all side by side will drop one or more down to the next free location.

NOTE

Of course, these methods for text and image sizing are intended to run automatically and therefore may not always result in exactly the sizes you want, but using them is a whole lot easier than rewriting your web pages for each and every browser and platform.

Using Rollovers and Tooltips

One word of advice: don't.

On devices that do not support a mouse, rollovers and tooltips are pointless. For example, on iOS and Android, users are restricted to pointing and dragging, and there is no alternative action to simulate a mouse hover.

On the other hand, if you intend your pages to also be used on non-touch devices, then go ahead and use rollover techniques, but don't rely on them for the interface—use them only as page enhancements.

Interactivity Navigation and User Input

Wherever possible, for touch devices you should replace textual inputs with point-and-click options such as radio buttons, check boxes, or, better still, your own graphical elements.

For sites that require user registration, you must ask for a username and password to log a user in, of course, but consider whether to use cookies to allow that user to remain logged in for the next few visits, or for as many days as you think is sensible to support. The longer you allow your users to stay logged in, the less your users will have to call up the onscreen keyboard.

Also try to avoid making users navigate around the screen. If you can, place segments of a page in separate <div> tags and give each an absolute position setting so that they can be overlaid on each other. Then make all layers except the current one invisible, and use tabs or some other simple system to change between them.

On long web pages, it helps to place multiple Home buttons or text links throughout the page so that the user can easily return to the top of the page. Or, with CSS3 and HTML5, you can always use statically located elements that remain onscreen to provide navigational access.

If you feel ambitious, you could also consider replacing a mobile device's screen-hogging, built-in, pop-up keyboard with one of your own (an example of how to do this is presented in Chapter 11), or use a third-party virtual keyboard such as the one at *greywyvern.com/code/javascript/keyboard* (see Figure 9-8).

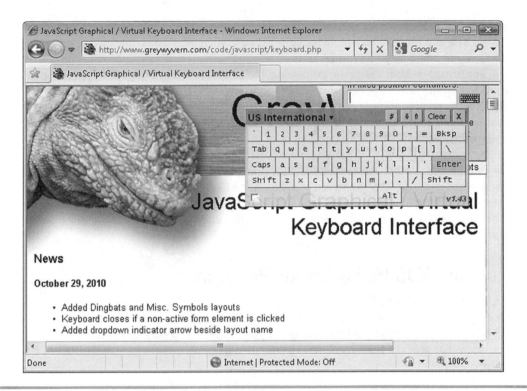

Figure 9-8   A virtual JavaScript keyboard that pops up next to an input field

Use sms: and tel: URLs

To accommodate mobile devices that are telephones, make sure that you include on your website the SMS and/or telephone number within a clickable link, like this:

```
Click to contact us via
   <a href='sms:0123456789'>SMS</a> or
   <a href='tel:0123456789'>telephone</a>.
```

This places a link under the text that, as with any `http://` or `mailto:` URL, when clicked, will call up the phone's SMS editor or telephone dialing screen.

Apple Home Screen Icons

You can provide to your iOS users an icon for use in identifying a web page when it is saved as a home screen icon. To do this, enter a line such as the following at the start of the web page, where `myicon.png` is the name of the icon to use:

```
<link rel="apple-touch-icon" href="myicon.png" />
```

For compatibility with all iOS devices, the icon should be a PNG image of 57×57 pixels. Create a strong image on a simple background and, when used as a home screen icon, Apple devices will add a nice shiny luster to it.

For example, after automatic processing, the image shown in Figure 9-9 appears on the third row of the iPhone home screen as shown in Figure 9-10. The image was added to the desktop by clicking the + button (or an arrow pointing out of a box on iOS 4.2) at the bottom middle of the browser and selecting Add to Home Screen.

Unfortunately, there is no equivalent of this for Android because all Android devices seem to deal differently with home page bookmarks. Generally, each Android device uses its own custom icons, and sometimes they don't even save the page's title, but instead enter a generic title like "Browser." I really hope Google reinstates this feature in a future release to create a unified experience, because the apple `<meta>` tag definitely used to work on pre-2.1 versions of Android—the functionality just seems to have disappeared since then.

Running iOS Home Screen Pages in Full Screen Mode

Once a user has saved a web page to an iOS home screen, when clicked it opens up just as if it had been selected from a bookmark. But if you would like to gain access to the navigation and status bar areas of the screen, you can use the following `<meta>` tag at the start of a web page:

```
<meta name="apple-mobile-web-app-capable" content="yes" />
```

When the iOS browser sees this tag during the loading of a home screen web page, it immediately disables both the navigation and status bars. For example, Figure 9-11 shows the same web page as Figure 9-7 but with this `<meta>` tag applied.

Figure 9-9   A simple but bold 57×57-pixel icon

Figure 9-10   The icon from Figure 9-9 on an iPhone home screen after processing

Creating an iOS Splash Screen

During the loading of a home screen web page, the screen display will not always be pretty, particularly if you have enabled full screen mode and it hasn't fully redrawn. To mitigate this, you can provide an image to iOS to display during loading, like this:

```
<link rel="apple-touch-startup-image" href="splashimage.png" />
```

Place this tag near the start of your web page, and the image (which must have a resolution of 320×460 pixels) will display until the page is fully loaded. A good image could be an enlarged version of the web page icon, along with the page title and possibly the text "Loading…"

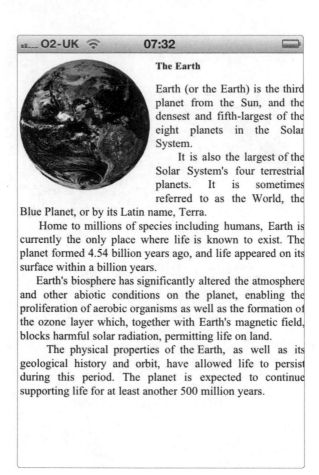

Figure 9-11   Releasing the navigation and status bar screen space to a web page

NOTE
On small and fast-loading web pages, you may never see the splash image because there is not time to load it. In such cases, try reducing the image size. Also, the splash image does not always display the first time a home screen icon is clicked, because it hasn't yet been downloaded, but, if it's going to display, it should thereafter.

Summary

If you use the tips detailed in this chapter when you're designing mobile friendly websites, your websites will be easier to use and look better than simple mobile websites—with very little extra work required to repurpose content from a website originally aimed at desktop users. And if you're developing from scratch, it should be a breeze.

In the next chapter I'll introduce the eML markup language for eBooks, which creates cross-browser and platform-independent eBooks and websites, and which was built using the techniques from this chapter.

Chapter 10

Using the eML eBook Platform

Key Skills & Concepts

- The basic structure of eML

- Creating the menu and chapters

- Using eML tags

- The three different types of tag

- Fonts, colors, and special symbols

- Basic and advanced formatting

- Overriding font sizes on iOS and Android

This chapter complements the previous one by showing you how to use a ready-made and free publication platform called eML (eBook Markup Language) that is already aware of the main different operating systems and browsers. It is especially suited to producing portable eBooks that work both as websites and as stand-alone applications, and is most useful for quickly getting your publications into the iOS and Android stores.

With eML you can place an entire eBook within a single HTML document, as shown in Figure 10-1. In fact, all the figures in this chapter have been captured using different devices displaying the eML software running, so that you can see how well they all reformat the publication to their own screen dimensions and capabilities.

Each eML document uses a JavaScript program file to process and display the book at its best according to the device and browser in which it finds itself. But eML is not just for eBooks, because you can also use the 150 special tags it provides as a content management system (CMS).

But the most importing thing about eML is that it works both as a website and as an application, which can be either a web app or a self-contained device app. This is achieved by keeping as much as possible of the website in a single file, and then using JavaScript to display a single page at a time, which cuts down on multiple page loads and server hits, and also makes eML eBooks and applications extremely fast to load and run.

NOTE

All the code and associated files you need for this chapter are available in the *examples.zip* file, which you can download from the companion website at *html5formobile.com*. You can also read the online eML manual at *nixonpublishing.com*, where you can always download the most up-to-date version of eML.

Figure 10-1   The front page of the eBook viewed on an iPhone

The Basic Structure of an eML Document

To create an eML publication, you start with a blank HTML file, into which you place the following header lines (possibly modified according to the filenames you use for the icons):

```
<!DOCTYPE html>
<!-- saved from url=(0014)about:internet -->
<html><head><meta name='viewport' content='width=980' />
<link rel='apple-touch-icon" href='apple-touch-icon.png' />
<link rel='apple-touch-startup-image' href='splashimage.png' />
<meta name='apple-mobile-web-app-capable' content='yes' />
```

All of this has been explained in previous chapters, but to recap, the first line defines the document type as HTML5; any non-HTML5 browsers will simply display the document using standards mode:

```
<!DOCTYPE html>
```

The second line is required if an eML publication is to be viewed locally on a Windows Internet Explorer browser; it ensures no pop-up security warnings are displayed:

```
<!-- saved from url=(0014)about:internet -->
```

After this, the HTML begins and the viewport of the browser is set to a width of 980 pixels:

```
<html><head><meta name='viewport' content='width=980' />
```

Next an image with the name *apple-touch-icon.png* is assigned as the icon to use when saving the publication to an iOS home screen:

```
<link rel='apple-touch-icon' href='apple-touch-icon.png' />
```

The following line then supplies a 320×460-pixel image called *splashimage.png* to use as a loading or splash screen when the application is started from an iOS home screen icon:

```
<link rel='apple-touch-startup-image' href='splashimage.png' />
```

And the last line of this group is used to make iOS browsers display the application in full screen mode when loaded from a home page icon:

```
<meta name='apple-mobile-web-app-capable' content='yes' />
```

Providing a Publication Title and Other Details

The next part of the document assigns a page title, enters JavaScript using the `<script>` tag, and assigns some global variables to be used by the publication:

```
<title>Example eBook</title><script>

PUBLICATION = 'Example eBook Title'
PUBIPAD     = 'Short Name'
PUBIPHONE   = 'Short Name'
SUBTITLE    = 'Subtitle'
AUTHOR      = 'Author Name'
PUBLISHER   = 'Publisher'
PUBLISHED   = 'Date'
ISBN        = 'If you have one... '
```

These are all pretty much self-explanatory except for the PUBIPAD and PUBIPHONE variables. These should contain the short name that will appear underneath the icon of publications that are saved to an iOS home screen. The PUBIPHONE string is the text that will be displayed under an icon on an iPhone and it should be just a few characters (maybe up to a dozen or so). The PUBIPAD string is the text that will be displayed on an iPad and it can be slightly longer due to larger screen and icon size.

Creating the Menu

In the next part of the document you create a menu of chapter names and titles, in the JavaScript array CHAPTERS, like this:

```
CHAPTERS =
{
   'Front Cover' : '',
   'Chapter 1'   : 'Chapter One Contents',
   'Chapter 2'   : 'Chapter Two Contents'
}

</script><script src='eML/eML.js'></script></head><body>
<div style='display:none'>
```

All but the final chapter should have a comma at the line end. If any strings require the use of a single quote character (such as an apostrophe), those strings should be contained in double quotes rather than single quotes.

The CHAPTERS array is followed by a closing </script> tag, and another <script> tag to load in the *eML.js* JavaScript program. Then the <head> section is closed and the <body> is opened. Finally, a <div> is started that will enclose all the chapters, but it is set to not display them because that will be handled by JavaScript.

NOTE

Assigning an empty string to a chapter title leaves a blank space, which is ideal for front pages because you can supply your own design in that space.

Adding the Chapters

Finally, all the chapters are listed in order, each within its own <div> tag, which must be given the ID assigned to its matching element in the CHAPTERS array, like this:

```
<div id='Front Cover'><pre>
#h:1|#center:Example eBook#-
#h:3|#center:By A N Author#-
#br:#center:#copy: Example Publishing#-
#br:#br:#br:#br:#br:#br:
#center:#color:#080;This eBook has been created using eML -
#br:the only digital publishing system that is both
#br:a website and an eBook at the same time.#-#br:#br:
</pre></div>
```

```
<div id='Chapter 1'><pre>
#p1:This is Chapter One
#p:Here are its contents...
</pre></div>

<div id='Chapter 2'><pre>
#p1:This is Chapter Two
#p:Here are its contents...
</pre></div>
```

For now you can ignore all the # tags (they will be explained shortly) and simply note the structure of each chapter, which is

```
<div id='Chapter Name'><pre>
...
</pre></div>
```

You place each chapter in a `<div>` tag, within which you surround its contents in `<pre>` and `</pre>` tags to allow the line feeds at the end of each file to be read by the JavaScript program (these tags state that the enclosed text is preformatted).

If you like, after the final chapter you can close the invisible `<div>` tag that contains all the chapters by adding a final `</div>`, but since there is nothing else in the document, this is optional as the tag will otherwise close itself on all browsers.

The eML Subfolder

You need to accompany each eML publication with a copy of the `eML` subfolder, which contains the various icons, a flash audio player, and the JavaScript used. You can place as many publications as you like in a folder, and they will all access only the single `eML` subfolder for their resources, so it's a quite efficient system.

And, as you'll see later, eML publications can also link to other eML publications, even when used as a self-contained application.

Bringing It All Together

When the preceding sections are brought together into a single eML document, it looks like this:

```
<!DOCTYPE html>
<!-- saved from url=(0014)about:internet -->
<html><head><meta name='viewport' content='width=980' />
<link rel='apple-touch-icon" href='apple-touch-icon.png' />
<link rel='apple-touch-startup-image' href='splashimage.png' />
<meta name='apple-mobile-web-app-capable' content='yes' />

<title>Example eBook</title><script>

PUBLICATION = 'Example eBook Title'
PUBIPAD     = 'Short Name'
PUBIPHONE   = 'Short Name'
```

```
SUBTITLE     = 'Subtitle'
AUTHOR       = 'Author Name'
PUBLISHER    = 'Publisher'
PUBLISHED    = 'Date'
ISBN         = 'If you have one... '

CHAPTERS =
{
    'Front Cover' : '',
    'Chapter 1'   : 'Chapter One Contents',
    'Chapter 2'   : 'Chapter Two Contents'
}

</script><script src='eML/eML.js'></script></head><body>
<div style='display:none'>
<div id='Front Cover'><pre>
#h:1|#center:Example eBook#-
#h:3|#center:By A N Author#-
#br:#center:#copy: Example Publishing#-
#br:#br:#br:#br:#br:#br:
#center:#color:#080;This eBook has been created using eML -
#br:the only digital publishing system that is both
#br:a website and an eBook at the same time.#-#br:#br:
</pre></div>

<div id='Chapter 1'><pre>
#p1:This is Chapter One
#p:Here are its contents...
</pre></div>

<div id='Chapter 2'><pre>
#p1:This is Chapter Two
#p:Here are its contents...
</pre></div>
```

Ask the Expert

Q: What if I want to create a website, not an eBook?

A: You are not restricted to using eML only for eBooks because, by simply avoiding use of the word "Chapter" in your chapter titles and instead using page titles, you can use the system to create a fully self-contained, multipage website. That is exactly what I have done with *nixonpublishing.com*, which is both a website and an eBook detailing how to use the eML language.

Using the eML Tags

The eML language is designed to be especially easy for authors to use when writing, and is also simple enough for formatting programs to be written to translate them into other formats. But more than that, it creates highly dynamic and interactive publications.

For example, you can fold or unfold entire sections with a single click, leaving only the parts you are currently reading displayed—making it very easy to browse through all the headings in a publication. The + and – buttons in the top navigation bar perform this function on *all* sections of a chapter.

The eML platform also enables you to display figures, tables, and examples such that all references are automatically renumbered if you move them; embed MP3 audio files and YouTube videos; add bookmarks (by clicking on a heading, and then clicking again on the star icon that appears); and enhance your program in many other ways.

All of this is achieved using a language based around the # symbol. For example, to start a new paragraph, you just precede it with a #p: tag, like this:

```
#p:This is a new paragraph. There is no need to mark the paragraph end
with anything. Just start each new one with the same tag.
```

There is also a universal closing tag, which is #-. If you open an italics tag in HTML using the <i> tag, you must close it with a matching </i>. But with eML, you can close most tags with the universal closer. You close all other eML tags either with a semicolon or by entering a line feed.

The Different Tag Types

The following three types of tag are supported by eML, their main difference being whether or not they support arguments, how they are closed, and whether they must be combined with other tags:

- Self-closing tags, which do not require a #- to close them and are complete in and of themselves

- Tags that require one or more arguments to be passed to them

- Multipart tags, in which two or more tags work together in combination

Self-Closing Tags

Self-closing tags are those like #p:, which, as you've already seen, simply starts a new paragraph whenever it is used. Other self-closing tags include #br: to create a line break, #caret: to display a ^ symbol, and so on.

Tags with Arguments

This type of tag requires one or more arguments, which are then closed when either a semicolon or the end of a line is reached. So, for example, to create a level 4 heading, the following combination of tag and text is used:

```
#h:4|This is a level 4 heading
```

The #h: sets up the heading tag, followed by the heading level, which is 4, and the | symbol, which indicates the end of the first part of the heading tag. Then follows the text to display in the heading, This is a level 4 heading, and the whole tag ends at the line end.

If you want to add another tag to the line in the preceding example, you could add a semicolon at the end of the line, which fulfills the function of a new line in eML, and then add the second tag. For example, this two-line pair of tags,

```
#fontsize:10pt
#alignment:justify
```

can be replaced with this single line:

```
#fontsize:10pt;#alignment:justify
```

Multipart Tags

These types of tag are slightly more complex in that they are composite or multipart, such as the tags used to create the following table:

Pet type	Pet name
Long haired cat	Rhubarb
Labrador dog	Emma
Goldfish	Mr. Bubbles

Only four tags are used to create this table: #example:, #th:, #td:, and #-, like this:

```
#table:example|A selection of pets and their names
#th:Pet type|Pet name
#td:Long haired cat|Rhubarb
#td:Labrador dog|Emma
#td:Goldfish|Mr. Bubbles
#-
```

Figure 10-2 shows the table section of the eML manual as it appears on an Android browser.

The first tag sets up a table with the ID example and the caption "A selection of pets and their names." Then the second line creates the table heading, giving it the two column titles of "Pet type" and "Pet name," while lines three through five contain the table data for each row.

As with the #h: heading tag, the | symbol is used to separate items of data. Because it is a reserved character, if you need to display a bar, you can use the #| tag.

Figure 10-2   Zoomed into the tables section on a Dell Streak running Android 2.1

Special Symbols and the Closing Tag

The eML language uses some characters in special ways, as follow:

- The | character is used to separate multiple arguments in a tag that takes arguments.

- The ; character is used to close the opening part of tags that take arguments. Alternatively, just like JavaScript, a line feed achieves the same result.

- The ^ symbol can be used as a quick shortcut for displaying the < symbol, rather than using the #lt; tag (or the HTML < tag).

- Because the # symbol prefaces tag names, when you wish to display the # symbol itself, you can use the ## tag.

- The #- tag closes all eML tags other than self-closing ones.

In Figure 10-3 a Galaxy Tab Android tablet is being used to display Chapter 3 of the eML manual in portrait mode.

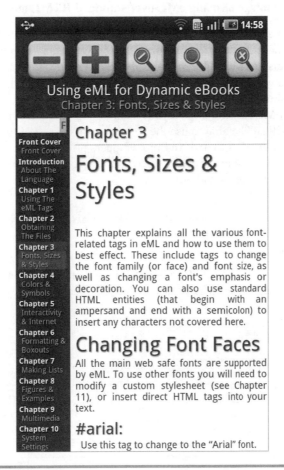

Figure 10-3   Displaying Chapter 3 on a Samsung Galaxy Tab running Android

The eML Tags

The eML tags can be divided into different categories, such as tags relating to fonts, tags for defining colors and symbols, Internet and interactivity tags, and so on. As you'll see in the following sections summarizing the most commonly used tags, they are very straightforward and easy to use, yet provide more flexibility than HTML tags.

Ask the Expert

Q: What is the advantage of using eML over standard HTML and JavaScript?

A: The main advantage is that the eML system automatically accounts for all the different types of iOS, Android, and other platforms and browsers, and formats its display accordingly. It also provides dozens of ready-made tags to access features that have been tested on a wide range of devices, so that you can quickly bring an eBook or self-contained website to market in the iOS or Android stores.

Of course, eML may not be everyone's cup of tea, and that's fine. If you don't wish to use it, you will still be able to use the techniques in the rest of this book to drop your own web pages into the iOS and Android wrappers provided, and create your own stand-alone apps. But you will also have to write your own code to take care of the differences between operating systems and browsers.

Managing Fonts

Whenever you wish to change font face in an eML document, you can simply refer to it by name, such as #arial:, and then, to resume the previous font face, you issue a #- closing tag, like this (see Table 10-1):

```
#arial:This text is in Arial font#-
```

Tag	Font Name	Tag	Font Name
#arial:	Arial	#helvetica:	Helvetica
#arialb:	Arial Bold	#impact:	Impact
#andale:	Andale Mono	#times:	Times
#comic:	Comic Sans MS	#timesnr:	Times New Roman
#courier:	Courier	#trebuchet:	Trebuchet
#couriern:	Courier New	#verdana:	Verdana
#georgia:	Georgia		

Table 10-1 The eML Font Tags—All Close with the #- Tag

Changing Font Size

To change font size, you use the `#size:` tag, which takes an argument following the `:`, followed by a semicolon, like this:

```
#size:12pt;This text is in 12 point#-
```

The `#-` tag resumes use of the previous font size. All CSS measurement types, such as em, pt, and px, are supported. Figure 10-4 shows how Chapter 3 of the eML manual looks on an iPad.

Changing Font Emphasis and Decoration

You can also easily change the way text displays using these tags (see Table 10-2), like this example, which changes the text to boldface:

```
#b:This text is in bold face#-
```

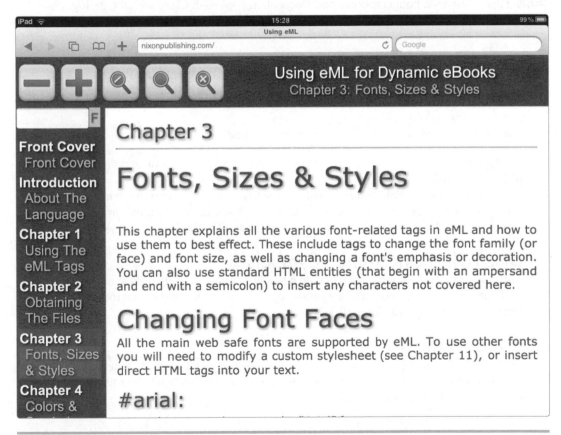

Figure 10-4   Displaying Chapter 3 on an iPad running iOS 4.1 in landscape mode

Tag	Action
`#lightshadow:`	Places a light shadow under the text
`#darkshadow:`	Places a dark shadow under the text
`#b:`	Enables boldface
`#i:`	Enables italics
`#l:`	Enables literal (monospace font)
`#s:`	Enables strikethrough
`#sub:`	Enables subscript
`#sup:`	Enables superscript
`#u:`	Enables underlining

Table 10-2 The eML Font Emphasis and Decoration Tags—All Close with the #- Tag

Changing Colors

To change the color of a section of text, you use the `#color:` tag (or `#highlight:` to change the background color), as in these examples:

```
#color:#ffff00;This is yellow text#-
#highlight:red;This has a red background#-
```

Figure 10-5 shows how the eML chapter on colors and symbols displays on another, different Android device.

A semicolon is required after the color value to close the first part of the tag, and the color can be restored to the previous one with the #- tag. You can use any three- or six-digit hex values preceded with a # character, or any supported CSS/HTML color names.

Displaying Uncommon Symbols

The eML system gives you easy access to a number of uncommonly used symbols—such as `#degree:` and `#euro:`. These symbol tags are self-closing and do not require using a semicolon or #- tag (see Table 10-3).

Basic Formatting

The eML language supports a wide range of formatting options, starting with the basics such as line breaks, centering, headings, indenting, and so on. For example, the following line displays a level 2 heading:

```
#h:2|This is a level 2 heading
```

Table 10-4 details some of the main formatting tags and how to use them.

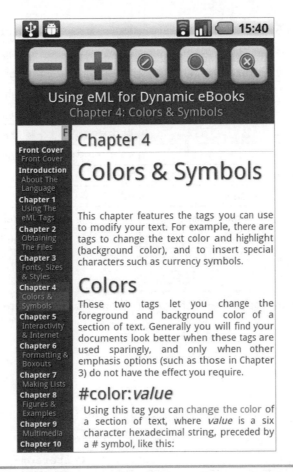

Figure 10-5 Displaying Chapter 4 on a Google Nexus One running Android 2.2

Tag	Symbol	Tag	Symbol
#bar:	|	#n:	(nonbreaking space)
#caret:	^	#nd:	– (en dash)
#cent:	¢	#pound:	#
#copy:	© (copyright)	#quarter:	¼
#degree:	°	#rb:	> (right bracket)

Table 10-3 The eML Symbol Tags—Self-Contained and Do Not Require Closing *(continued)*

Tag	Symbol	Tag	Symbol
`#divide:`	÷	`#reg:`	® (registered trademark)
`#euro:`	€ (Eurozone euro)	`#rq:`	" (right quote)
`#feet:`	'	`#rs:`	' (right single quote)
`#half:`	½	`#sc:`	; (semicolon)
`#hash:`	#	`#threeq:`	¾ (three-quarters)
`#inches:`	"	`#ukpound:`	£ (British pound)
`#lb:`	< (left bracket)	`#yen:`	¥ (Japanese yen)
`#lq:`	" (left quote)	`##`	#
`#ls:`	' (left single quote)	`#...`	. . . (ellipsis)
`#md:`	— (em dash)	`^`	< (left bracket)
`#multiply:`	×		

Table 10-3 The eML Symbol Tags—Self-Contained and Do Not Require Closing

Tag	Action	Example	Closing Tag
`#br:`	Apply line break	`End of line#br:`	none
`#center:`	Center text	`#center:I'm Centered#-`	`#-`
`#h:n|text`	Display heading	`#h:1|Level 1 heading`	; or a new line
`#hr:n`	Draw horizontal rule	`#hr:75%`	; or a new line
`#indent:n`	Indent section	`#indent:30px;Indented#-`	; or a new line for opener, #- to close
`#p:`	Indent first line of paragraph by 20 pixels	`#p:Indented text`	`#p:` or `#p1:`
`#p1:`	Start unindented new paragraph	`#p1:Unindented text`	`#p:` or `#p1:`
`#tab:`	Indent section by 20 pixels	`#tab:Indented block#-`	`#-`

Table 10-4 Some of eML's Basic Formatting Tags

The different #p: and #p1: tags are provided to support indented and nonindented paragraphs, so that #p1: displays a paragraph without the first line indented, while #p: displays one with the first line indented. Since paragraphs are so common, there is no tag to close a paragraph; instead, by starting a new paragraph, the previous one is automatically closed.

Advanced Formatting

To help you lay out publications professionally, eML supports several more-advanced formatting features such as boxouts and sidebars. For example, to place a section of a document within a sidebar on the left of the screen, you use the #lsidebar: tag like this (see Figure 10-6):

```
#lsidebar:200;This is a sidebar, which is placed all the way over on
the left of the page.#-
```

Figure 10-6 A screen grab showing how boxouts and sidebars display

Tag	Action
`#boxout:`	Display in a boxout
`#code:`	Display as code
`#input:`	Display as user input
`#lsidebar:n;`	Display in left sidebar
`#note:`	Display as a note
`#output:`	Display as program output
`#quote:`	Display as a quote
`#rsidebar:n;`	Display in right sidebar
`#text:`	Display as sample text
`#tip:`	Display as a tip
`#warn:`	Display as a warning

Table 10-5 The Advanced Formatting Tags Provided by eML

The value before the `;` character is the number of pixels to allocate to the sidebar's width. Table 10-5 lists the advanced formatting tags that are available, all of which close with the `#-` tag. Only the `#lsidebar:` and `#rsidebar:` tags require the additional value of a width in pixels, followed by a semicolon.

The `#boxout:` tag displays its contents in a simple bordered box with a light background, while `#note:`, `#tip:`, and `#warn:` do the same thing but also display a suitable icon to the left of the boxout. The remaining tags format their contents indented and preceded with a vertical dotted line, along with other formatting to emphasize their content type.

NOTE
Many other advanced formatting options are supported, such as a wide variety of list types, tables, and figures; page number management; citations and footnotes; embedding audio, video, images, and maps; and much more. Please read the online manual in the *examples.zip* download available from *html5formobile.com*, or at *nixonpublishing.com*, for full details.

Overriding Font Sizes on iOS and Android
In the previous chapter I introduced some code to let you change font size on-the-fly according to the device in use. With eML, similar code has been used but if you wish you can override the defaults using the `#androidfontsize:`, `#iphonefontsize:`, and

`#ipadfontsize:` tags, like the following line, which sets the base font size for Android devices to 18 pt:

`#androidfontsize:18pt`

These tags are closed either by a new line or with a semicolon.

Summary

This chapter explained how to use eML as a way to quickly bring a project to fruition, ready to place in the iOS and Android app stores (as detailed in Part III). Using the platform is a great way to get started, and I recommend you give it a try.

But using eML is only one way of preparing a website for distribution on mobile devices. In the next chapter I'll explain exactly what you need to do if you intend to go it alone with your own HTML and JavaScript, by showing you how to create both a database-driven web app and a simpler web app that is easily turned into a stand-alone mobile app.

Chapter 11

Developing Web Applications

Key Skills & Concepts

- Creating a suitable MySQL database

- Ensuring that the Ajax calls will work

- Verifying a username and password

- Logging users in and out

- Posting and retrieving chat messages

- Sending personal messages

- Managing the virtual keyboard

- Preventing iOS and Android from also processing tap events

- Customizing for saving to the iOS home screen

- The PHP side of the Ajax communication

This entire chapter is devoted to a single project called "Rob's Place" (see Figure 11-1), comprising client and server software for running a simple chat room. In this chapter, you will learn how to create a permanent onscreen keyboard (to avoid having to constantly pop a device's own soft keyboard up and down), manage the input returned by the keyboard, connect the input and viewing screens to a web server using Ajax, create and manage a MySQL database, and process the Ajax requests on the server side.

Once the project is complete, we will then use it as one example for building a professional-looking and self-contained iOS or Android app. And along the way, I'll be pointing out many techniques you can use, and pitfalls to avoid, when developing web apps for touch devices.

About This Project

There's quite a lot of code in this project, but I have tried my best to keep it to the bare minimum that will at least present quite decently, and I have kept the main JavaScript code to well under 500 lines.

The project is divided into multiple files, as follows:

- *robs.htm* The main HTML page of the project
- *login.php* PHP program from Chapter 8

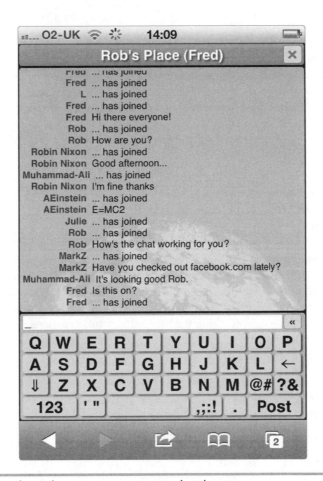

Figure 11-1   Rob's Place chat running on an Apple iPhone

- *robslogin.php*   PHP program to verify/log in a user via Ajax

- *robsgetchat.php*   PHP program to return chat messages via Ajax

- *robspost.php*   PHP program to post a message via Ajax

All these files are available in the *examples.zip* file at *html5formobile.com*. You can also point your iOS or Android browser (or, if you zoom right out, the latest PC or Mac version of any major browser) at the following URL to try the project out for yourself, using the *html5formobile.com* server to store the MySQL database and handle the Ajax calls:

html5formobile.com/examples/robs.htm

Setting Up MySQL

Before we look at the code for the chat room project, you first need to set up a MySQL database and table. If you have a web server with MySQL installed and have worked through Chapter 8, you should already have a database with the name phpdb (if not, you'll need to create a MySQL database before proceeding with this chapter), which you can use by entering the MySQL command line and typing:

```
use phpdb;
```

Next you need to create the table that will hold all the users' login details. I have called the table users. It needs both a username field and a password field, as well as a third field called latest, which will store an unsigned integer value between 0 and 4.3 billion, to hold the number of the user's most recently viewed message, so that only newer ones are displayed. It is highly unlikely that this chat room will get anything like 4 billion posts, but it only takes up 4 bytes to store this value.

To be able to quickly look up users in the table, you need to assign its username field an index and have chosen to give this index a length of seven characters, which is about a third of the maximum username length of 20 characters. The password field will store a 32-character string created from the password using the PHP md5() function, as explained in Chapter 8.

To create the table with these specifications, enter the following lines at the MySQL command line (see Figure 11-2):

```
CREATE TABLE users(
    username VARCHAR(20),
    password CHAR(32),
    latest INT UNSIGNED,
    UNIQUE INDEX(username(7))
);
```

Next you need to create the table to contain the chat messages. It will contain an unsigned integer field called num to uniquely identify each message. This field will be set as a primary key for indexing and will also auto-increment after each message insertion.

The table also needs sender and recip fields to hold the sender and recipient usernames for each message, and the first seven characters of each need to be indexed for quick searching. Finally, the table needs a message field to hold the message itself (of up to 1,000 characters). The message field does not need to be indexed because there are no plans to allow searching by message contents in this project.

To create the table, issue the following lines at the MySQL prompt, as shown in Figure 11-3:

```
CREATE TABLE chat(
    num INT UNSIGNED NOT NULL AUTO_INCREMENT,
    sender VARCHAR(20),
    recip VARCHAR(20),
    message VARCHAR(1000),
```

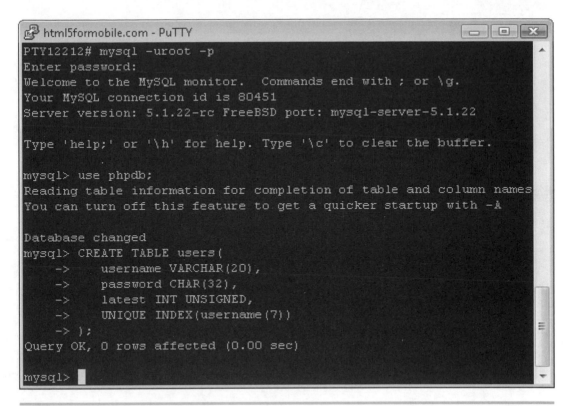

Figure 11-2 Creating the MySQL table named `users`

```
    PRIMARY KEY (num),
    INDEX(sender(7)),
    INDEX(recip(7))
);
```

The reason for including both the `recip` field and the `sender` field is to allow for private messaging. In the project, any message with a recipient username of `ALL` is deemed to be posted for everyone to read. But if `recip` is any other username, then only the sender and recipient will be able to view it. Therefore, we need to lock out the username `ALL` as a possible choice for new users to select by entering the following line to reserve the username, as shown in Figure 11-4:

```
INSERT INTO users VALUES('ALL', '', 0);
```

Because the password provided is the empty string, `' '`, it can never match an `md5 ()` hash string, and so that username is now reserved.

Figure 11-3 Creating the chat table

The HTML

The HTML for this project is quite short but the file is fairly long as it also includes the CSS and JavaScript code, to minimize server hits. Having all three elements in a single HTML page also reduces the risk of Android caching either the CSS or JavaScript if they were in separate files, so that any updates you might make to them could end up being ignored by a browser until the cache updates, making them almost impossible to properly debug.

The file, shown next, comprises the standard heading lines (discussed in Chapter 1), a section to create an onscreen keyboard, another for the login screen, and a couple of others for the personal messaging pop-up window. Particular things to point out in the following web page are the `<div>` with the ID of `main`, which contains the top part of the screen above the keyboard, and the `<div>` with the ID of `keyboard`, which contains the keyboard.

```
<!DOCTYPE html> <!-- robs.htm -->
<!-- saved from url=(0014)about:internet -->
<html><head><meta name='viewport' content='width=980' />
<link rel='apple-touch-icon' href='robs.png' />
```

```
html5formobile.com - PuTTY                                    □ □ ✕
    ->      username VARCHAR(20),
    ->      password CHAR(32),
    ->      latest INT UNSIGNED,
    ->      UNIQUE INDEX(username(7))
    -> );
Query OK, 0 rows affected (0.00 sec)

mysql> CREATE TABLE chat(
    ->      num INT UNSIGNED NOT NULL AUTO_INCREMENT,
    ->      sender VARCHAR(20),
    ->      recip VARCHAR(20),
    ->      message VARCHAR(1000),
    ->      PRIMARY KEY (num),
    ->      INDEX(sender(7)),
    ->      INDEX(recip(7))
    -> );
Query OK, 0 rows affected (0.01 sec)

mysql> INSERT INTO users VALUES('ALL', '', 0);
Query OK, 1 row affected (0.00 sec)

mysql>
```

Figure 11-4   Reserving the username ALL

```html
<meta name='apple-mobile-web-app-capable' content='yes' />
<html>
   <head>
      <title>Rob's Place</title>
      <link href="robs.css" rel="stylesheet" type="text/css" />
   </head>
   <style>
      // The contents of this section are listed separately
   </style>
   <body bgcolor='black'>
      <table id='table' border='0' cellpadding='0' cellspacing='0'
         height='100%' width='100%'>
      <tr><td><div id='title'>Rob's Place</div>
      <div id='logout'>&times;</div>
      </td></tr><tr><td height='100%'>
```

```
            <div id='main'>
                <div id='mainoverlay'></div>
                <div id='pmoverlay'></div>
                <div id='pmoverlay2'></div>
            </div>
        </td></tr><tr><td height='338'>
        <div id='keyboard'>
            <div id='inpcontainer'>
                <textarea id='input' rows='1'>_</textarea><div
                    id='clear'>&laquo;</div>
                <div id='inpoverlay'></div>
            </div>
            <div id='keybcontainer'>
                <div id='board'>
                    <div class='k' id='q'>Q</div><div class='k' id='w'>W</div>
                    <div class='k' id='e'>E</div><div class='k' id='r'>R</div>
                    <div class='k' id='t'>T</div><div class='k' id='y'>Y</div>
                    <div class='k' id='u'>U</div><div class='k' id='i'>I</div>
                    <div class='k' id='o'>O</div><div class='k' id='p'>P</div>
                    <div class='k' id='a'>A</div><div class='k' id='s'>S</div>
                    <div class='k' id='d'>D</div><div class='k' id='f'>F</div>
                    <div class='k' id='g'>G</div><div class='k' id='h'>H</div>
                    <div class='k' id='j'>J</div><div class='k' id='k'>K</div>
                    <div class='k' id='l'>L</div>
                    <div class='k' id='del'>&#8592;</div>
                    <div class='k' id='shift'>&dArr;</div>
                    <div class='k' id='z'>Z</div><div class='k' id='x'>X</div>
                    <div class='k' id='c'>C</div><div class='k' id='v'>V</div>
                    <div class='k' id='b'>B</div><div class='k' id='n'>N</div>
                    <div class='k' id='m'>M</div>
                    <div class='k' id='at'>@#</div>
                    <div class='k' id='ques'>?&amp;</div>
                    <div class='k' id='alt'>123</div>
                    <div class='k' id='apos'>' "</div>
                    <div class='k' id='space'></div>
                    <div class='k' id='comma'>,;:!</div>
                    <div class='k' id='period'>.</div>
                    <div class='k' id='post'>Post</div>
                </div>
            </div>
        </div></td></tr></table>
        <script>
            // The contents of this section are listed separately
        </script>
    </body>
</html>
```

This web page loads into the browser from either a local or remote URL, is then styled using CSS, and the chat code is called up in the `<script>` section at the end.

The CSS

Although the HTML looks (and is) quite straightforward, this project has an awful lot going on in it, such as pop-up windows for entering private messages, objects fading in and out, smooth gradient fills, and other effects such as shadows and transitions.

But it's beyond the scope of this book to explain every aspect of the project, particularly since you will probably be writing your own web apps, rather than expanding on this one (which you are welcome to do if you wish, but please use a name other than Rob's for it), so you should take the following CSS as is and use it primarily for reference when examining the JavaScript or PHP code:

```
/* Rob's Place CSS Rules from the <style> section of the page */
      body, html {
          padding      :0;
          margin       :0;
          height       :100%; }
      .inp {
          width        :14em;
          max-width    :14em;
          height       :1.2em;
          padding      :0 10px;
          margin-bottom:20px;
          color        :#000;
          overflow     :hidden;
          border       :10px solid #ccc;
          background   :#fff; }
      .k {
          float        :left;
          width        :88px;
          height       :65px;
          margin       :4px;
          text-align   :center;
          font-size    :3.5em;
          color        :#000;
          background   :#e0e4cc;
          -webkit-box-shadow:4px 4px 4px #444;
          -moz-box-shadow   :4px 4px 4px #444; }
      .pm {
          background   :#e0e4cc; }
      .cont {
          width        :400px;
          margin       :50px;
          font-size    :1.3em;
          text-shadow  :5px 5px 5px #444;
          -webkit-box-shadow:6px 8px 8px #444;
          -moz-box-shadow   :6px 8px 8px #444; }
      .user {
          white-space  :nowrap;
```

```
        padding-right:2%;
        font-weight  :bold;
        color        :#22b;  }
#alt, #post {
    width         :184px;  }
#clear {
    float         :right;
    width         :56px;
    height        :50px;
    margin-right  :12px;
    text-align    :center;
    font-size     :2.5em;
    color         :#000;
    background    :#e0e4cc;  }
#comma {
    width         :104px;  }
#del {
    font-size     :4.5em;
    line-height   :.7em;  }
#inpcontainer, #keybcontainer {
    position      :relative;  }
#inpoverlay {
    width         :892px;
    height        :56px;
    left          :0px;
    top           :0px;
    margin-left   :.5%;
    z-index       :10;
    opacity       :0;  }
#input {
    width         :886px;
    height        :50px;
    padding       :0 0 0 4px;
    margin-left   :.5%;
    font-size     :2.5em;
    overflow      :hidden;  }
#keyboard {
    width         :970px;
    height        :336px;
    padding       :4px 0px 20px 4px;
    opacity       :0;  }
#logout {
    top           :7px;
    right         :10px;
    width         :60px;
    height        :60px;
    text-align    :center;
    line-height   :1.1em;
```

```
          font-size     :3.5em;
          color         :#f00;
          background    :#e0e4cc;
          opacity       :0; }
#main {
          width         :958px;
          height        :100%;
          padding       :8px;
          margin-bottom:5px; }
#mainoverlay {
          width         :97%;
          height        :96%;
          top           :10px;
          left          :0px;
          font-size     :4em;
          padding       :10px;
          z-index       :10;
          opacity       :0; }
#period {
          width         :72px; }
#pminput {
          width         :90%;
          height        :335px;
          margin-top    :10px;
          padding       :3%;
          font-size     :1em;
          font-family   :helvetica;
          -webkit-box-shadow:10px 10px 10px #888;
          -moz-box-shadow   :10px 10px 10px #888; }
#pmoverlay {
          width         :80%;
          height        :500px;
          top           :9%;
          left          :9%;
          padding       :10px;
          text-align    :center;
          font-size     :3em;
          background    :#e0e4cc;
          background    :-webkit-gradient(linear, left top,
                         left bottom, from(#e0e4cc), to(#a7dbd8));
          background    :-moz-linear-gradient(top, #e0e4cc, #a7dbd8);
          z-index       :-1;
          opacity       :0;
          -webkit-box-shadow:20px 20px 10px #888;
          -moz-box-shadow   :20px 20px 10px #888; }
#pmoverlay2 {
          width         :83%;
          height        :525px;
```

```
    top          :9%;
    left         :9%;
    z-index      :-1; }
#pmtip {
    width        :100%;
    text-align   :center;
    font-size    :.6em;
    font-style   :italic; }
#post {
    width        :184px; }
#shift {
    font-size    :2.8em;
    line-height  :1.3em; }
#space {
    width        :280px; }
#title {
    width        :958px;
    height       :58px;
    padding      :8px;
    margin-bottom:5px;
    text-align   :center;
    font-size    :3em;
    text-shadow  :5px 5px 5px #444; }
.k, .cont, #clear, #inpoverlay, #input, #logout, #mainoverlay,
#pmoverlay, #title {
    font-weight  :bold;
    font-family  :helvetica; }
.cont, #title {
    color        :#fff;
    background   :#fa6900;
    background   :-webkit-gradient(linear, left top, left
                  bottom, from(#f38630), to(#fa6900));
    background   :-moz-linear-gradient(top, #f38630, #fa6900); }
#keyboard, #main {
    position     :relative;
    border       :1px solid black;
    background   :#69d2e7;
    background   :-webkit-gradient(linear, left top, left
                  bottom, from(#69d2e7), to(#a7dbd8));
    background   :-moz-linear-gradient(top, #69d2e7, #a7dbd8); }
.pm, #clear, #logout, #pminput, #pmoverlay, #title {
    border       :1px solid #000; }
.inp, .k, .cont, .user, #clear, #logout, #pmoverlay2 {
    cursor       :pointer; }
#inpoverlay, #logout, #mainoverlay, #pmoverlay,
#pmoverlay2, #pmtip {
    position     :absolute; }
```

```
.inp, .k, .pm, .cont, #clear, #keyboard, #logout, #main,
#pminput, #pmoverlay, #title {
   border-radius      :10px;
   -moz-border-radius:10px; }
.k, #keyboard, #logout, #mainoverlay, #pmoverlay {
   -webkit-transition:opacity,color,background 0.25s linear;
   -moz-transition    :opacity,color,background 0.25s linear; }
```

The JavaScript Program

I have refactored the JavaScript several times, stripping it back from in excess of 1,000 lines of code, so it is now as simple as it can reasonably be made. But you don't need to understand all the code anyway; nor am I going to explain it to you in detail. Instead I am going to simply give you an outline of the code, mainly covering what each function does so that you can learn about the types of things you will need to bear in mind when writing your own web apps.

Also, the code has been written to support both touch and mouse input, and you can run the project from any recent browser version on a PC or Mac, as long as you use maximum zoom out (as shown in Figure 11-5). This makes it easy to modify and quickly retest the code on a desktop computer.

The Global Variables

The initial dozen or so lines of code set up some of the global variables used by the project. These include file names and locations and the variable BROWSER, which will be accessed whenever device-dependent code is required.

Also, the first few assignments after the window.onload = function() definition create a number of additional global variables used throughout the project, and a few more are created a little further on. All global variables are easily recognized as such because they are in uppercase, listed in Table 11-1.

Here is the first section of the code prior to the function definitions:

```
// Rob's Place JavaScript from the <script> section of the page
BASEURL       = 'http://html5formobile.com/examples/'
MAINPAGE      = BASEURL + 'robs.htm'
LOGIN         = BASEURL + 'robslogin.php'
GETCHAT       = BASEURL + 'robsgetchat.php'
POSTCHAT      = BASEURL + 'robspost.php'
UNDEF         = 'undefined'
LOCALSTORAGE = true
RECIP         = 'ALL'
TAIL          = window.location.search.substring(1)

if (TAIL.length > 0) TAIL = '?' + TAIL
```

Figure 11-5 Logging into the chat using Google Chrome on a PC

Global Variables	Purpose
BASEURL	URL of the web server folder containing the program files and data
MAINPAGE	URL of the main HTML web page
LOGIN	URL of the PHP login page
GETCHAT	URL of the PHP page to return the latest chat messages
POSTCHAT	URL of the PHP program to post new messages

Table 11-1 The Global Variables Used and Their Purposes *(continued)*

Global Variables	Purpose
UNDEF	Shorthand variable for the string "undefined"
LOCALSTORAGE	Boolean variable with the value `true` if HTML5 local storage is available
RECIP	String containing the current recipient's username
BROWSER	String variable containing the browser type out of "iOS" for Apple devices, "Streak" for the Dell Streak Android device, "Android" for other Android devices, and "Other" for all other devices and desktop/laptop PCs
ALPHA	Array containing the names of all the `<div>` sections used for displaying letter keys and other keys in the virtual keyboard
UPPER	String containing the uppercase letters A–Z, used for switching the keyboard to uppercase
NUMBERS	String containing the alternative characters viewable when the "123" key is tapped. Note the use of the escape sequence \\ within the string assignment, which results in only a single \ character being inserted
OLDBUT	Style object copy of the most recently tapped key
MAXINP	Integer containing the maximum input length
SMARTPERIOD	Boolean variable that is `true` if a space should be added to the input after the period key is tapped, and otherwise `false`
FIRST	Boolean variable that is `true` the first time a request is made for the latest chat message from the server, in which case up to 50 of the most recent messages are returned. If `false`, only unread messages are returned from the server
GETFREQ	Integer containing the frequency, in milliseconds, between polling the server for new messages. The default value is 2000 milliseconds, or 2 seconds
USERNAME	The username as entered by the user
PASSWORD	The password as entered by the user
CHATTOUT	A handle returned by the repeating Ajax interrupts, and which can be used to disable them
TOUT	A handle used by the `HighlightButton()` function to remove the highlight applied to a key after two seconds
THEFIELD	If the keyboard data is to be transferred to an external field, this holds its ID

Table 11-1 The Global Variables Used and Their Purposes

```
if (self.location != MAINPAGE + TAIL ) self.location = MAINPAGE + TAIL

if (NavCheck('iPod') || NavCheck('iPhone') || NavCheck('iPad'))
                                   BROWSER = 'iOS'
else if (NavCheck('Dell Streak'))  BROWSER = 'Streak'
else if (NavCheck('Android'))      BROWSER = 'Android'
else                               BROWSER = 'Other'

document.onkeypress = function(e)
{
    var key = ''

    switch(e.keyCode)
    {
        case  8: key = 29; break
        case 13: PostMessage(RECIP); return false
    }

    var p = String.fromCharCode(e.charCode)

    switch(p)
    {
        case ' ': key = 26; break
        case "'":
        case '"': key = 27; break
        case '.': key = 30; break
        case '@':
        case '#': key = 32; break
        case '?':
        case '&': key = 33; break
        case ',':
        case ';':
        case ':':
        case '!': key = 34; break
    }

    c = ALPHA.indexOf(p)
    if (c > -1)
    {
        key = c
        DoToLower()
    }

    c = UPPER.indexOf(p)
    if (c > -1)
    {
        key = c
        DoToUpper()
    }
```

```
      c = NUMBERS.indexOf(p)
      if (c > -1)
      {
         key = c
         DoToNumbers()
      }

      ProcessKey(key)
      return false
}

window.onload = function()
{
   ALPHA = new Array('a', 'b', 'c', 'd', 'e', 'f', 'g', 'h', 'i', 'j',
      'k', 'l', 'm', 'n', 'o', 'p', 'q', 'r', 's', 't', 'u', 'v', 'w',
      'x', 'y', 'z', 'space', 'apos', 'alt', 'del', 'period', 'shift',
      'at', 'ques', 'comma')
   UPPER           = 'ABCDEFGHIJKLMNOPQRSTUVWXYZ'
   NUMBERS         = '(|¥_3%+-8*/=\\~9014)57€2£6$'
   OLDBUT          = O('space')
   BUFFER          = ''
   MAXINP          = 0
   SMARTPERIOD     = true
   FIRST           = true
   GETFREQ         = 2000
   S('board').height = '280px';

   if (BROWSER == 'iOS')
   {
      S('logout').lineHeight = '.9em'
      S('shift' ).fontSize   = '3.5em'
      S('shift' ).lineHeight = '1.1em'
      O('del'   ).innerHTML  = ' &#8592;'
   }

   O('inpoverlay').ontouchstart =
   O('keyboard'  ).ontouchstart = StopDefaultAction

   for (j = 0 ; j < ALPHA.length ; ++j)
      eval('ActivateObject(O(ALPHA[j]), function(e) ' +
         '{ ProcessKey(' + j + ', e) })')

   ActivateObject(O('clear'), SetUpClearBut)
   window.scrollTo(0, 1)

   wh = window.innerHeight
   ww = window.innerWidth
   if (ww > wh) wh = ww / wh * ww
```

```
S('table').height = wh + 'px'
S('table').width  = '100%'
S('main').height  = '100%'

if (BROWSER != 'Other') setTimeout(function()
   { window.scrollTo(0, 1) }, 500)

try
{
   USERNAME = localStorage.getItem('username')
   PASSWORD = localStorage.getItem('password')
}
catch(e)
{
   LOCALSTORAGE = false
   USERNAME     = ProcessCookie('read', 'username')
   PASSWORD     = ProcessCookie('read', 'password')
}

if (USERNAME && PASSWORD)
{
   display = "<table height='100%' width='100%' border='0'><tr>" +
      "<td align='center' valign='absmiddle'>Welcome back "      +
      USERNAME + "<div id='login' class='cont'>Continue</div>"    +
      "<br /><br /></td></tr></table></center>"

   O('mainoverlay').innerHTML = display
   S('mainoverlay').opacity    = '1'
   S('keyboard'   ).opacity    = '.5'

   ActivateObject('login', Login)
} else DoLogin()
}
```

After setting up the various global variables, the first particularly interesting piece of code is in the document.onkeypress = function(e) section, which attaches to the browser's onkeypress event and processes the keypresses as if they are taps on the virtual keyboard. This allows devices with attached keyboards to also use them to post chat messages.

The following code for setting up the virtual keyboard is also worth highlighting:

```
for (j = 0 ; j < ALPHA.length ; ++j)
   eval('ActivateObject(O(ALPHA[j]), function(e) ' +
      '{ ProcessKey(' + j + ', e) })')
```

This is a for() loop that iterates through the ALPHA array of keyboard key <div> sections, and uses the ActivateObject() function to assign a key tap to the ProcessKey() function, where it will be processed.

NOTE

The use of the `eval()` function is to enable the current value of the variable `j` to be used in each iteration, rather than simply passing the variable `j` itself, to be evaluated only when the event is clicked. It's quite advanced JavaScript, so if it confuses you, don't worry—you can just copy and paste the code to use it in your own web apps.

Also note the use of HTML5 local storage in these lines:

```
USERNAME = localStorage.getItem('username')
PASSWORD = localStorage.getItem('password')
```

Using them, if the user has previously logged in (and not logged out), the login details are pulled from local storage, saving the user from having to reenter them, as with the following `if()` statement, which simply presents a Continue button in a `<div>` with the ID of `login` for tapping, instead of a login screen, as shown in Figure 11-6, a screen grab taken from a Dell Streak. Notice that the keyboard is grayed out at this point because there is nothing that can currently be entered with it.

NOTE

By the way, since it's nonessential, I am considering removing the image of Earth if I find that it slows down instant loading of the page when run as an app, so if it doesn't make it to the *examples.zip* file on the website, you'll know why.

The two calls to the `getItem()` function are placed within a `try` section so that browsers that do not support HTML5 local storage do not issue an error, but instead fall through to the `catch` section, in which standard browser cookies are used instead.

The final two lines in this segment are also of interest:

```
    ActivateObject('login', Login)
} else DoLogin()
```

The first line attaches to the login `<div>` so that when it is tapped, the `Login()` function will be called to verify the details submitted and log the user in.

The second line runs only if the local storage did not return a saved username and password. It calls the `DoLogin()` function, which is detailed after the following section.

Preparing for Using Ajax

Before moving on to the functions, we need to look back at one of the first lines of code in this section:

```
TAIL = window.location.search.substring(1)

if (TAIL.length > 0) TAIL = '?' + TAIL
if (self.location != MAINPAGE + TAIL ) self.location = MAINPAGE + TAIL
```

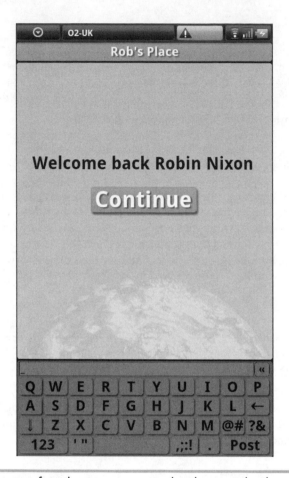

Figure 11-6 To save users from having to reenter details, users that have not logged out are automatically logged back in when they return.

What this does is ensure that if the current web page is not at the URL in the variable MAINPAGE, then the URL in MAINPAGE is loaded in to replace the current one. The use of the TAIL string is to keep in place any query string that may have been attached to the URL.

The page change is made for the simple reason that the chat code uses Ajax and, for security reasons, Ajax communication can take place *only* between a server and a web page that was loaded from that server. If, for example, the web page were downloaded and run locally, the Ajax would fail and the page would not run correctly. But, by always ensuring that the page is served from the same server and folder as the PHP files, the Ajax should run without issues.

The DoLogin() Function

This function is called if the preliminary code could not retrieve a saved username and password from HTML5 local storage. It simply displays a short web form and attaches the username and password inputs (uname and pword) to the GetInput() function, and the Continue button to the LoginCheck() function.

To get things going, the final line calls GetInput() with a value of uname so that the keyboard is automatically activated on that field:

```
function DoLogin()
{
   display = "<table height='100%' width='100%' border='0'><tr><td "   +
      "align='center' valign='absmiddle'><div id='unameinp'>Username"   +
      "<div id='uname' class='inp'></div></div><div id='pwordinp'>"    +
      "Password <div id='pword' class='inp'></div></div><div id="      +
      "'login' class='cont'>Continue</div><div style='font-size:.8em;" +
      "'><i>Please enter your existing or<br />desired login details " +
      "to continue</i></div></td></tr></table></center>"

   S('mainoverlay').opacity   = '1'
   S('mainoverlay').fontSize   = '4em'
   O('mainoverlay').innerHTML = display

   ActivateObject('unameinp', function() { GetInput('uname') } )
   ActivateObject('pwordinp', function() { GetInput('pword') } )
   ActivateObject('login', LoginCheck())
   GetInput('uname')
}
```

The LoginCheck() Function

When the Continue button is tapped, the function LoginCheck() is called to verify the USERNAME and PASSWORD variables. It makes a simple test, which is to ensure that both variables have been given a value. If one or the other hasn't, then an alert box pops up with a message, as shown in Figure 11-7. But if both have values, then the Login() function is called.

```
function LoginCheck()
{
   USERNAME = O('uname').innerHTML
   if (USERNAME.length == 0) alert('Please Enter a Username')
   else
   {
      PASSWORD = O('pword').innerHTML
      if (PASSWORD.length == 0) alert('Please Enter a Password')
      else Login()
   }
}
```

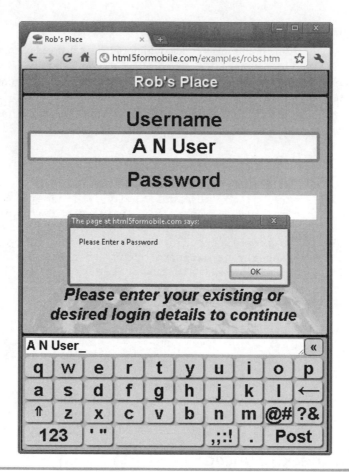

Figure 11-7 An alert is popped up because no password has been entered

The Login() Function

This function uses Ajax to query the web server with the values in the variables USERNAME and PASSWORD. The server sends back the single word "Error" if there was a problem on the server, the word "Invalid" if the username does not exist or the password does not match the username, or the word "Valid" if the username and password validated.

```
function Login()
{
    PostAjaxRequest(result, LOGIN, 'u=' + USERNAME + '&p=' + PASSWORD)
    S('mainoverlay').opacity = ''
```

```
function result()
{
    if (this == 'Error')
    {
        alert('There was an error - please try again.')
        DoLogin()
    }
    else if (this == 'Invalid')
    {
        alert('That Username is taken or the Password is incorrect' +
            ' - please try again')
        DoLogin()
    }
    else
    {
        O('title').innerHTML = "Rob's Place (" + USERNAME + ')'
        S('logout').opacity  = '1'

        if (LOCALSTORAGE)
        {
            localStorage.setItem('username', USERNAME)
            localStorage.setItem('password', PASSWORD)
        }
        else
        {
            ProcessCookie('save', 'username', USERNAME, 31556926)
            ProcessCookie('save', 'password', PASSWORD, 31556926)
        }

        ActivateObject('logout', Logout)
        PostMessage('ALL', '... has joined')

        BUFFER                      = ''
        SMARTPERIOD                 = true;
        MAXINP                      = 1000
        S('mainoverlay').fontSize   = '2em'
        S('mainoverlay').fontWeight = 'normal'
        S('mainoverlay').overflow   = 'auto'
        S('keyboard'   ).opacity    = '1'
        O('input'      ).value      = '_'
        O('mainoverlay').innerHTML  = ''

        GetChat()
        DoToUpper()
        SetPostRecipient('ALL')
    }
}
}
```

The Ajax call, `PostAjaxRequest()`, which is on the first line, uses a POST request, passing the contents of USERNAME in the field u and PASSWORD in p. The variable LOGIN contains the URL of the PHP program to call for this.

Upon completion the local function `result()` (constituting the remainder of the function code) is called by the Ajax routine. If there was an error or the credentials did not validate, a message is displayed and the function `DoLogin()` is called to ask for input again. Otherwise, the username and password validated, so the `else` section of code changes the page's title to include the username, and a Logout button is added to the title bar by changing the opacity of the button from 0 to 1. Because a CSS transition is applied to this button in the CSS rules, the button fades in gently.

Then the username and password contents are saved in local storage (or cookies if that is not available) to allow quick access in the future until (or unless) the user logs out, the logout button is attached to the `Logout()` function, and the message "… has joined" is posted to the chat using the username.

After this, the input buffer, BUFFER, is reset, SMARTPERIOD is set to `true` to allow automatic spaces after periods, the maximum input length in MAXINP is set to 1,000 characters, and various CSS properties are modified to present the chat at its best.

The final three lines set up the repeating Ajax calls to the server to keep fetching new messages, switch the keyboard to uppercase letters, and set the default recipient for posts to the user ALL, which means all messages will be public.

The GetChat() Function

This function sets up an Ajax call to the web server using the `PostAjaxRequest()` function. It passes both the username and password each time in the fields u and p, so that every Ajax request verifies the user's credentials.

If the variable FIRST is `true`, then the field f is also passed to the web server, which will then return up to 50 of the most recent messages to populate the chat screen with the latest chatter. Otherwise, after this first time, FIRST is set to `false`, and the server will thereafter return only those messages that haven't been read.

```
function GetChat()
{
   var args = 'u=' + USERNAME + '&p=' + PASSWORD

   if (FIRST)
   {
      args += '&f=1'
      FIRST = false
   }

   PostAjaxRequest(ShowChat, GETCHAT, args)
}
```

The variable GETCHAT contains the URL of the PHP program on the server to call, and the `ShowChat()` function is specified as the target for the data returned by the Ajax call.

The ShowChat() Function

The returned data from the web server is received by the ShowChat () function in the pseudo variable this. If there were not any new messages, then this contains the empty string. Otherwise, the variable text is assigned a copy of the contents of this so that any instances of the ontouchstart event returned by the web server can be replaced with onclick for browsers that do not support the ontouchstart event.

Then the innerHTML property of the mainoverlay <div> has the contents of text appended to it and the <div> is scrolled down to the 100,000th line—this line will almost certainly never be reached, so the call has the effect of simply scrolling the chat screen so that the most recent message(s) can be seen.

```
function ShowChat()
{
   if (this.length > 0)
   {
     var text = this

     if (BROWSER == 'Other')
        text = text.replace(/ontouchstart/g, 'onclick')

     O('mainoverlay').innerHTML += text
     O('mainoverlay').scrollTop  = '100000'
     S('mainoverlay').opacity    = '1'
     GETFREQ                     = 2000;
   } else GETFREQ += 17;

   CHATTOUT = setTimeout(GetChat, GETFREQ)
}
```

If no messages were returned, then the pseudo variable this has no contents and so GETFREQ is incremented by 17. This has the effect that every time nothing is returned by the server, an additional 17 milliseconds is added to the delay before trying again. Therefore, on a slow day in the chat room, if no messages are returned for 60 seconds, the gap of 2,000 milliseconds between message checks will have increased to 3,020 milliseconds, or just over 3 seconds—and after an hour of no messages being retrieved, the server will now be polled only once per minute, and so on.

But as soon as any message is received, the delay frequency returns to two seconds, so this is a great way of minimizing bandwidth use both for your server and your users when little or no chatting is occurring.

The final line in this function sets up an interrupt to call the GetChat () function once again in two seconds using the setTimeout () function, whose return value is saved in the global variable CHATTOUT so that the timeouts can be disabled if the user logs out. Otherwise, the flow continues indefinitely in the background between GetChat () and ShowChat () via Ajax calls, so that the chat screen will update with new messages while the user is doing other things such as entering a message to post.

Figure 11-8 shows the chat on an Apple iPad, just after logging in, and after sending and receiving a pair of private messages, shown highlighted and with borders.

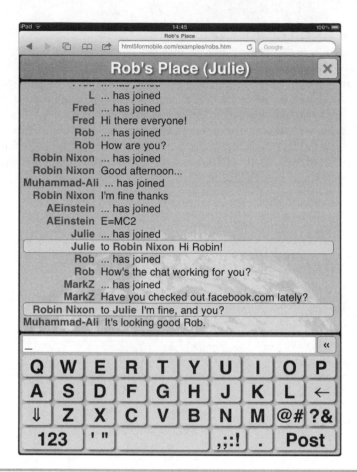

Figure 11-8 How public and private messages are displayed

The SetPostRecipient() Function

This function is called in function `Login()` to attach the `PostMessage()` function to the Post button on the virtual keyboard. The function is short and sweet and simply ensures that whatever username is in the variable `to` is set as the default recipient for any messages.

```
function SetPostRecipient(to)
{
   RECIP = to
   ActivateObject('post', function() { PostMessage(to) } )
}
```

The global variable `RECIP` is also set to the value in `to` so that if the ENTER key on an attached keyboard is pressed, the current recipient value can be looked up and the message can be posted.

The PostMessage() Function

After being attached to the Post button, this function is called when the button is tapped. It uses the contents of the to and mess arguments to post a message via Ajax.

The to argument is the username of the message recipient, which is ALL if the message is public. If mess has a value, then it contains the message to be posted. Otherwise, the message held in the virtual keyboard variable BUFFER is the message. The reason for the mess argument is to allow quick posts to be made such as "Fred … has joined" when a user logs in.

As long as the message to post is not the empty string, it is sent to the server using the PostAjaxRequest() function. Then the keyboard BUFFER variable is cleared, as is the <textarea> with the ID input (used to display the contents of BUFFER).

Finally, the RemovePMWindow() function is called to close the window in case the post came from the Private Message window, and the keyboard is reset to uppercase letters.

```
function PostMessage(to, mess)
{
   if (typeof mess != UNDEF) BUFFER = mess
   else HighlightButton('post')

   if (BUFFER.length > 0)
   {
      PostAjaxRequest(function() {}, POSTCHAT,
         'u=' + USERNAME + '&p=' + PASSWORD + '&t=' + to + '&m=' +BUFFER)
      BUFFER          = ''
      O('input').value = '_'
      RemovePMWindow()
      DoToUpper()
   }
}
```

NOTE

In the second line of code, the HighlightButton() function is called if the message to post has come from the keyboard. This has the effect of changing the key's color, which will then change back when another key is tapped or after two seconds without any further key taps.

The SendPM() Function

I briefly referred to the Private Message (PM) window in the previous section. This pops up whenever a username is tapped and enables a private message to be sent to that person. This is achieved by an ontouchstart event being attached to each username via the chat HTML returned by the server.

When activated, this function brings the PM window (the <div> with the ID pmoverlay) to the forefront by changing its CSS z-index property, as shown in Figure 11-9, a screen grab taken from a Samsung Galaxy Tab.

Figure 11-9 Sending a private message

A second overlay is also brought above this to place the `<textarea>` underneath it. This prevents the iOS or Android built-in virtual keyboard from popping up if the `<textarea>` is tapped, a behavior we don't want because we have already provided a keyboard.

To send the keyboard input to the `<textarea>`, its ID of `pminput` is passed to the `GetInput()` function. The default recipient is then set to the username that was tapped using a call to `SetPostRecipient()`.

```
function SendPM(to)
{
   S('pmoverlay' ).zIndex    = '20'
   S('pmoverlay2').zIndex    = '30'
   S('pmoverlay' ).opacity   = '1'
   O('pmoverlay' ).innerHTML = 'PM ' + to + "<textarea id='pminput'>" +
```

```
        "</textarea><div id='pmtip'>Use keyboard to send message, or "  +
        "tap to close.</div>"

    GetInput('pminput')
    SetPostRecipient(to)
    ActivateObject('pmoverlay2', RemovePMWindow)
}
```

In the final line, the `ontouchstart` event (or `onclick` on a non-iOS or -Android device) of the `<div>` that was placed over the PM window is assigned to the `RemovePMWindow()` function so that if it is tapped, the PM window simply disappears.

The RemovePMWindow() Function

This function is called either when the `<div>` overlaid on the PM window is tapped or when a post is sent using the `PostMessage()` function. It removes the window (and its second overlay) by clearing its `innerHTML` and changing the `z-index` properties to place it behind all other objects. The `opacity` of the window is also set to `0`, and the virtual keyboard buffer is cleared.

```
function RemovePMWindow()
{
    O('pmoverlay' ).innerHTML = ''
    S('pmoverlay' ).zIndex    = '-1'
    S('pmoverlay2').zIndex    = '-1'
    S('pmoverlay' ).opacity   = '0'
    O('input'     ).value     = '_'
    BUFFER                    = ''

    SetPostRecipient('ALL')
    GetInput(null)
}
```

The final two lines restore the default recipient to the username `ALL`, so that posts will be public, and call the `GetInput()` function. A value of `null` is passed in this instance because there is no field in which to place a copy of the virtual keyboard input, such as the login or PM inputs. If the keyboard input buffer input were required to be copied elsewhere, the argument would be the ID of the field to which it should be copied.

The GetInput() Function

This function is called whenever input is wanted from the virtual keyboard. The argument `field` specifies a field (such as the username and password inputs—`uname` and `pword`— during login) to which the input should be assigned. If its value is `null`, then there is no field external to the keyboard to which the input should be copied. In this case the Post button will be directed to simply submit directly to the web server via Ajax.

If `field` refers to either `uname` or `pword` (the username and password input fields), then the field is styled, `SMARTPERIOD` is set to `false` so that automatic spaces after periods are disabled, and the `MAXINP` variable is set to 20, the maximum supported length for either a username or password.

```
function GetInput(field)
{
    if (field == 'uname' || field == 'pword')
    {
        S('uname').borderColor =
        S('pword').borderColor = '#ccc'
        SMARTPERIOD            = false
        MAXINP                 = 20
    } else MAXINP = 1000

    if (field != null)
    {
        BUFFER                = O(field).innerHTML
        S(field).borderColor  = '#fa6900'
    }

    O('input'   ).value   = BUFFER + '_'
    S('keyboard').opacity = '1'
    THEFIELD              = field
    DoToUpper()
}
```

The middle section of code ensures that if there is an external field to populate, it is styled with an orange border. In the final four lines of code, the input `<textarea>` is set to the contents of `BUFFER`, followed by an underline character to act as a cursor; the keyboard's `opacity` is set to 1, which will fade it in due to a transition effect that is enabled on it in the CSS; a copy of the value in `field` is placed in the global variable `THEFIELD` for use in other functions; and the keyboard keys are reset to uppercase.

The ProcessKey() Function

This function is called whenever one of the keys in the virtual keyboard is tapped. The first thing it does is call `StopDefaultAction()` to prevent iOS or Android from doing anything further with the key tap. Then the local variables `last` and `ch` are assigned the length of the input in `BUFFER` and the last character entered, respectively. Also, any timeout event set to occur to remove a key highlight after two seconds of inactivity is cancelled with a call to `clearTimeout()`.

Then follows a `switch()` statement with nine `case` sections to deal with special keys such as the period, comma, and space keys, and a final `default` section to handle all other keys.

```
function ProcessKey(key, e)
{
   if (e) StopDefaultAction(e)

   var last = BUFFER.length - 1
   var ch   = BUFFER[last]

   if (typeof TOUT != UNDEF) clearTimeout(TOUT)

   switch(ALPHA[key])
   {
     case 'period':
        if (BUFFER.length >= MAXINP) return
        DoToUpper()
        BUFFER += '.'
        if (ch != '.' && SMARTPERIOD) BUFFER += ' '
        break
     case 'comma':
        if      (ch == ',') BUFFER = BUFFER.substr(0, last) +  ';';
        else if (ch == ';') BUFFER = BUFFER.substr(0, last) +  ':';
        else if (ch == ':') BUFFER = BUFFER.substr(0, last) +  '!';
        else if (ch == '!') BUFFER = BUFFER.substr(0, last) +  ',';
        else if (BUFFER.length < MAXINP)              BUFFER += ','
        break
     case 'del':
        if (BUFFER.length > 1)
        {
           BUFFER = BUFFER.substr(0, BUFFER.length - 1)
           ch     = BUFFER[BUFFER.length - 1]
           if      (ch == '.')               DoToUpper()
           else if (NUMBERS.indexOf(ch) > -1) DoToNumbers()
           else                              DoToLower()
        }
        else
        {
           BUFFER =  ''
           DoToUpper()
        }
        break
     case 'space':
        if (BUFFER.length >= MAXINP) return
        if (ch == '?' || ch == '!') DoToUpper()
        BUFFER += ' '
        break
     case 'ques':
        if      (ch == '?') BUFFER = BUFFER.substr(0, last) +  '&';
        else if (ch == '&') BUFFER = BUFFER.substr(0, last) +  '?';
        else if (BUFFER.length < MAXINP)              BUFFER += '?'
        break
```

```
        case 'at':
            if      (ch == '@') BUFFER = BUFFER.substr(0, last) +  '#';
            else if (ch == '#') BUFFER = BUFFER.substr(0, last) +  "@";
            else if (BUFFER.length < MAXINP)            BUFFER += '@'
            break
        case 'apos':
            if      (ch == "'") BUFFER = BUFFER.substr(0, last) +  '"';
            else if (ch == '"') BUFFER = BUFFER.substr(0, last) +  "'";
            else if (BUFFER.length < MAXINP)            BUFFER += "'"
            break
        case 'shift':
            if (O('a').innerHTML != 'A') DoToUpper()
            else                         DoToLower()
            break
        case 'alt':
            if (O('a').innerHTML == '(') DoToUpper()
            else                         DoToNumbers()
            break
        default:
            if (BUFFER.length >= MAXINP) return
            BUFFER += O(ALPHA[key]).innerHTML
            if (O('a').innerHTML == 'A') DoToLower()
            break
    }

    O('input').value     = BUFFER + '_'
    O('input').scrollTop = 10000

    HighlightButton(ALPHA[key])

    if (THEFIELD)
    {
        O(THEFIELD).innerHTML = BUFFER
        O(THEFIELD).scrollTop = 10000
    }
}
```

After the switch() statement, the value of the input <textarea> is updated with the contents of BUFFER plus an underline character for a cursor. Then its scrollTop property is set to a very high value such that only the most recently entered characters are seen.

After this, the HighlightButton() function is called to highlight whichever key was tapped. Then, if the global variable THEFIELD has a value, it is also given a copy of the contents of BUFFER and has its scrollTop property set to a value that will ensure only the most recently entered characters are in view. This is the part of the function that copies the keyboard input to an external field.

The DoToUpper() Function

This function ensures that the uppercase characters A through Z are displayed in the virtual keyboard. The SHIFT key is also changed to a down arrow and the ALT key is set to display 123.

```
function DoToUpper()
{
   for (var j = 0 ; j < 26 ; ++j) O(ALPHA[j]).innerHTML = UPPER[j]

   O('shift').innerHTML = '&dArr;'
   O('alt'  ).innerHTML = '123'
}
```

The DoToLower() Function

This function ensures that the lowercase characters a through z are displayed in the virtual keyboard (see Figure 11-10). The SHIFT key is also changed to an up arrow and the ALT key is set to display 123.

```
function DoToLower()
{
   for (var j = 0 ; j < 26 ; ++j) O(ALPHA[j]).innerHTML = ALPHA[j]

   O('shift').innerHTML = '&uArr;'
   O('alt'  ).innerHTML = '123'
}
```

Figure 11-10 The lowercase keyboard

The DoToNumbers() Function

This function ensures that the numbers 0 through 9 and a collection of punctuation, currency, and other symbols are displayed in the virtual keyboard (see Figure 11-11). The SHIFT key is also changed to an up arrow and the ALT key is set to display ABC.

```
function DoToNumbers()
{
    for (var j = 0 ; j < 26 ; ++j) O(ALPHA[j]).innerHTML = NUMBERS[j]

    O('shift').innerHTML = '&uArr;'
    O('alt'  ).innerHTML = 'ABC'
}
```

The HighlightButton() Function

This function highlights one of the keys in the virtual keyboard. It then makes a copy of the key in the global variable OLDBUT so that the highlight can be later cancelled via the setTimeout() call, which sets up an interrupt to an anonymous function to occur in 2,000 milliseconds (2 seconds).

```
function HighlightButton(button)
{
    but            = S(button)
    but.background = '#fa6900'
    but.color      = '#fff'
```

Figure 11-11 The numeric, currency, and punctuation keyboard

Figure 11-12 The 7 key has just been tapped.

```
if (OLDBUT != but)
{
    OLDBUT.background = '#e0e4cc'
    OLDBUT.color     = '#000'
    OLDBUT           = but
}

TOUT = setTimeout(function()
{
    but.background = '#e0e4cc'
    but.color      = '#000';
}, 2000)


}
```

Before OLDBUT is assigned a copy of but, it is first compared with it. If it is not the same, then a different key is currently highlighted, so it is first unhighlighted. Figure 11-12 shows the keyboard in numeric mode with the 7 key currently highlighted.

The Logout() Function
This function is attached to the Logout button displayed at the right of the title bar. When the Logout button is tapped, a dialog box pops up asking the user to confirm whether they wish to log out, as shown in Figure 11-13.

If the user response is Cancel, then the function simply exits and nothing happens. Otherwise, the variable FIRST is set to true, ready to load up to 50 lines of chat if the user (or another) logs in again, and the USERNAME and PASSWORD variables are set to the empty string. The Logout button is also removed, as is the username following the title.

Figure 11-13 The logout confirmation dialog box viewed on a Nexus One phone

```
function Logout()
{
   if (confirm("Logout from Rob's?"))
   {
      S('mainoverlay').overflow = 'hidden'
      S('logout'     ).opacity  = '0'
      O('title').innerHTML      = "Rob's Place"
      FIRST                     = true
      USERNAME = PASSWORD       = ''

      if (LOCALSTORAGE)
      {
         localStorage.removeItem('username')
         localStorage.removeItem('password')
      }
```

```
        else
        {
            ProcessCookie('erase', 'username')
            ProcessCookie('erase', 'password')
        }

        PostMessage('ALL', '... has left')
        clearTimeout(CHATTOUT)
        DoLogin()
    }
}
```

Before returning, the function also clears out the local storage copies of the username and password (or the cookies if local storage is not supported) to prevent automatic logging back in, a message such as "Mary ... has left" is posted in the chat, the repeating Ajax calls to fetch the latest chat messages are cancelled with a call to `clearTimeout()`, and the `DoLogin()` function is called to allow the user (or a new user) to log back in.

The NavCheck() Function

This function is called right at the start of the program to determine the type of device or browser in use according to the User Agent string the browser supplies.

```
function NavCheck(check)
{
    return navigator.userAgent.indexOf(check) != -1
}
```

The ActivateObject() Function

This function attaches the function in `func` to the object in `object` via an `ontouchstart` event if the device is iOS or Android, or via an `onclick` event on any other hardware.

```
function ActivateObject(object, func)
{
    if (BROWSER != 'Other') O(object).ontouchstart = func
    else                     O(object).onclick      = func
}
```

The `ontouchstart` event is preferred for iOS and Android devices because it triggers immediately after an object is tapped. On these devices, the `onclick` event is triggered only after a wait of about 300 milliseconds while the operating system tries to detect a drag or double-tap action, before defaulting to a single click event. The `onclick` event is activated immediately on all other devices.

The StopDefaultAction() Function

This function is needed because when the `ontouchstart` event of a touch device occurs that we wish to deal with, we also want to prevent iOS or Android from further processing it, possibly turning two single taps on the keyboard into an unwanted double tap to zoom in.

By calling this function within an object's event handler, the underlying operating system will take no further action on the touch event.

```
function StopDefaultAction(e)
{
    e.preventDefault()
    e.stopPropagation()
    return false
}
```

The SetUpClearBut() Function

This function attaches to the button that looks like <<, to the right of the keyboard's input field. When this button is tapped, the entire contents of the input is discarded and the keyboard, if it is displaying either lowercase or numeric/punctuation characters, is switched to display uppercase letters.

```
function SetUpClearBut()
{
    HighlightButton('clear')
    BUFFER          = ''
    O('input').value = '_'
    DoToUpper()

    if (typeof THEFIELD != UNDEF && THEFIELD != null)
        O(THEFIELD).innerHTML  = ''
}
```

The `if()` statement also clears the global variable `THEFIELD` if it has a value.

The O() Function

This function is used to replace dozens of `getElementById('id')` function calls and make the code much shorter and simpler. It takes either the ID of an object or an object itself, and returns the object to which it refers. It has handy error checking, too, in that unrecognized objects cause an alert box to pop up, which is very useful during debugging should you misspell an object ID, for example.

```
function O(id)
{
    if (typeof id == 'object') return id
    try      { return document.getElementById(id) }
    catch(e) { alert('Unknown ID: ' + id)         }
}
```

The S() Function

This is a companion to the O() function in that it takes the same argument (either an ID or an object), except it then returns the style subobject to which it refers. The function therefore replaces the use of getElementById('id').style and also substantially shortens the program. It also reports via an alert if an object is not found.

```
function S(id)
{
   if (typeof id == 'object') return id.style
   try     { return O(id).style        }
   catch(e) { alert('Unknown ID: ' + id) }
}
```

The CreateAjaxObject() Function

This function, described in Chapter 7, is used by PostAjaxRequest() to create an Ajax object and then fetch some information from the server in the background.

```
function CreateAjaxObject(callback)
{
   try      { var    ajax = new XMLHttpRequest()                    }
   catch(e1) { try { ajax = new ActiveXObject("Msxml2.XMLHTTP")   }
   catch(e2) { try { ajax = new ActiveXObject("Microsoft.XMLHTTP") }
   catch(e3) { ajax = false }}}

   if (ajax) ajax.onreadystatechange = function()
   {
      if (this.readyState   == 4   &&
          this.status       == 200 &&
          this.responseText != null)
      callback.call(this.responseText)
   }

   return ajax
}
```

The PostAjaxRequest() Function

This function, also detailed in Chapter 7, handles the posting of arguments via Ajax to a web server and then returns the data provided by the server to the function named in the argument callback:

```
function PostAjaxRequest(callback, url, args)
{
   var ctype = 'application/x-www-form-urlencoded'
```

```
        var ajax   = new CreateAjaxObject(callback)
        if (!ajax) return false

        ajax.open('POST', url, true)
        ajax.setRequestHeader('Content-type',    ctype)
        ajax.setRequestHeader('Content-length', args.length)
        ajax.setRequestHeader('Connection',       'close')
        ajax.send(args)
        return true
    }
```

The ProcessCookie() Function

This function is used for saving, reading, and retrieving cookies. It takes the action to perform in the first argument (save, read, or erase), the cookie name for the second argument, its value in the third argument, and its expiry time in seconds. Optionally, a path, domain, and secure options can also be passed.

```
function ProcessCookie(action, name, value, seconds,
    path, domain, secure)

{
    if (action == 'save')
    {
        var date = new Date()
        date.setTime(parseInt(date.getTime() + seconds * 1000))

        var expires     = seconds ? '; expires=' + date.toGMTString() : ''
        path            = path    ? '; path='    + path               : ''
        domain          = domain  ? '; domain='  + domain             : ''
        secure          = secure  ? '; secure='  + secure             : ''
        document.cookie = name + '=' + escape(value) + expires + path
    }
    else if (action == 'read')
    {
        if (!document.cookie.length) return false
        else
        {
            var start = document.cookie.indexOf(name + '=')

            if (start == -1) return false
            else
            {
                start  += name.length + 1
                var end = document.cookie.indexOf(';', start)
```

```
            end     = (end == -1) ? document.cookie.length : end

            return unescape(document.cookie.substring(start, end))
        }
      }
    }
    else if (action == 'erase')
        ProcessCookie('save', name, '', -60)
}
```

Using the Web Page

Once the web application has been loaded into a browser in portrait mode, if you find that the keys of the virtual keyboard are too small to easily use on a particular device, you can rotate the device, as shown in Figure 11-14. This will usually quadruple the size of the keyboard and still leave the most recent few messages in view—simply drag the page down and up to view previous messages or the PM window.

Ask the Expert

Q: Why do some of the keys in the virtual keyboard have more than one character?

A: The reason for this is to avoid having several alternative screens of characters. For example, the @ and # characters share a key on the main keyboard layout since they are commonly used when referring to e-mail addresses and twitter messages. Likewise, the ? and & characters are also commonly used and need to be in the main layout for easy access, so they also share a key.

Using these combination keys is similar to texting a message using a numeric phone keypad, which many people are used to doing. The first tap selects the first character and a second tap selects the second character. Thereafter, each time you tap the same button, it toggles between the two characters and is finally selected only when another key is pressed.

This toggle action also happens with the single and double quote characters on the key to the left of the spacebar, and the comma, semicolon, colon, and exclamation characters on the key to the right of the spacebar. Between these four combination keys, you have access to most of the characters you would otherwise have to switch to a second keyboard layout to select.

Figure 11-14   Viewing the chat in landscape mode on an iPhone

Using a Home Screen Icon

When a web page is saved to the home screen on an iOS device, if you have a line of HTML such as the following near the start of your web page, the icon specified (in this case *robs.png*) will be used for the home screen icon:

```
<link rel='apple-touch-icon' href='robs.png' />
```

Figure 11-15 shows a very simple icon I created for this program on an iPhone home screen (on the third row), after rounded borders and a glossy sheen have been automatically added.

Unfortunately, Android will not use this icon (although it used to in some earlier versions).

Providing Extra Screen Space to the Web App

Unlike Android, which has a back button and menu button built into the hardware, the iOS web browser takes up 86 pixels' depth of prime screen real estate with its button row. But if

Figure 11-15   The icon has been transformed into an iOS home screen icon.

you include the following line of HTML at the start of a web page, if the page is saved to an iOS home screen, the space the button row used to occupy is freed up, and this project will notice the fact and enlarge the chat area accordingly:

```
<meta name='apple-mobile-web-app-capable' content='yes' />
```

NOTE
Figure 11-14 was captured from an iPhone running as web app capable as you can see, there is no bottom button bar. In Chapter 12 I'll show you how you can also free up the top Info bar when turning the project into a local application.

The PHP Programs

On the server side of the equation, there are four PHP files, which handle logging into the MySQL database (*login.php*), verifying and logging in users (*robslogin.php*), retrieving messages from the chat (*robsgetchat.php*), and posting messages to it (*robspost.php*).

The login.php Program

This program, introduced in Chapter 8, is used only by the other PHP programs to log into the MySQL database. On your web server, you will have to change one or more of the values assigned to $db_database, $db_username, and $db_password according to how you have set it up, and the database username and password you have assigned to PHP.

```php
<?php // login.php
$db_hostname = 'localhost';
$db_database = 'phpdb';
$db_username = 'php';
$db_password = 'a_password';

$db_server = mysql_connect($db_hostname, $db_username, $db_password)
    or die('Cannot connect to MySQL: ' . mysql_error());
mysql_select_db($db_database)
    or die('Cannot select database: ' . mysql_error());
?>
```

The robslogin.php Program

This program is called by the web browser using Ajax to either verify or create a given username and password pair. If the provided username (posted as the field u) is not found in the database and if there is a matching password (posted as the field p), then a new user is added to the database and the die() command is called to output the word "Valid" and exit—but if there is any error, then the word "Error" is returned.

If the username does exist in the database and the supplied password matches it, then the word "Valid" is also returned. Otherwise, the world "Invalid" is returned to indicate that the password did not match.

```php
<?php // robslogin.php
require_once 'login.php';

if (isset($_POST['u'])) $uname = MySQL_Sanitize($_POST['u']);
if (isset($_POST['p'])) $pword = MySQL_Sanitize($_POST['p']);

if (strlen($uname) == 0 || strlen($pword) == 0) die ('Error');

$query  = "SELECT password FROM users WHERE username='$uname'";
$result = mysql_query($query);
```

```
$rows    = mysql_num_rows($result);
$pw      = md5('salt_1' . $pword . 'salt_2');

if (!$rows)
{
    $query = "INSERT INTO users VALUES('$uname', '$pw', 0)";
    if (mysql_query($query)) die('Valid');
    die('Error');
}
else
{
    $row = mysql_fetch_row($result);
    if ($pw == $row[0]) die('Valid');
    else                die('Invalid');
}
```

As also explained in Chapter 8, a pair of *salt* strings are used as a security measure; they are placed before and after the password, before converting it to a 32-character string using the md5() function.

Then, to compare each user-supplied password with the database, it is also passed through the salting process followed by the md5() function, and only the result of this is compared with the value in the database. This ensures that an uncrackable value is stored in the database, rather than the password itself, which would be very dangerous because, if the database were successfully hacked, it could reveal usernames and password pairs that the chat users might also use to access other services. By storing the passwords in this way, no indication of the actual passwords used could be gained by a hacker.

The MySQL_Sanitize() Function

The MySQL_Sanitize() function is used to remove any malicious characters a hacker may try to send to the server, replacing them with safe ones. The function is at the end of the file, so following the function the file is closed with a final ?> tag.

```
function MySQL_Sanitize($string)
{
    if (get_magic_quotes_gpc())
        $string = stripslashes($string);
    return mysql_real_escape_string($string);
}
?>
```

The robsgetchat.php Program

This is the program that returns chat messages to the web browser. It has two modes. In the first mode it returns up to the most recent 50 messages to populate the browser's chat screen, and in the second mode it returns only unread messages.

The mode to use is determined by whether a field with the name f (for first) has been posted. If it hasn't, then the condition in $cond (which ensures only unread messages are returned) is inserted into $query; otherwise, $cond is set to the empty string and this extra condition is not applied, allowing all messages up to the most recent 50 to be returned.

```php
<?php // robsgetchat.php
require_once 'login.php';

$latest = VerifyUser();
$output = '';
$cond   = "num>$latest AND";

if ($latest < 0) die('Error');
if (isset($_POST['f'])) $cond = '';

$query = "SELECT * FROM chat WHERE $cond (sender='$uname' OR " .
         "recip='$uname' OR recip = 'ALL') ORDER BY num DESC LIMIT 50";
$result = mysql_query($query);
```

Inside the if() Statement

The result of performing the query using mysql_query() is placed into the variable $result. If it has a value, then an if() statement is entered and the number of rows returned is placed into the variable $rows.

If the value is less than 1, then no messages were returned; otherwise, a for() loop iterates through each message, displaying only those that have been posted to the user ALL or to either the sender or recipient. In the former case, one type of HTML table is used to display the message; in the latter case, a different table, with a colored background and a border, is used. Each message is then appended to the variable $output.

NOTE

I chose to use tables here because they are a quick way to ensure that all parts of the messages display in tightly constrained areas—in other words, tables keep the display neat without the need for lots of CSS. After all, chat can be viewed as a form of tabular data, so using tables here is quite legitimate.

Once all the messages have been processed, the value in $latest, which contains the number of the most recent message returned, is inserted into the latest field for the user in the table users. This is used to ensure only new messages are returned.

```php
if ($result)
{
    $rows = mysql_num_rows($result);
```

```
    if ($rows < 1) return;

    for ($j = 0 ; $j < $rows ; ++$j)
    {
        $row  = mysql_fetch_row($result);
        $from = $row[1];
        $to   = $row[2];
        $mess = $row[3];

        if ($j == 0) $latest = $row[0];

        if ($to == 'ALL')
            $output = "<table border='0' cellpadding='0' cellspacing="       .
                "'0' width='100%'><tr valign='top'><td width='25%' align="   .
                "'right' class='user' ontouchstart=\"SendPM('$from');\">"    .
                "$from</td><td>$mess</td></tr></table>\n" . $output;
        else if ($uname == $from || $uname == $to)
            $output = "<table class='pm' border='0' cellpadding='0' "         .
                "cellspacing='0' width='100%'><tr valign='top'><td width="   .
                "'25%' align='right' class='user' ontouchstart=\"SendPM("   .
                "'$from');\">$from</td><td>to <span class='user' "           .
                "ontouchstart=\"SendPM('$to');\">$to</span>$mess</td>"       .
                "</tr></table>\n" . $output;
    }

    $query = "UPDATE users SET latest='$latest' WHERE
username='$uname'";
    mysql_query($query);
}

die ($output);
```

After all the processing, the value in $output is returned to the web browser and the program exits, both of which actions are achieved with the die() function. If no messages were found then because $output will contain the empty string, no data will be returned to the web browser.

The VerifyUser() Function
This function is a modified version of the *login.php* program and is used to ensure that every request made to the server is being made by an authorized user. It returns either −1 (if the username and password do not verify) or the value of the field latest in the users table, which contains the highest message the user has so far viewed.

```
function VerifyUser()
{
   global $uname;

   if (isset($_POST['u'])) $uname = mysql_sanitize($_POST['u']);
   if (isset($_POST['p'])) $pword = mysql_sanitize($_POST['p']);

   if (strlen($uname) == 0 || strlen($pword) == 0) return -1;

   $query  = "SELECT password,latest FROM users WHERE username='$uname'";
   $result = mysql_query($query);
   $row    = mysql_fetch_row($result);
   $pw     = md5('salt_1' . $pword . 'salt_2');

   if ($pw != $row[0]) return -1;
   return $row[1];
}
```

The MySQL_Sanitize() Function

This is the same function as used in the *robslogin.php* program.

```
function MySQL_Sanitize($string)
{
   if (get_magic_quotes_gpc())
      $string = stripslashes($string);
   return mysql_real_escape_string($string);
}
?>
```

The robspost.php Program

This program is actually very short and sweet when you take out the functions it uses. What it does is verify the user and then post a new message into the chat table.

```
<?php // robspost.php
require_once 'login.php';
if (VerifyUser() < 0) die('Error');

if ($mess != '' )
{
   $query = "INSERT INTO chat VALUES(null, '$uname', '$to', '$mess')";
   mysql_query($query);
}
```

The VerifyUser() Function

This is similar to the function of the same name used by *robsgetchat.php*, except that it also processes the posted fields t and m into the global variables $to and $mess.

```
function VerifyUser()
{
    global $uname;
    global $to;
    global $mess;

    if (isset($_POST['u'])) $uname = MySQL_Sanitize($_POST['u']);
    if (isset($_POST['p'])) $pword = MySQL_Sanitize($_POST['p']);
    if (isset($_POST['t'])) $to    = MySQL_Sanitize($_POST['t']);
    if (isset($_POST['m'])) $mess  = MySQL_Sanitize($_POST['m']);

    if (strlen($uname) == 0 || strlen($pword) == 0) return -1;

    $query  = "SELECT password,latest FROM users WHERE username='$uname'";
    $result = mysql_query($query);
    $row    = mysql_fetch_row($result);
    $pw     = md5('salt_1' . $pword . 'salt_2');

    if ($pw != $row[0]) return -1;
    return $row[1];
}
```

The MySQL_Sanitize() Function

This is similar to the function of the same name used by two of the other PHP programs, except that it includes a call to an additional function, htmlentities(), which removes any HTML from a posted message so that users cannot mess about with the chat screen by using huge fonts, try to hack into it, or annoy other users with JavaScript, and so on.

```
function MySQL_Sanitize($string)
{
    if (get_magic_quotes_gpc())
        $string = stripslashes($string);
    return mysql_real_escape_string(htmlentities($string));
}
?>
```

Summary

This chapter has taken you through many different aspects of building a web application targeted to iOS and Android devices. Of course, your apps are likely to be very different from the one presented in this chapter, but they will need to use many of the same strategies as this project.

So now you have two example projects (in this and the previous chapter) that can run as web apps. In the final part of this book, I'll show you how you can easily drop them into ready-made wrappers provided on the companion website, to turn them into self-contained apps you can offer in the Apple App Store and Android Market.

Part III

Creating Self-Contained Applications

In this part of the book you'll learn how to install and use both the Apple Xcode and Google Eclipse SDKs (software development kits) and how to connect your iOS and Android devices to them to download and test your apps.

You'll also learn how to drop your web apps into ready-made wrappers, supplied on the companion website, and turn them into self-contained apps—without having to learn any more than a few basic aspects of the Objective C (for iOS) and Java (for Android) languages used for writing native apps.

These self-contained apps will use the same web applications outlined in Chapters 10 and 11 (or any that you write), and you won't have to tweak them for either iOS or Android (since both platforms have been taken into account during their writing). This means you'll be able to write a web app once, and then easily convert it to both an iOS and an Android app in a matter of minutes.

Chapter 12

Setting Up the Apple SDK

Key Skills & Concepts

- Registering as an Apple Developer
- Using the Member Center
- Joining the iOS Developer Program
- Installing the iOS SDK
- Provisioning iOS devices for development

To develop apps for iOS devices, you must first become a registered Apple Developer. This is a completely free and simple process. However, to publish your apps, you have to pay a $99 fee each year, even if your apps will be free. The only alternative to this is to offer your apps to "jailbroken" devices via a service such as Cydia, which is not covered in this book.

In this chapter I'll take you step by step through everything you need to do to get the iOS software development kit (SDK) up and running, ready for dropping web apps into ready-made wrappers, outlined in the following chapter, to turn them into self-contained apps.

Registering as an Apple Developer

If you don't already have an Apple Developer account, you need to get one by visiting the following URL and clicking the Get Started button, shown in Figure 12-1:

developer.apple.com/programs/register

Figure 12-2 shows the first screen of the registration process, in which you are asked about your Apple ID. You can continue the process by using an existing Apple ID to log in (such as one you use on iTunes), or you can create a new one, which is the recommended course if you wish to separate your business development from your personal Apple account.

If you opt to create a new Apple ID, a new screen will be displayed (shown in Figure 12-3), in which you'll need to choose an ID and password, enter your birthday and a security question, and provide your name, company, address, and phone number. If you choose to use an existing Apple ID, you'll be presented with the screen shown in Figure 12-4; after logging in, you'll be shown your personal details, which you can update if necessary.

Whether you create a new Apple ID or use an existing Apple ID, the next screen in the registration process asks you to complete your professional profile, as shown in Figure 12-5. Check the boxes that apply to you. Depending on the boxes you check in the first section, other subsections may open, in which you should provide additional details. Once you have completed the professional profile, you must read and agree to be bound by the Registered Apple Developer Agreement terms on the following screen (see Figure 12-6).

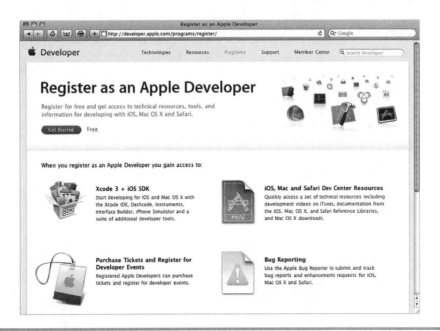

Figure 12-1   Registering as an Apple Developer on the *apple.com* website

Figure 12-2   The first screen of the Apple Developer registration process

Figure 12-3 Creating a new Apple ID

Figure 12-4 Signing in with an existing Apple ID

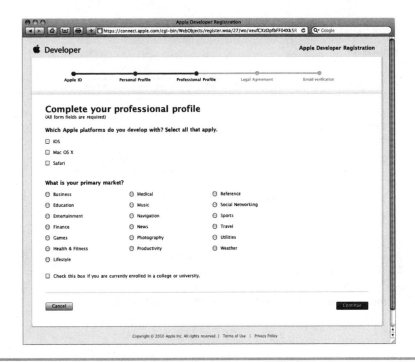

Figure 12-5 Completing your professional profile

Figure 12-6 Agreeing to the terms and conditions

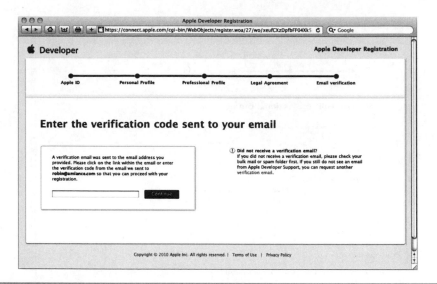

Figure 12-7 Enter the verification code you receive in this screen

In the final step, you must wait for Apple Developer Support to send you an e-mail with the title "Please verify your email address." When you receive it, copy the code it contains into the field shown in Figure 12-7, or you can click the code in the e-mail. Once completed, you'll be shown the screen in Figure 12-8, where you can click the Continue button to move on to the Member Center.

The Member Center

The Member Center is your start page for Apple development. It provides a comprehensive range of resources, videos, support, and news updates (see Figure 12-9). The URL to get here directly in the future is

developer.apple.com/membercenter

The first thing you need to do is download the latest SDK, so click the iOS link in the Dev Centers section to bring up the screen shown in Figure 12-10, where you should then click the link in the Downloads section with the title similar to "Xcode 4.02 and iOS SDK 4.3," depending on the latest version available. The download will be around 3.5 GB (see Figure 12-11), so it could take up to four or five hours on an average 2-Mbps connection.

While waiting for the download to complete, you can spend your time constructively by viewing some of the documents and videos in the iOS Dev Center, or by browsing the iOS Reference Library, How-To's, and Sample Code categories.

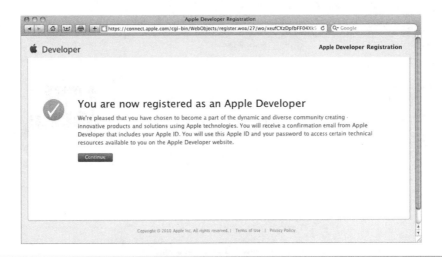

Figure 12-8   Confirmation that you are now a registered Apple Developer

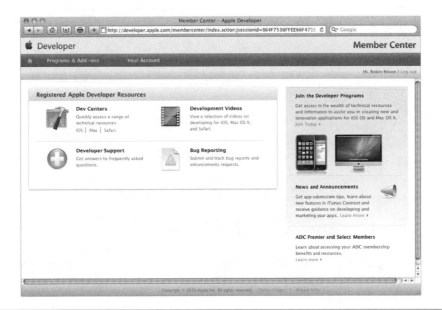

Figure 12-9   The Apple Developer Member Center web page

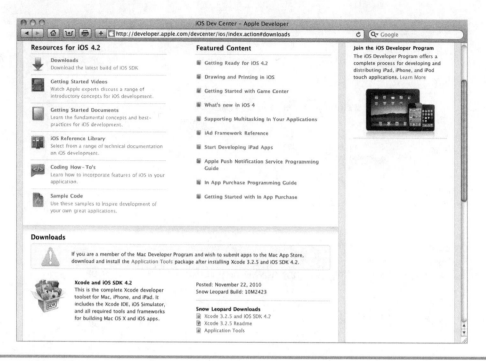

Figure 12-10 The iOS Dev Center with the Downloads section at the screen bottom

Figure 12-11 Depending on your broadband speed, you may have a wait of several hours before the SDK download completes.

Joining the iOS Developer Program

Another thing you can do while waiting for the download is join the iOS developer program if you intend to offer apps in the Apple App Store (whether free or for a price). The cost is $99 a year, but the program also enables you to provision iOS devices to run development code, so you can try out your code on actual devices rather than on the iOS emulator.

You can join the program by clicking the Programs link at the top of the iOS Dev Center or by visiting the following URL:

developer.apple.com/programs

Simply click the iOS Developer Program link, followed by the Enroll Now link on the next screen. You will then need to choose whether to enroll as an individual or company by clicking the appropriate button, as shown in Figure 12-12. Then, enter the various details required in the subsequent screens to review your details, agree to the license, purchase a subscription to the program, and activate it.

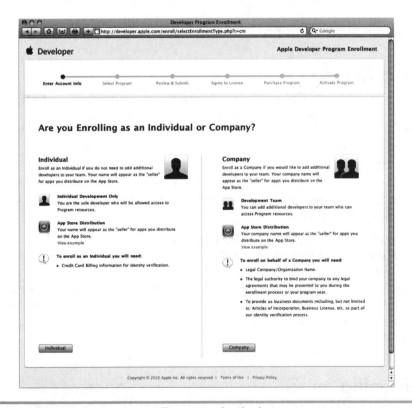

Figure 12-12   Choose whether to enroll as an individual or a company.

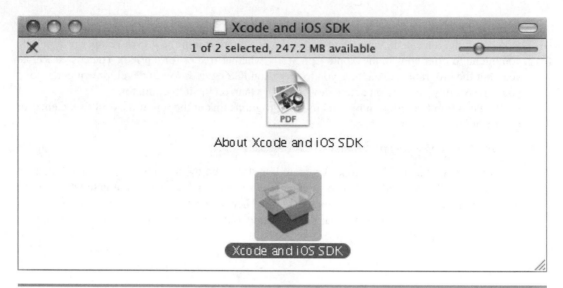

Figure 12-13 Running the Xcode and iOS SDK installer

Installing Xcode

Once it has finished downloading, the Xcode installer *.dmg* file "Xcode and iOS SDK" should mount and open the window shown in Figure 12-13. Before installation, you may wish to read the instructions by double-clicking the top About file. When you are ready, double-click the bottom file and follow all the instructions until installation is completed.

TIP

Ensure that iTunes is not running during the installation of Xcode or the process will be interrupted until you close iTunes.

For the installation, you should probably accept all the default options whenever prompted, as you can always come back and reinstall with different options later. The whole installation will take up to 15 minutes.

After the installation completes you may wish to use the Go menu of Finder to open the Macintosh HD folder, then from in there open the Developer folder, and inside that open the Applications folder, and from in there use your mouse to copy the Xcode application to the Dock bar for easy access.

The SDK is now installed and ready for use.

Provisioning an iOS Device for Development

In order to use an iOS device to test your software, you must first provision the device. This simply enables it to be connected to your computer via USB so that you can transfer apps to it for testing. To do this, go to your iOS Dev Center screen, which will look like Figure 12-14

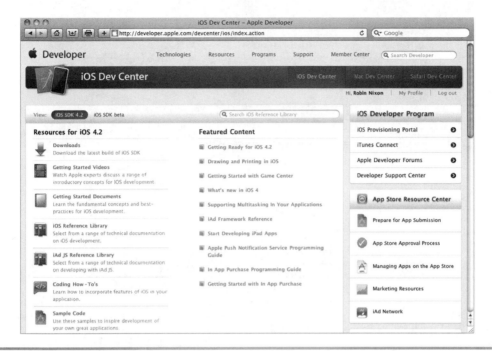

Figure 12-14 The iOS Dev Center viewed using a iOS developer profile

after you have registered as a iOS developer. In the iOS Developer Program box at the top right, click the first item, iOS Provisioning Portal, to open the screen shown in Figure 12-15.

NOTE
Don't worry about tying up your favorite iPad, iPod Touch, or iPhone when you provision it, because when you unplug a provisioned iOS device from your Mac, it will be just as useable in the normal way as it was before the provisioning. The only difference you may notice is a warning that will appear a few days before the provisioning is due to expire.

To begin the provisioning process, click the Launch Assistant button at the bottom of the screen to open the Development Provisioning Assistant, shown in Figure 12-16. Click the Continue button to move to the next screen (see Figure 12-17), where you can create a new App ID or use an existing one you may have created.

Because this will be the first time you use this assistant, you will want to create a new ID. I recommend you use a short name that identifies you or your business, such as "janedoedev."

TIP
Don't take too long running the assistant or it may log you out without warning and become unresponsive, in which case you'll need to go back and log in again.

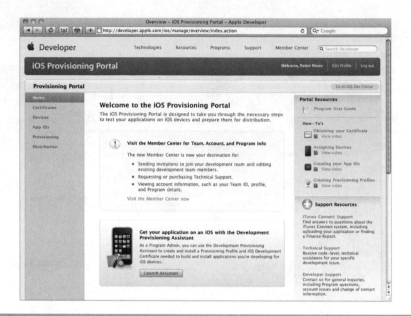

Figure 12-15 The iOS Provisioning Portal

Figure 12-16 The Development Provisioning Assistant

Figure 12-17 Choosing an App ID

Once you have created the new ID (or selected an existing one), the screen in Figure 12-18 is displayed, in which you can assign provisioning to a new iOS device, or use a device that has previously been provisioned. Assuming you are provisioning for the first time, choose Assign a New Apple Device and click Continue.

This takes you to the screen shown in Figure 12-19, in which you should enter a name for the device, such as "Fred iPhone 4," avoiding punctuation characters like apostrophes and so on. You will also need to provide the Unique Device ID (UDID) of the device.

You can retrieve the UDID from the Xcode Organizer, or via a free app you can get by searching for and installing "My Device ID" at the Apple App Store. After you install and run the app, it will open a new e-mail message containing the UDID. Simply enter your e-mail address into it and tap Send to e-mail it to yourself.

Then, whichever means you used to obtain it, copy and paste the UDID into the Provisioning Assistant Device ID field and click Continue to move on to the screen shown in Figure 12-20.

The next thing you are going to do is send a Certificate Signing Request (CSR) to Apple. To do this, click the Applications folder, open the Utilities folder inside it, and launch the

Figure 12-18 Choosing an Apple device to provision

Figure 12-19 Naming a device and supplying its Unique Device ID

Figure 12-20   Generating a Certificate Signing Request

Keychain Access program. Then, from the drop-down menu at the top of the screen, select Certificate Assistant followed by Request a Certificate from a Certificate Authority to open the Certificate Assistant screen shown in Figure 12-21.

In the Certificate Information fields, enter your e-mail address and name, choose the Saved to Disk option, and then click the Continue button. In the Save As dialog box that appears, choose where to save the request—for easy access, the Desktop is a good idea. You can then click Done and close the Keychain Access program.

Now click the Continue button in the Provisioning Assistant to proceed to the screen shown in Figure 12-22, in which you should click the Choose File button and select the file *CertificateSigningRequest.certSigningRequest* that you just saved.

Next click the Continue button in the Provisioning Assistant to move on to the screen shown in Figure 12-23, which will display your App ID, Device, and Certificate Name in the blank areas shown.

Choose a description for the provisioning profile such as "Jane Doe Provisioning" and click the Generate button. There will then be a delay of up to a minute or so while the request is processed, followed by the message "Your provisioning Profile has been generated."

When ready, click the Continue button to move on to the next screen (see Figure 12-24), where you should click the Download button, which will save the provisioning profile to your computer, ready to install in Xcode.

Figure 12-21 Entering your certificate information

Figure 12-22 Submitting the Certificate Signing Request

Figure 12-23   Naming the provisioning profile

Figure 12-24   Downloading and installing a provisioning profile

All you need to do now is ensure that your device is connected to the Mac and, assuming you copied the Xcode application to the Dock bar, drag-and-drop the provisioning profile onto the Xcode program to install it. This results in Xcode running; after a possible prompt or two about updating files on your iOS device, it will display the window shown in Figure 12-25, in which I have blurred the Serial Number, ECID, and Identifier.

The Provisioning section in the Organizer should show the provisioning profile you created. If it doesn't, click the + button, locate the profile where you saved it, and click it; it should then appear in the Provisioning section.

Now go back to the Provisioning Assistant and click Continue twice to display the screen shown in Figure 12-26, and then click the Download button to download the certificate.

After it has downloaded, double-click the .cer file to install it into the Keychain Access program. You can then click Continue followed by Done in the Provisioning Assistant to finish.

You will now be able to use your iOS device to test your apps. You can use the same process covered in this section to add provisioning to any other iOS devices you wish to use to test your apps.

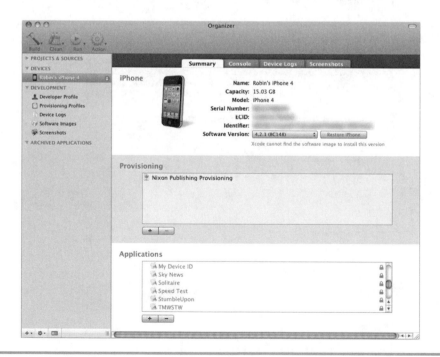

Figure 12-25　The Xcode device Organizer window

Figure 12-26   Downloading the development certificate

Ask the Expert

Q: What is the purpose of the device provisioning process?

A: Provisioning is Apple's way of keeping tight control over everything to do with app development for its devices. It means that Apple knows about every single device that has been set up for use in development. It also restricts nonprovisioned iOS devices from being able to download and run apps from anywhere else other than the Apple App Store.

Supposedly this is all about quality control, and there is some merit to that claim. However, the real reason would appear to be to restrict the emergence of alternative (and competing) app stores. The only way around this is to "jailbreak" your iOS device, which is not supported by Apple and could void your warranty.

At the other end of the spectrum, as you will see with its SDK in Chapter 14, you can connect any Android device to a computer in USB debugging mode and copy any apps you write to that device without any further to-do. To my mind, this stands as evidence that Apple's provisioning is not actually needed and is more of an unnecessary and complicated annoyance than anything.

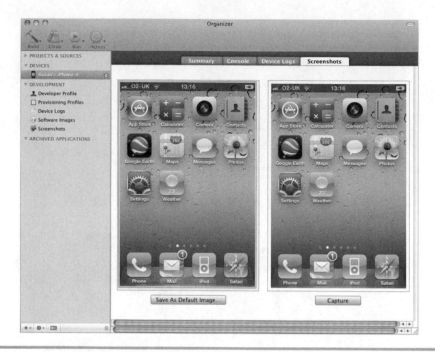

Figure 12-27 Grabbing the screen from an attached iPhone

Using the Xcode Organizer for Taking Screen Grabs

Screen grabs of your apps will be required (or at least asked for) when you submit them to the Apple App Store. Normally, the way to create them is to click the top and front buttons on an iOS device at the same time, and then locate the screen grab in the camera roll and e-mail it to yourself.

But you can sidestep all this palaver using the Xcode Organizer by clicking the Screenshots tab, as shown in Figure 12-27. From there you can use the standard CMD-SHIFT-3 or CMD-SHIFT-4 key combination to grab the image from the screen to a file on the desktop.

Summary

At this point, you should have the iOS SDK downloaded and installed and you should be signed up as an iOS developer. If you have also signed up as an iOS developer, you now are able to provision your iOS devices for development purposes, and you'll also be able to upload your apps to the Apple App Store. If you are not signed up, you can still develop apps, but you will have to test them in the SDK emulator, and you will not have access to the Apple App Store either.

But whichever options you chose, you are now ready to create stand-alone iOS apps using the information in the following chapter.

Chapter 13

Creating iOS
Stand-alone Apps

Key Skills & Concepts

- Creating a Hello World app
- Using the iOS emulator
- Saving apps to attached devices and running them
- Tweaking the Objective C code
- Obtaining a distribution certificate and provisioning profile
- Building an app for distribution
- Using the iTunes Connect website
- Submitting details on your app to Apple
- Uploading icons and screen grabs
- Using the Application Loader

Turning your web apps into stand-alone iOS apps is very easy using the Wrapper project supplied on the companion website. With it you simply rename a few items; copy some icons, HTML, and other files to the right folder; change a few settings; and click a button. But there's also a fairly complicated process of obtaining distribution certificates and provisioning profiles that this chapter takes you through step by step, so that doing so is as quick and simple as possible.

You'll also learn how to use the iTunes Connect website to send Apple information about your apps, set app prices, sign contracts, provide tax and bank details so you can be paid (if you are submitting paid apps), and so forth.

By the time you finish the chapter (in which three different apps are created), you will have learned everything you need to know to build and submit your apps to iTunes.

Preparing Your Mac for the Xcode Wrapper Project Files

Having installed Xcode following the instructions in Chapter 12, you are now ready to start creating your own self-contained iOS apps, starting with a very simple "Hello World" program.

To do this you will need to download the *examples.zip* file from the *html5formobile.com* companion website. Within this archive you'll find the following folders, which you need to extract and copy to your Mac's desktop:

- *iOS Wrapper* The Xcode Objective C wrapper used as the basis for the apps
- *eML Files* The files for creating the eML eBook app
- *Rob's Files* The files for creating the Rob's Place app

Once all three folders are on the desktop, hold down the Mac's ALT key and drag the *iOS Wrapper* folder to another part of your desktop to make a copy, which will be given the title *iOS Wrapper 2*. Then press CTRL, click the new folder and select Get Info, rename the folder to *Hello World*, and then close the window. You can now double-click the new *Hello World* folder to open it, revealing the contents shown in Figure 13-1.

The files you will be changing when dropping your own code into this project are the three PNG images (*icon50.png*, *icon57.png*, and *icon72.png*) and the *index.htm* file. You can ignore all the other files for now, except for the file *Wrapper.xcodeproj*, which you should now double-click to call the project up in Xcode to display the window shown in Figure 13-2. In

Figure 13-1 The contents of the Hello World folder

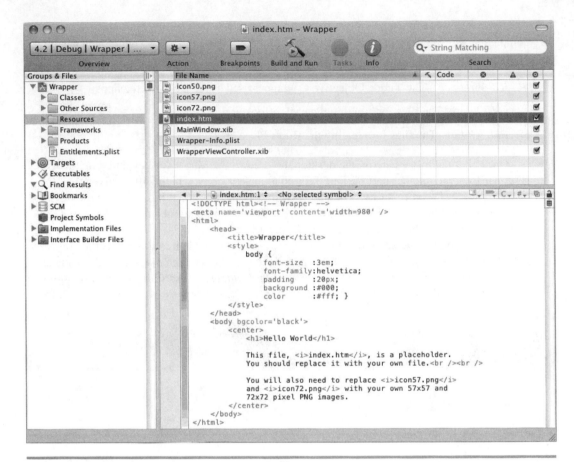

Figure 13-2 The default *index.htm* file of the Wrapper project is selected.

the figure, the *Resources* folder in the Groups & Files pane at the left of the window has been clicked, followed by the *index.htm* file in the top-right pane, the contents of which are being displayed in the bottom pane.

At the moment this project has the name "Wrapper," so you need to rename it to "HelloWorld" (without a space); select Project from the pull-down menu at the top of the desktop, followed by Rename, provide the new name **HelloWorld**, and click the Rename button. Once you have completed the renaming, click the OK button to close the window.

CAUTION

It is important that you use the Wrapper project files only on version 3.2 or higher of Xcode, so you must ensure that you have downloaded and installed the latest version. Xcode versions 3.1 and lower use different file formats that can cause unpredictable errors when used with the files supplied in the Wrapper project folder.

Running the App on the Xcode Emulator

Because the Wrapper project comes with a default *index.htm* file, you are now ready to test it by clicking the Overview button at the top left of the Xcode window and ensuring that both Simulator and Debug are checked, and that you have chosen iPhone Simulator 4.2, as shown in Figure 13-3. You can then click the Build and Run button at the top center of the Xcode window, and, all being well, the emulator will pop up and display the screen shown in Figure 13-4.

And that's all there is to it—you've created a working iPhone application. However, one of the neat things about the wrapper is that it is designed to also support iPads, so click the top-left button again, but this time select iPad Simulator 4.2, and then click Build and Run again.

After replying OK to the alert that pops up about stopping the executable, the emulated iPhone will disappear and be replaced with an emulated iPad, as shown in Figure 13-5.

Figure 13-3   Selecting a target type and device

Figure 13-4 Your first iOS application

Running the App on a Real Device

If you have already provisioned an iOS device for development by following the procedure presented in Chapter 12, you can now install this app onto that device by ensuring that the device is connected to your Mac via USB, clicking the top-left Overview button in Xcode, and selecting the Device option at the top of the menu, as shown in Figure 13-6, as well as the device that is connected, which should be listed toward the bottom of the menu, under Active Executable.

Now click Build and Run, and (after clicking OK if prompted to stop the executable) your iOS device will download and run the app, displaying it in exactly the same way as shown in either Figure 13-4 or Figure 13-5.

Figure 13-5   The app also runs on iPads.

Changing the App's Title

If you click the front button on either the emulator or actual iOS device, you'll see that the app has been installed to its home screen with an icon and the title Wrapper. To change the title, you need to click the *Resources* folder in the left pane of the Xcode window and then click the file *HelloWorld-Info.plist* in the top-right pane. This will display the file in the bottom pane, where you should click Wrapper in the Bundle Display Name field and change it to Hello World, as shown in Figure 13-7.

Figure 13-6   Choosing an iOS device as the target

Now you can click Build and Run again, click OK to stop the executable, and then click Save All to save the change you just made. The app will then download and run on whichever target you selected (either an emulator or actual device). When you click the Home button on the emulator or device screen to close it, you'll see that the application now has the correct title, Hello World, as shown in Figure 13-8.

Changing the App's Icon

You can also change the icon used by the application, but, because the iPhone, iPod Touch, and iPad are all supported, there are three icons to replace for the differently sized screens, *icon50.png*, *icon57.png*, and *icon72.png*, which should be 50×50, 57×57, and 72×72 pixels, respectively.

NOTE

The *icon72.png* file is used by the iPad for an app's home screen icon, and *icon50.png* is used for spotlight search on the iPad. The *icon57.png* file is used as a home screen icon on the iPhone and the iPod Touch.

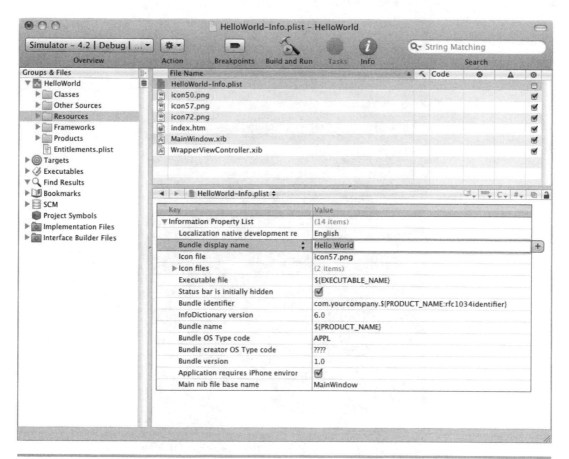

Figure 13-7 Changing the application's title

Once you have prepared the icons you'll be using, you can get rid of the default ones, by clicking the *Resources* folder in the left pane of the Xcode window, then select the three icon files in the top-right pane, press CTRL and click the files. Now select Delete from the pop-up menu, and click Also Move to Trash when the dialog box pops up, and they will be removed from the folder.

You can now drag-and-drop the replacement icons you made onto the *Resources* folder in the left pane of the Xcode window, which will bring up the dialog box shown in Figure 13-9, in which you should ensure that the Copy Items into Destination Group's Folder check box is checked and then click the Add button.

Click Build and Run and then click the front button on the emulator or iOS device to see that the icon has been updated.

Figure 13-8 The application's title has been successfully renamed.

Turning the eML Web App into a Self-Contained App

Let's now look at how to create a more useful app by taking the eML eBook from Chapter 10 and compiling it into a stand-alone app. To do this, once again make a copy of the *iOS Wrapper* folder on your Mac desktop by holding down the ALT key and dragging it to a new location, and then rename the new folder to *eML eBook*. Double-click the folder to open it. It will look like the window shown earlier in Figure 13-1 but with the title eML eBook.

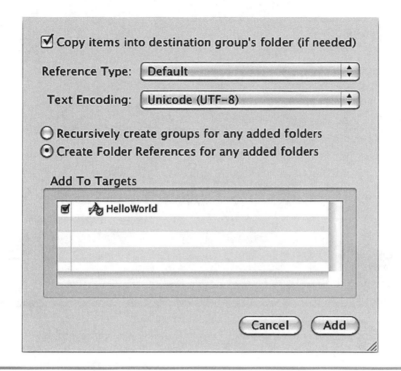

Figure 13-9 Copying the two new icons into the project

Now open up the folder *eML Files* that you also previously copied to the desktop, select the three icon files (*icon50.png*, *icon57.png*, and *icon72.png*) and the *index.htm* file, hold down the ALT key, and drag-and-drop the files into the new *eML eBook* folder. When prompted, check Apply to All and click Replace (see Figure 13-10). The resulting folder will look like Figure 13-11.

TIP

Remember during these instructions that this could also be your own eBook created using the eML system—just change the *index.htm* file, icons, and any supporting files, but do make sure the *eML* subfolder is always included.

Now double-click the *Wrapper.xcodeproj* icon to open it in Xcode. When it is open, select Project from the menu bar at the top of the desktop, followed by Rename, and rename

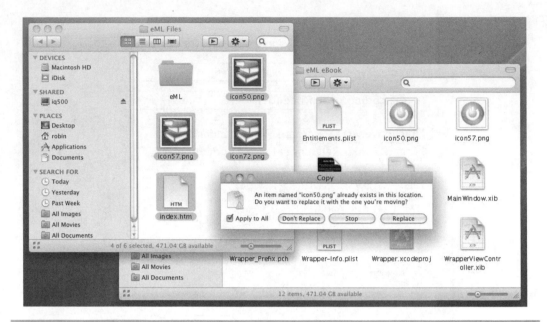

Figure 13-10 Copying the files from *eML Files* to the new *eML eBook* folder

the project to eMLeBook (without a space). When you are finished renaming the project, click OK.

You now need to update the project by adding the eML folders (*eML* and *usingeML*) to it by dragging-and-dropping them from the *eML Files* folder onto the *Resources* folder in the left pane of the Xcode window. When the dialog box pops up, check Copy Items into Destination Group's Folder (as shown previously in Figure 13-9) and click Add.

Handling .js Files

There's probably a good reason for it (although I cannot figure out what it is, so it could be a bug), but JavaScript *.js* files have to be treated differently in Xcode because they do not automatically get copied to the *Targets* folder (further down the left pane of the Xcode window). The workaround for this took a lot of research, so let me save you the hassle with the following solution.

To get the *eMLsmall.js* file into the *Targets* folder, you must manually copy it. To do so, first click the *Targets* folder in the left pane and open it to reveal the *eML eBook* subfolder, and then open that to show the *Copy Bundle Resources* folder. Click the *Resources* folder and locate *eMLsmall.js* in the *eML* subfolder. When you have it in view, uncheck its check box at

Figure 13-11   The contents of the *eML eBook* folder

the right side of the window (when checked, the check box tells Xcode to automatically copy the file to the *Target* folder, but since this doesn't work for *.js* files, you need to disable this option for them).

To copy the file, drag-and-drop it from the *Resources* folder to the *Copy Bundle Resources* folder (see Figure 13-12). Both folders may unfold and extend the left pane downward, but you can click the arrow next to each to fold it back up. Afterward, if you view the *Resources* folder again, you'll see that the *eMLsmall.js* file is once again checked—this is correct and confirms that the manual copying worked.

NOTE

The uncompressed *eML.js* file is also in the *eML Files* folder. It is identical to *eMLsmall.js* but is larger and the source is easier to read. This file is included so that you can view and/or modify it and use it in place of *eMLsmall.js* if you make any enhancements. And even though it copies to the *Resources* folder when you drag-and-drop the files, it will not copy to the *Targets* folder unless you copy it manually. This default is exactly what you want because (to keep the application size down) only the *eMLsmall.js* file is used by the *index.htm* file.

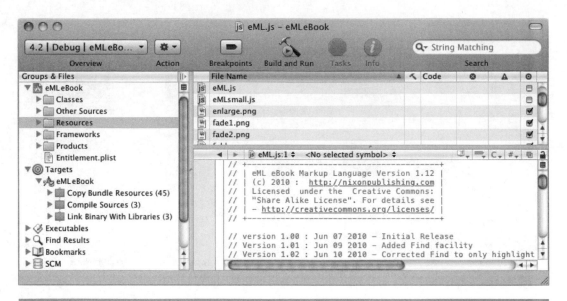

Figure 13-12 Manually copy the *eMLsmall.js* file to the Target folder.

CAUTION

In Xcode there is no support for subfolders in a target application; therefore, the contents of all the subfolders that are dropped into the *Resources* folder end up in the root of the *Target* folder. Because of this, any references to subfolders in the *index.htm* file must be removed. For example, in this particular application, where *eML/eMLsmall. js* is referenced, the *eML/* preface should be removed—as has already been done for you with the *index.htm* file supplied in the *eML Files* folder.

Renaming the Application

As with the Hello World app, this app is still called Wrapper, as it was built on the Wrapper skeleton, so you need to rename it. Click the *Resources* folder and locate and click the *eMLeBook-Info.plist* file to open a screen similar to the one shown earlier in Figure 13-7—with the file opened for editing in the bottom pane. Click the word Wrapper in the Bundle Display Name field and rename it eML eBook.

Building the Application

The app is now ready to be built, so click the top-left Overview button and choose either Simulator or any provisioned iOS device connected to the Mac, and then click the Build and Run button. The eBook should open, as shown in Figure 13-13.

Figure 13-13   The eML eBook application is now compiled.

Of course, it's unlikely that you'll want to publish this particular eBook, as it's already published in the iTunes and Android stores, but these instructions will enable you to turn any web app you create with the eML software into an iOS stand-alone app.

Turning the Rob's Place Web App into an iOS App

To illustrate how to create a stand-alone application with a third web app, let's now create a Rob's Place application by copying the *iOS Wrapper* folder again and this time renaming it to *Rob's Place*. Then open the *Rob's Files* folder and copy the three icons and *index.htm* file into the new *Rob's Place* folder, checking the Apply to All check box and clicking Replace when prompted.

Now double-click the file *Wrapper.xcodeproj* to open it in Xcode, and then use the Project | Rename option to rename the project RobsPlace (with no spaces or punctuation).

About the index.htm File

Interestingly, if you click the *index.htm* file to view it, you'll see that it doesn't contain all the Rob's Place HTML from Chapter 11; instead, it reads simply as follows:

```
<!DOCTYPE html>
<html>
   <head>
      <script>
         self.location = 'http://html5formobile.com/examples/robs.htm'
      </script>
      <style>
         body { font-size:3em; font-family:helvetica; padding:20px; }
      </style>
   </head>
   <body>
      <center>
         <h1>Loading...</h1>
      </center?>
   </body>
</html>
```

The reason for this is that the Rob's Place project uses Ajax to communicate with the web sever, and therefore restrictions are in place so that only web pages that are loaded from a server can communicate with it via Ajax. The only way around this limitation is to force the Rob's Place web page to load directly from the server. This is achieved by changing the `self.location` property to provide it with the location of the web page. Therefore, only the three icon files and short *index.htm* file are required for this app.

Building the App

So all you need to do now is click the *RobsPlace-Info.plist* file and rename the Bundle Display Name from Wrapper to Rob's Place, select either Simulator or a connected iOS device using the top-left button, and then click Build and Run to test the new app, which should appear as shown in Figure 13-14 on an iPad—although it will run equally well on an iPhone or iPod Touch.

Tweaking Applications

Did you notice that we got all the way through creating three iOS apps without encountering a single line of Objective C code? This section describes a couple of other things you can do to tweak your iOS apps without understanding the workings of the Objective C language.

For example, if you click the *Classes* folder in the left pane of the Xcode program and then click the *WrapperViewController.m* file in the top-right pane, the file opens in the bottom pane

Figure 13-14   Rob's Place running as a stand-alone iPad application

and should look like this:

```
#import "WrapperViewController.h"

@implementation WrapperViewController

- (void) viewDidLoad
{
    NSBundle *bundle   = [NSBundle mainBundle];
    NSString *path     = [bundle bundlePath];
    NSString *fullPath = [NSBundle pathForResource:@"index"
                          ofType:@"htm" inDirectory:path];
```

```
      [webView loadRequest:[NSURLRequest requestWithURL:
                            [NSURL fileURLWithPath:fullPath]]];
}

- (BOOL) shouldAutorotateToInterfaceOrientation:
  (UIInterfaceOrientation)interfaceOrientation
{
    return YES;
}

- (void) didRotateFromInterfaceOrientation:
  (UIInterfaceOrientation)fromInterfaceOrientation
{
    webView.scalesPageToFit = YES;
    webView.backgroundColor = [UIColor blackColor];
}

- (void) didReceiveMemoryWarning
{
    [super didReceiveMemoryWarning];
}

- (void) dealloc
{
    [super dealloc];
}

@end
```

This is the program that loads the *index.htm* file into what is known as a WebView, which is an instance of the iOS browser embedded within an app.

Disabling Autorotation

One of the things you can do with *WrapperViewController.m* is comment out the following function by placing /* and */ tags before and after it to disallow autorotating of the view:

```
/* - (BOOL) shouldAutorotateToInterfaceOrientation:
     (UIInterfaceOrientation)interfaceOrientation
{
    return YES;
} */
```

Once recompiled, the app will display only in portrait mode. You can verify this on a connected iOS device by rotating it; the display should stay locked. On the emulator use the CMD key and the left and right arrows to rotate the emulated device.

Disabling Scaling and Changing Background Color

Or, if you wish to prevent iOS from scaling pages to fit the screen in a WebView, you can comment out the top line in the following function with the // tag:

```
- (void) didRotateFromInterfaceOrientation:
  (UIInterfaceOrientation)fromInterfaceOrientation
{
// webView.scalesPageToFit = YES;
   webView.backgroundColor = [UIColor blackColor];
}
```

You can also change the default background color displayed during loading by modifying the bottom line. Simply change the word blackColor to blueColor or any other common color name.

Distributing an App on iTunes

In order to be able to upload apps to the iTunes App Store, Apple requires you to obtain another certificate, called an iOS Distribution Certificate, by opening the Keychain Access program in *Applications/Utilities* and choosing Keychain Access | Certificate Assistant | Request a Certificate from a Certification Authority.

The person responsible for submitting applications is called the Team Agent, so enter that person's e-mail address and name into the relevant fields, select the Saved to Disk option, and click Continue to save the request to disk.

Now point your web browser to *developer.apple.com*, click iOS Dev Center followed by Log In, and enter your developer ID and password to see the screen shown in Figure 13-15. Click the iOS Provisioning Portal link at the top right of the page to view the screen shown in Figure 13-16.

Next click the Certificates link on the left side, followed by the Distribution tab (which will display the screen shown in Figure 13-17), and click the Request Certificate button. On the page that follows (see Figure 13-18), scroll down and click the Choose File button, select the signing request that you just saved, and click the Submit button.

It shouldn't take long for the certificate to be issued, and to see when it has been issued, click the Development and Distribution tabs alternately until the certificate shows as having been issued (see Figure 13-19), at which point you can click the Download button to save it on your computer as the file *distribution_identity.cer*.

Now drag-and-drop the downloaded certificate into the Keychain Access program and it will be applied—Figure 13-20 shows the program with both a developer and a distribution certificate in place.

Building a Distribution Provisioning Profile

Next you need to create a distribution provisioning profile, which associates your new distribution certificate with your Xcode application. Click Provisioning on the left side of the

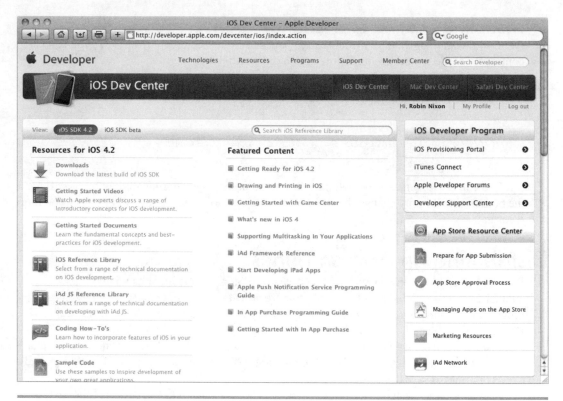

Figure 13-15 The iOS Dev Center

iOS Provisioning Portal, click the Distribution tab, and then click the New Profile button to open the screen shown in Figure 13-21. Enter a Profile Name such as "Jane Doe Distribution," select your App ID from the pull-down list, and click the Submit button.

Again, you can click the Development and Distribution tabs alternately until the profile is assigned, at which point click the Download button to save the profile to your Mac—it will have a name such as *Jane_Doe_Distribution.mobileprovision*. Drag-and-drop the profile into the Xcode window or onto the Xcode icon in the Dock bar to install it.

Now you need to double-click the name of the application in the far top left of the Xcode program (such as *RobsPlace*), which will bring up the Project Info window, from where you should click the Build tab to see the window shown in Figure 13-22.

Click the pull-down input next to Configuration at the top left and ensure that it says either Distribution or Active (Distribution). Also, in the Any iOS field, select the iPhone Distribution option if it isn't already selected. You can now close the window; if you are asked to accept any changes to your Keychain, do so.

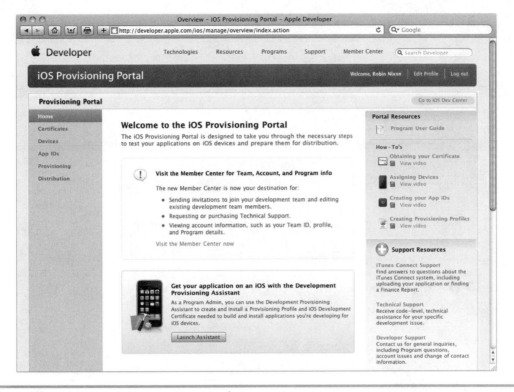

Figure 13-16   The iOS Provisioning Portal

Ask the Expert

Q: What is the difference between the Standard (armv6 armv7) and Optimized (armv7) options in the Architectures field of the Project Info window?

A: Apple's iOS devices initially used the armv6 processor architecture, but newer devices now use armv7, and code optimized for the new architecture will not run on the earlier one. Therefore, if you wish to target all devices, you should use only the Standard (armv6 armv7) option. If you are certain that you need to support only the newer architecture, you can select the Optimized (armv7) option.

When using the Standard option, your app is compiled twice—once for armv6 and once for armv7—and then both binaries are placed next to each other in a single app. When this app is run on an iOS device, only the binary the app requires will be used.

But when you use the Optimized option, only the armv7 code is compiled and placed into the app, so the app is half the size—but it also means that older devices cannot run it.

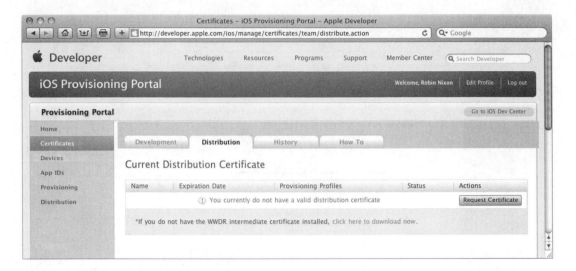

Figure 13-17 The Distribution Certificate page

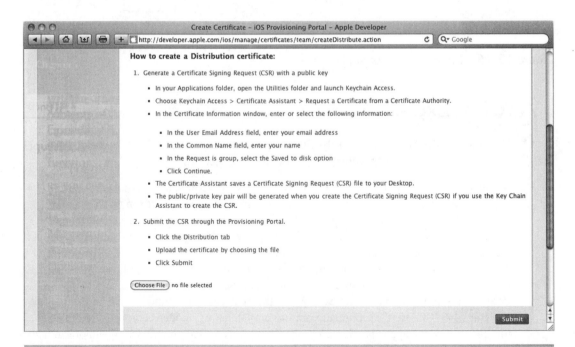

Figure 13-18 Choosing the certificate request to upload to Apple

Figure 13-19   The certificate has been issued.

Figure 13-20   The distribution certificate is now installed.

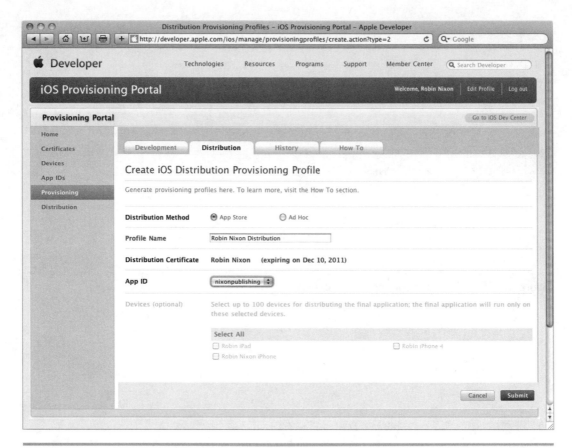

Figure 13-21 Creating a distribution provisioning profile

Updating the Bundle Identifier

Now click the *Resources* folder in the left pane of the Xcode window and click the file with the *.plist* extension (such as *RobsPlace.plist*) in the top-right pane to open it in the bottom pane. Then locate the Bundle Identifier field, which will contain a value such as the following:

```
com.yourcompany.${PRODUCT_NAME:rfc1034identifier}
```

You must replace the string `yourcompany` with the company ID you use to log into the iOS Dev Center (such as `janedoedev`), like this:

```
com.janedoedev.${PRODUCT_NAME:rfc1034identifier}
```

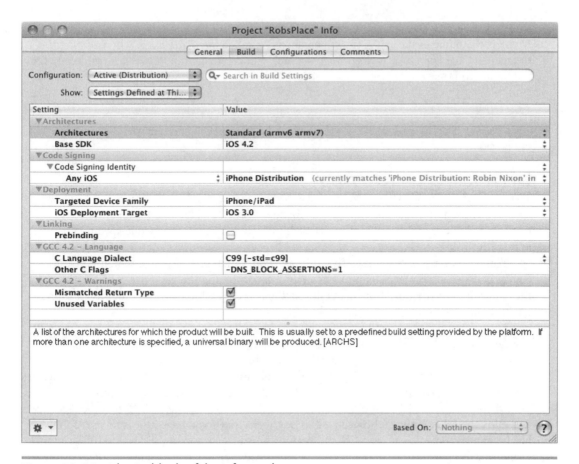

Figure 13-22   The Build tab of the Info window

CAUTION

It is important that *janedoedev*, or whatever you enter, is the same as your company ID or iTunes will refuse to accept the app when it is uploaded.

Building the App for Distribution

Now click the top-left button in the Xcode program, select Device in the top section and Distribution in the second section, and then select the Build option from the Build menu at the top of the desktop to build the application without running it.

The application will now be built and you will find it in the *build/Distribution-iphoneos* subfolder of the project folder, saved as *appname.app*. For example, the Rob's Place app will be stored at *Rob's Place/Distribution-iphoneos/RobsPlace.app*. So locate the app, press the

CTRL key and click the app, and then select Compress *Application Name*, where *Application Name* is the name of the app. This will create a file called *application.zip*, where *application* is the name of the app (such as *RobsPlace*—which will create the file *RobsPlace.zip*), ready for uploading to iTunes.

CAUTION

Compressing the app is essential because iTunes will not accept an uncompressed application.

Distributing an iOS App

To distribute an app via iTunes, you will also need to create a high-resolution 512×512-pixel icon to represent it in the store. Simply upsizing a 57- or 72-pixel icon for this is not recommended because it will look really bad. Instead you should create one specifically at this resolution.

You should also create up to five iPhone/iPod Touch screen grabs, which you can easily do via the emulator, using SHIFT-CMD-4 and dragging the cursor to outline just the inner area of the emulator that contains the screen—which will then be saved to the desktop as a PNG image.

These screen grabs should be 320×480 pixels; you can use landscape grabs, but they will display in portrait mode and users will have to rotate their phone to view them. You should also take up to five iPad screen grabs, which must be 768×1024 pixels.

The iPad emulator doesn't display at full resolution by default, so (if you don't have access to an iPad) you have to either resize a grab from the emulator—which is not optimal—or (if your display has at least 1024 pixels depth) click the Window menu at the top of the desktop and click the Scale option followed by 100%. Otherwise (if you have access to an iPad that has been provisioned) you can click the Window menu at the top of the desktop followed by Organizer to open the Xcode Organizer, and then click the link for a connected iPad, followed by the Screenshots tab to grab its screen.

All grabs should be 72 pixels per inch, flattened and without transparency. The first grab you take for each device will be used as the main image on your product page. In my experience, the more grabs you provide, the better your chance of the app being downloaded.

Once the artwork is ready, it's time to sign in to iTunes Connect (using your Apple developer ID and password) at *itunesconnect.apple.com*, which will display the page shown in Figure 13-23.

It's not really within the scope of this book to teach you how to manage your iTunes Connect account, but one of the first things you must do to enable the uploading of apps is click the Contracts, Tax, and Banking link and agree to all the various paid and unpaid app contracts, and set up your tax and banking details.

TIP

Once you have apps accepted into the iTunes Store, the Payments and Financial Reports link provides a wealth of information about downloads and revenue generated.

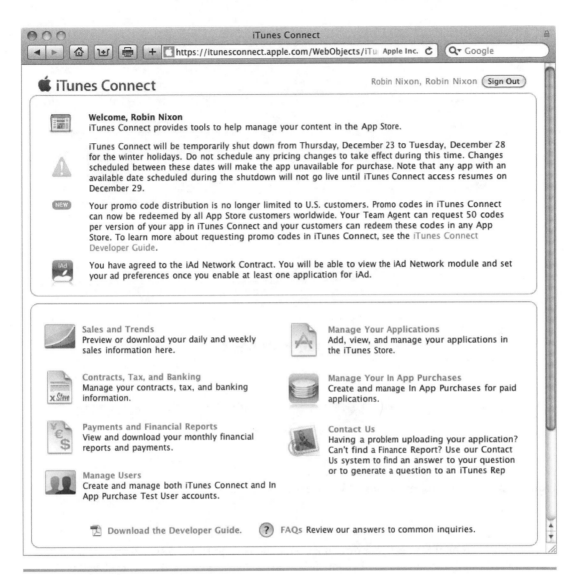

Figure 13-23 The iTunes Connect main page

Once you have done all of that, you can click the Manage Your Applications link to get started with uploading. In my case, I already have five applications on iTunes, so the screen shown in Figure 13-24 is what I see.

To tell iTunes about a new app, click the Add New App button at the top left to display the App Information screen shown in Figure 13-25, in which you must enter the app's title, enter an SKU number, which is any number you like for your own tracking purposes (at least

Figure 13-24 The iTunes Connect Manage Your Apps screen

two digits, though), select your developer ID in the Bundle ID section, and provide a Bundle ID Suffix by typing in the word "com" followed by your developer ID, a period, and the app name.

For example, if your developer ID is *janedoedev* and the app name is *RobsPlace*, then the Bundle ID Suffix is *com.janedoedev.RobsPlace*. Now click Continue.

Next you must decide on the date from which you would like the application published, whether to charge for the app or offer it for free, and whether to give educational institutions a discount (see Figure 13-26).

When you click Continue, a Metadata page appears, in which you'll have to enter a lot of information about the app. As shown in Figure 13-27, I have started to enter information about the Rob's Place app.

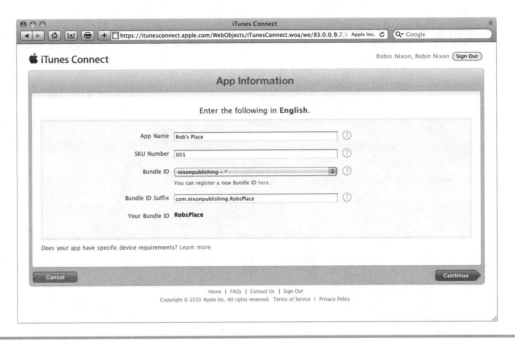

Figure 13-25   The iTunes Connect App Information screen

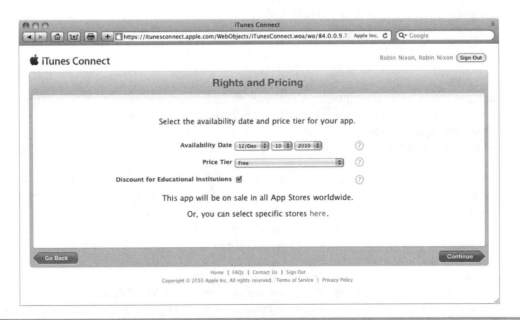

Figure 13-26   Specifying the app's rights and pricing

Figure 13-27 Filling in the app's details

Further down the page, you'll also need to check several boxes to define the app's audience based on whether it features violence, profanity, mature themes, and so on. This is all quite simple and doesn't need to be illustrated here. After that is the section where you upload the icons and screen grabs, as shown in Figure 13-28, in which a very simple large icon has been uploaded, and the first of the five iPhone/iPod Touch and iPad grabs have also been uploaded.

When you have finished uploading at least one of each file type, click the Save button. You'll be taken to a summary screen for the app, where you can then click Done to return to the App Management screen, where your new app will now be displayed.

Click the app icon to go back to its information screen, and then click the View Details button next to its icon. On the next screen, click the button at the top right called Ready to Upload Binary, which opens the Export Compliance screen (if you are allowing your app to be downloaded outside the United States, which is usually the case).

If your app uses encryption from a source other than iOS or Mac OS X, click Yes and follow the prompts; otherwise click No and then click Save. Now click the Continue button to finish, and you're done.

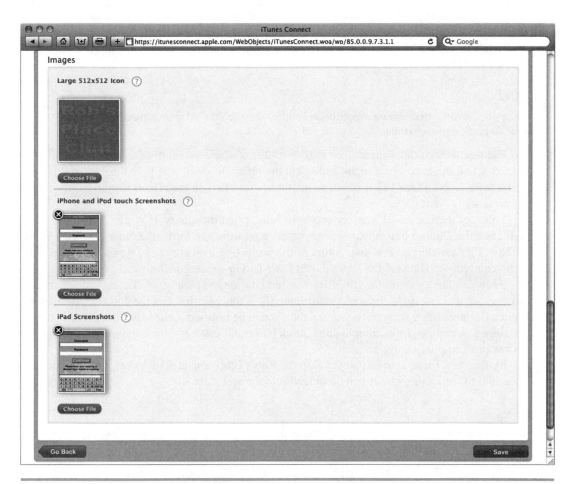

Figure 13-28   Uploading the large icon and the screen grabs

NOTE
Whenever your application changes state, such as becoming ready for you to upload (or later, when/if it is approved, or if there are problems with it), the iTunes Store will send you an e-mail to let you know.

Uploading the App
You are now ready to use the Xcode Application Loader built into Xcode to send the app to iTunes. So, using Finder, open the *Developer* folder on your hard disk, followed by the *Applications* folder, and then the *Utilities* folder, in which you'll find the program *Application Loader.app* (which you may wish to drop into the Dock bar next to the Xcode app for future

easy access). Double-click the program, click the Next button to enter the Login window, where you need to enter your Apple Developer ID and password, and then click Next again at the following screen.

NOTE
Once you have logged into the Application Loader, you should not be prompted for your ID and password again.

The next screen that appears (see Figure 13-29) is where you choose the app binary to upload. Click the drop-down menu and select the binary to send, which, in the case of this example, is Rob's Place 1 (1 is the version number supplied on the iTunes Connect website). Then click the Next button.

You may then be asked whether you have fully tested the binary. If you have, click Yes and then click the Choose button that appears on the next screen to locate the binary, which will be in the *build/Distribution-iphoneos* folder of the project. In the case of the Rob's Place app, this is the compressed file saved at *Rob's Place/Distribution-iphoneos/RobsPlace.zip*.

Once you have located the file, click the Send button to upload it to iTunes. If there are any errors, such as a mismatch between the Bundle ID in the *.plist* file and the one you provided on iTunes Connect (they must be the same), then you'll be notified. Otherwise, the file will start uploading. When has finished uploading, click Next, and that's it—the app is now awaiting review prior to publication.

By the way, I intend to further develop the Rob's Place app at some point, so I ask you to rename it to something else if you do upload it to the app store.

Figure 13-29 Selecting the binary to upload

Summary

In this chapter you've seen three examples of using the Wrapper project files supplied on the companion website to turn web applications into stand-alone iOS apps. Hopefully, the ease of doing this will spur you on to creating and uploading many successful apps to the iTunes Store.

In the following chapter I'll introduce the Android SDK, which I think you'll find even easier to use than Apple's SDK.

Chapter 14

Setting Up the Android SDK

Key Skills & Concepts

- Downloading and installing the Android SDK
- Downloading and installing the Eclipse IDE
- Adding the Android plug-in to Eclipse

Having worked through the process of installing and using the iOS SDK in Chapters 12 and 13, when you follow through the steps in this chapter, I think you're going to be very pleased with how the Android SDK compares in terms of ease of use and speed of development.

Of course, there are pros and cons to everything, and some aspects of installing the Android SDK are a bit trickier than they are for the iOS SDK (such as installing on 64-bit PCs, as you'll see), but this is only to be expected. On the whole, though, the entire installation and development process is much quicker and easier on Android than on iOS.

Downloading and Installing the Android SDK

To install the Android SDK, you must visit *developer.android.com/sdk* (see Figure 14-1) and choose the version you require, Windows, Mac OS X, or Linux. This chapter discusses only the Windows SDK, but the other versions are quite similar and you should be able to follow the instructions I give as long as you change path names and other machine-dependent items where necessary.

Before you start, if you don't already have it, you'll first need to download and install the Java Development Kit (JDK), available at the following URL:

oracle.com/technetwork/java/javase/downloads

Once you have downloaded it, run the installer and accept all the default options—the process is quite straightforward. After installing the JDK (if necessary), download the Android SDK and open the installation file to begin installing it.

NOTE
On a 64-bit computer, if the installer reports "Java SE development kit not found" don't worry, simply click the Back button followed by the Next button and this time it will find Java and the installation can continue.

During installation of the Android SDK, accept the defaults offered to you. Click Finish when you are done, but make sure that the Start SDK Manager check box is checked before you do. This opens the window shown in Figure 14-2, from which you can choose the

Figure 14-1 The SDK download page on the Android Developers website

packages to install. For complete flexibility when developing for Android, I recommend that you install all available packages by clicking the Accept All radio button followed by Install.

The download process will then take up to half an hour or longer depending on your bandwidth speed, after which you'll be shown the packages that have been installed. Click the Close button.

Downloading and Installing the Eclipse IDE

Now you need to install the Eclipse IDE (Integrated Developing Environment) from *eclipse .org/downloads*. Choose the package called *Eclipse IDE for Java Developers*, which is a zip file of about 100MB in size that you will need to extract after downloading. The extraction will result in a folder with a long filename that starts with the string *eclipse-java-helios*. Within

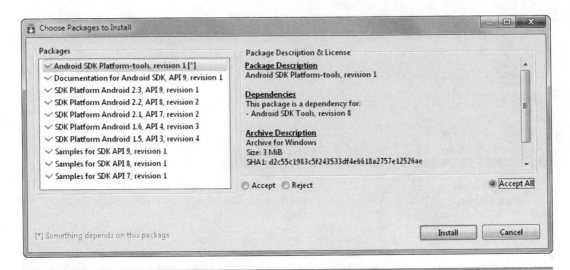

Figure 14-2 Downloading all the available Android packages

this folder is another folder, simply called *eclipse*, which you should drag-and-drop to its permanent destination, such as the root of your *C:* drive.

Navigate to the new *eclipse* folder and double-click the file *eclipse.exe* to start the program, which will then ask you to decide which folder to use to store your workspace (see Figure 14-3). Generally, the default offered is probably the best option. To avoid seeing the message again, you can check the box at the bottom left of the window.

TIP

For future ease of use, you may wish to hold down the ALT key and drag the *eclipse.exe* file to your desktop to create a shortcut icon.

After you choose the location and click OK, Eclipse will continue to load and will eventually display the Welcome screen, shown in Figure 14-4.

Adding the Android Plug-in

Lastly, you need to install the Android plug-in for Eclipse (called ADT). Choose Help | Install New Software, which opens the screen shown in Figure 14-5. In the Work With field, where it says "type or select a site," enter the following URL, click the Add button, give the resource a name such as "Android Repository" when prompted, and then click OK.

https://dl-ssl.google.com/android/eclipse/

The Name field should then change to show the heading Developer Tools, next to which is a check box that you should ensure is checked (see Figure 14-6). Then click the Next button,

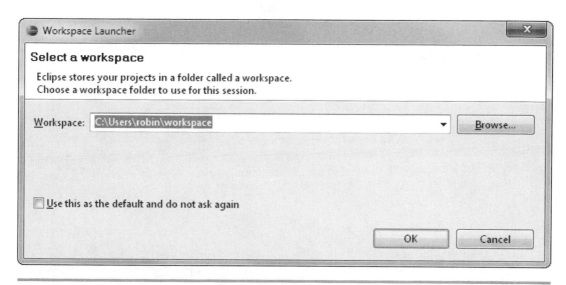

Figure 14-3   Decide where your workspace folder should be located.

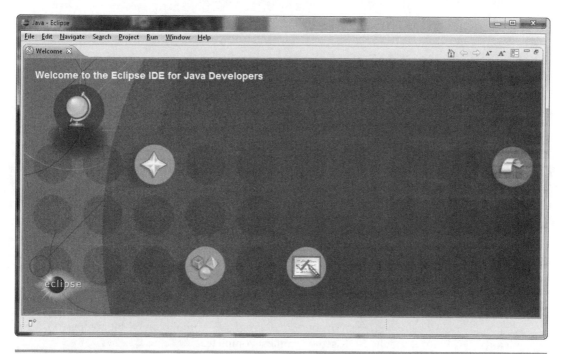

Figure 14-4   The Eclipse Welcome screen

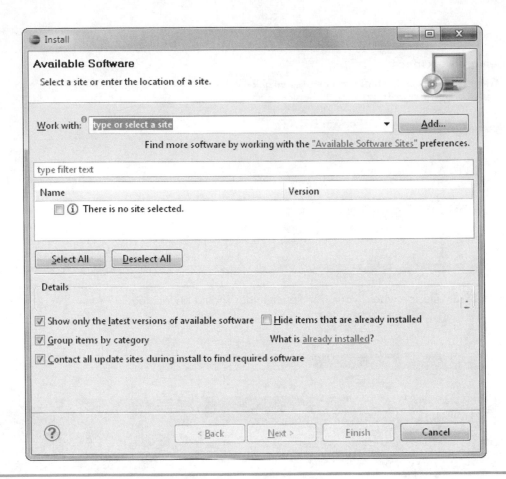

Figure 14-5 The Eclipse software installation screen

followed by the Next button on the following screen. On the screen after that, choose the radio button labeled "I accept the terms of the license agreements" and click the Finish button.

Another window will open to show the progress of the repository download; if a security window pops up warning that the software contains unsigned content, click OK to close it. When the download has finished, click the Restart Now button to restart Eclipse.

When the program opens back up, choose Window | Preferences. Then, at the top left of the Preferences screen, click the Android heading, and then click the Browse button to locate the Android SDK folder, which by default will be *C:\Program Files\Android\android-sdk-windows* (or *C:\Program Files (x86)\Android\android-sdk-windows* on 64-bit computers). Now click the OK button, and the SDK setup is almost complete.

Finally. On a 32-bit computer you should open the Window menu from the Eclipse menu bar, then click Preferences to open up a new window. In the left half of this window, click the

Figure 14-6   The Android repository has now been added and selected.

Android heading and then in the SDK Location input field that appears at the top right ensure one of the following paths is listed, depending on whether you are using a 32-bit or 64-bit computer, respectively:

```
C:\Program Files\Android\android-sdk
C:\Program Files (x86)\Android\android-sdk
```

If not, use the Browse… button to locate the folder, or type the path in directly and remember to replace the C: with another disk name if you installed the Android SDK somewhere other than on drive C.

Now click the OK button to enter the path into Eclipse's preferences and then close the program and reopen it before proceeding with the next chapter to ensure all settings are up to date.

Ask the Expert

Q: This installation process really does seem much easier than with iOS. Why is that?

A: The simple answer is probably that Android is an open platform rather than a proprietary platform. The Android operating system is open source, as are all the tools used to develop with it, and Google has fewer concerns than Apple about keeping tight control over third-party developers.

That said, the Android Market has picked up a reputation for including a high proportion of very buggy and somewhat pointless programs. And the Android operating system itself has become quite fragmented as different companies tailor it to their needs. So there is a downside to all this openness.

However, Google is putting pressure on phone manufacturers to not change Android too much, and the platform is rapidly growing as a consequence—with a reported 300,000 Android smart phones being activated every day at the time of this writing, which is a huge market to which you can pitch your apps.

Summary

Believe it or not, you have now installed the Android SDK, with no certificates to obtain or profiles to provision. You are ready to move on to Chapter 15, in which I'll show you how to compile matching Android apps from the three web apps that were turned into iOS apps in Chapter 13.

Chapter 15

Creating Android Stand-alone Apps

Key Skills & Concepts

- Creating a Hello World app
- Using the Android emulator
- Saving apps to attached devices and running them
- Building an app for distribution
- Signing your apps
- Using the Android Market website
- Submitting your app to the Market
- Uploading icons and screen grabs

In this final chapter of the book I show you how to use the Android Wrapper project on the companion website to turn your web applications into stand-alone Android apps, or to use the project and SDK to build new apps.

In it I focus on creating three different apps, illustrating how easy and relatively straightforward the process is—in fact you should find it a lot quicker than building iOS apps.

By the time you finish the chapter you will have completed your iOS and Android development toolkit and will be ready to start building and uploading your own apps.

Preparing Your PC for the Android Wrapper Project Files

Similar to the iOS Wrapper project for turning your web apps into iOS applications, there is also an *Android Wrapper* folder in the *examples.zip* file available at *html5formobile.com*. Once you have extracted the zip file, copy the *Android Wrapper* folder to your desktop, from where you will be copying it to the Android SDK a few times over the course of the rest of the chapter.

While you are at it, you should also copy the *eML Files* and *Rob's Files* folders to your desktop, as you'll be using them later. Once you have copied them to the desktop, you should conduct the following procedure each time you wish to make a new Android app.

Creating a New Android Project from the Wrapper

To create a new Android app, you now need to copy the Android Wrapper project from the desktop into the workspace folder you assigned during setup of the SDK in Chapter 14. By default this will be in the home folder for your username on the computer—in my case it's in *robin/workspace*.

Once you have dragged the *Android Wrapper* folder into the *workspace* folder, you should rename it to match the app you are building. So, for this example, right-click the folder, select Rename, and rename the folder to Hello World.

Now run the Eclipse program and, when it opens, select File | Import to open the dialog box shown in Figure 15-1. Click the General folder and then select Existing Projects into Workspace from the sub-options that displays. Then click the Next button to open the screen shown in Figure 15-2, where you should click the Browse button at the top right and locate the *Hello World* folder.

Once you have the folder loaded, click the Finish button to move on to the Eclipse main screen, as shown in Figure 15-3, in which I have closed all windows except for the Package

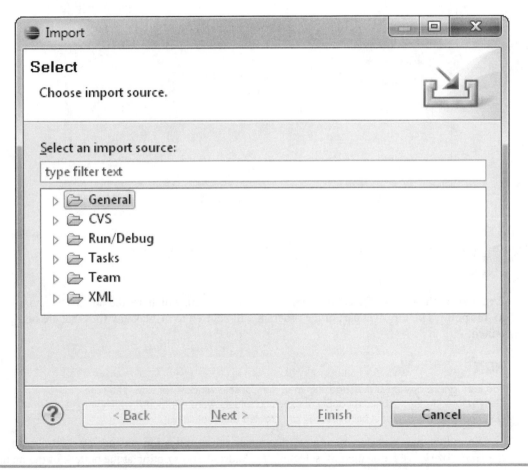

Figure 15-1 Selecting an import source

Figure 15-2 The *Hello World* folder has been selected as the source.

Explorer on the left and the Console Window at the bottom, which are the only two required at this point. The top-right part of the program will be used to display any files that are being edited.

NOTE
You can ignore any error message shown in the Console window for now. They are likely related to the fact that a couple of expected folders were not found, which you don't have to worry about because they are created automatically.

From this main screen, you now need to rename the application package by right-clicking the *Hello World* folder on the left, selecting the Android Tools option at the bottom of the menu

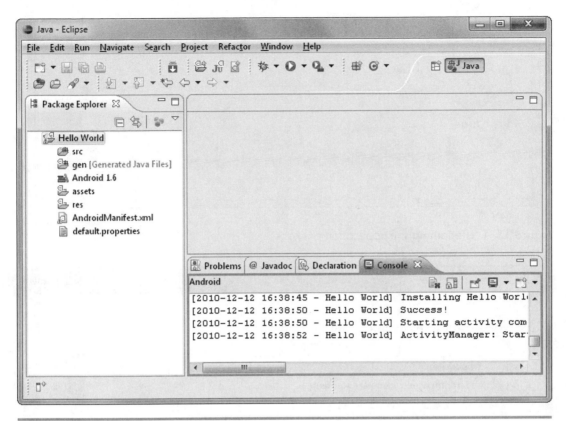

Figure 15-3 The Eclipse main screen

that appears, and then clicking Rename Application Package. This will bring up the dialog box shown in Figure 15-4, in which you should replace the string com.yourcompany .wrapper with a string such as com.janedoedev.helloworld, in which janedoedev is the developer ID you will use and helloworld is the app ID.

When you click OK, the screen shown in Figure 15-5 will be displayed, listing the items that will get modified. Just click the Finish button to make the changes and, when asked about updating the Launch Configuration, click the Yes button.

Renaming the Home Screen Icon

Back in the Eclipse main screen, click the *res* folder in the left pane to reveal three subfolders, the last of which is *values*. Open this folder and you'll see the file *strings.xml*, which you should double-click to open in the top-right pane (see Figure 15-6).

Double-click app_name (String) in the box under Elements, and (to the right) the fields Name and Value will be shown, with app_name and Wrapper for their values, respectively. To rename the home screen icon from Wrapper, replace that word with

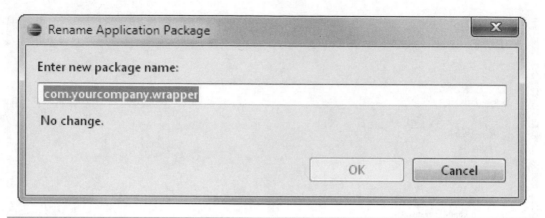

Figure 15-4 Renaming the application package

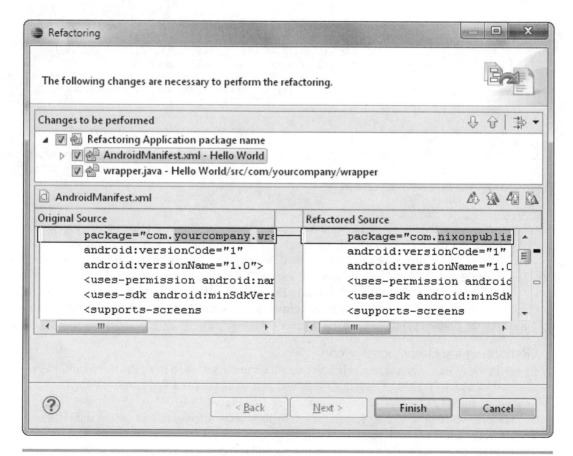

Figure 15-5 Confirming the items to be modified

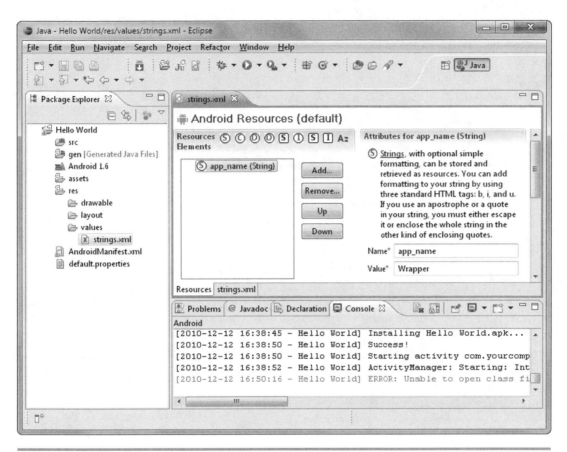

Figure 15-6 Updating the *strings.xml* file

Hello World in the Value field. Then click the icon of a single floppy disk at the top left of the program to save the updated file.

Updating the Manifest File

Since this is the first time you have created the application, it will have a default Version code of 1 and a Version name of 1.0, which you can see by double-clicking the *AndroidManifest.xml* file in the left pane (see Figure 15-7).

At this point you do not need to edit the file, but, once you have successfully uploaded an app to the Android Market, you must increment the Version Code field if you update the app, or the Market will reject the app. The Version Name string enables you to name your versions in a similar way to how Android is named after desserts such as Gingerbread, Honeycomb, and Ice Cream.

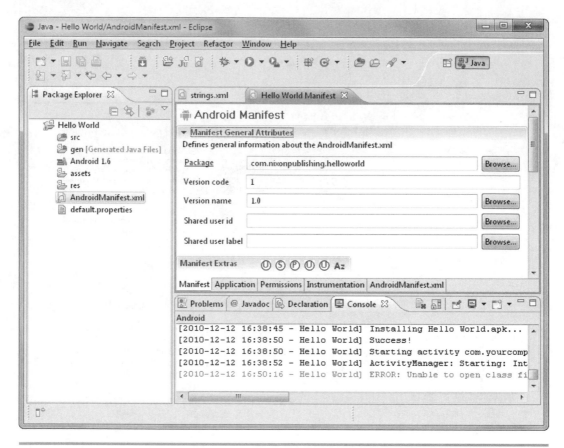

Figure 15-7 Updating the *AndroidManifest.xml* file

Running the Application

You are now ready to build and run the application, so click the green, round button with a right-pointing white triangle in it at the top center of the program (the Build and Run button). When the Run As dialog box pops up, select Android Application and click OK. If no Android device is connected to your PC (and we'll get to that in a minute), a dialog box will pop up telling you that no compatible targets were found and asking you whether you would like to add a new Android Virtual Device (AVD). Click Yes to enter the AVD Manager.

When the AVD Manager opens, click the New button at the top right to bring up the window shown in Figure 15-8, in which I have entered a Name of Android2.2 (no spaces are allowed in the name), selected a Target of Android 2.2 - API Level 8, entered a Size value of 1000, and specified a Resolution of 480×800 pixels. Complete the information for your virtual device in a similar manner and then click the Create AVD button.

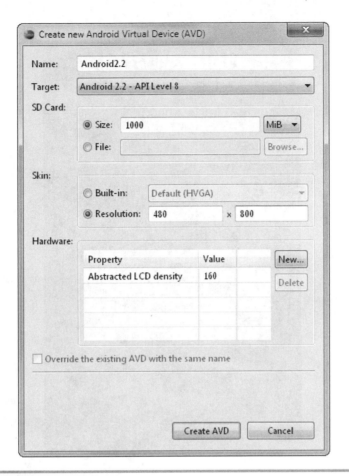

Figure 15-8   Creating a virtual device

After a few seconds, the new device will be displayed in the AVD Manager screen; click the virtual device and then click the Start button. If prompted, you can choose to scale the display to real size, or simply click the Launch button to start the device running.

Booting up the emulator could take a minute or two. After it completes the bootup, once again click the Build and Run button at the top center of the SDK to compile and run the application in the virtual device, which should then display as shown in Figure 15-9.

If you see this screen, then you have successfully compiled and run your first Android application. To return to the virtual device's main screen, you can exit from the app by pressing the ESCAPE key. If you do this and then click the Applications button, you'll see the new Hello World icon, which you can click and hold to open the home screen if you like.

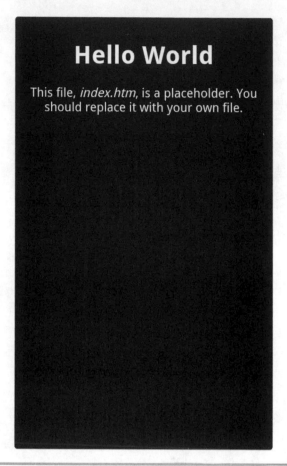

Figure 15-9 The Hello World app has successfully compiled and run.

Connecting Android Devices

To install apps directly to a real Android device, you first need to install the drivers supplied with the device. Most Android devices come with the drivers you need, so follow the instructions supplied by the device manufacturer. Alternatively, Windows automatically searches for and installs the drivers for many devices when you connect them to your computer. If that doesn't work, you can also try to locate and download the drivers from your device manufacturer's website.

TIP

In the case of the Galaxy S, Galaxy Tab, and other Samsung Android devices, in the United Kingdom I have successfully been able to use the drivers included as part of the distribution available from *samsung.com/uk/support*. Enter (for example) "Galaxy Tab" in the Search Product Support field and then click the software link on the following page, from where you can then download the Samsung Kies and PC Sync programs, which contain the drivers you need.

In the United States, the counterpart URL is *samsung.com/us/support/downloads*, where you will need to pull down (for example) Galaxy Tab from the Category menu, followed by choices from the Sub-Category, Model Name, and Model Code menus, and then click Find It and click the Software link on the following screen.

Once the drivers for your device have been installed, you must then tell the device to allow you to place apps on it, rather than simply browse its file system from your PC. To do this, select Settings on the device and then tap Applications, tap Development, check the USB Debugging check box, and tap the OK button.

Your device is now ready to use to run your apps—wasn't that easier than setting up provisioning profiles and so forth, as you have to do with iOS?

Saving Apps to Android Devices

Now that you have a device connected and set to USB Debugging mode, it will appear in the SDK (as shown in Figure 15-10) when you click the Build and Run button. You can now double-click the device to download and install the application onto it, which will display in a similar way to the example shown in Figure 15-9.

TIP
If the SDK seems to be stuck in automatic mode and always selects the same target device or virtual device without offering you the opportunity to choose between them, select Run | Run Configurations, click the Target tab, choose the Manual radio button, and then click the Apply button. After that, click Close to close the window.

Building an eML eBook Application

Having successfully compiled and run the Hello World application, here's how to turn an eML publication into an app. First, right-click the *Hello World* folder and select Close Project.

Now, once again, follow the process outlined earlier and copy the *Android Wrapper* folder to your *workspace* folder, but this time rename it to *eML eBook*. Then import the project into the SDK using the Existing Projects into Workspace option. Next, right-click the *eML eBook* folder at the top left, select Android Tools, and rename the package to a string such as com.janedoedev.emlebook. Then edit the *strings.xml* file in *res/values*, changing the word Wrapper to eML eBook.

Copying the eML Files to the Project

Now open up the *eML Files* folder that you copied to your desktop. Press the CTRL key and click to select the two folders (*eML* and *UsingEML*) and the file *index.htm*, and then drag-and-drop them into the *assets* folder in the left pane of the SDK. When prompted, ensure that the

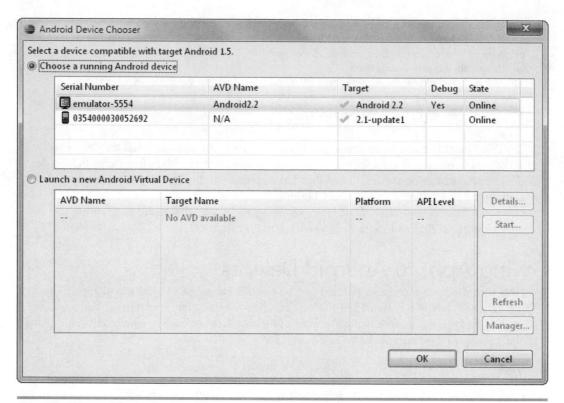

Figure 15-10 The top frame of the Android Device Chooser now also shows a connected device.

Copy Files and Folders radio button is selected and click OK. Also, click Yes when you are asked whether to overwrite the *index.htm* file.

Next, because the line of code in the *index.htm* file that refers to the *eMLsmall.js* file is optimized for iOS, you need to right-click the *index.htm* file and select Open With followed by Text Editor. When the file displays in the right pane, scroll down until you find the following line, and insert the string eML/ just before eMLsmall.js:

```
</script><script src='eMLsmall.js'></script></head>
```

The result should look like this:

```
</script><script src='eML/eMLsmall.js'></script></head>
```

Then click the floppy disk icon at the top left of the program to save the file. You must do this because iOS doesn't support folders and paths in applications, but Android does, so it needs to know which folder the JavaScript file is located in.

Running the Application

You can now test the app by clicking the Build and Run button and then selecting either the virtual device you created before or an attached device for the target. After the app has been compiled and transferred to the device, it should display the screen shown in Figure 15-11.

Updating the Home Screen Icon

Now that the app has been verified, you need to change the home screen icon by dragging-and-dropping the file *icon72.png* from the *eML Files* folder on your desktop into the *res/drawable* folder in the left pane of the SDK. When prompted, ensure that Copy Files is checked and click OK.

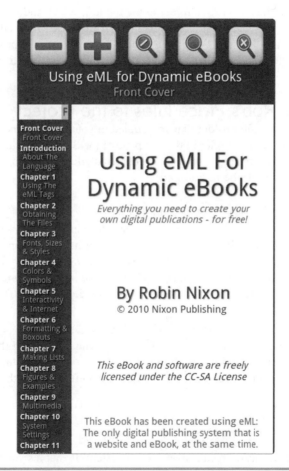

Figure 15-11   The eML eBook compiled and running as an app

Now open the *res/drawable* folder, right-click the old icon (*icon.png*), and select Delete. Then right-click *icon72.png* and select Refactor | Rename, and rename the file to *icon.png*. Run the application again to reinstall it, and you will see that the application icon is updated.

Building the Rob's Place Application

To build the Rob's Place app, right-click the *eML eBook* folder and select Close Project, then follow the process outlined earlier and copy the *Android Wrapper* folder to your *workspace* folder, but this time rename it to *Robs Place* (unfortunately, you cannot use the apostrophe that should be in the name, since Android will not let you export your apps if you do). Then import the project into the SDK using the Existing Projects into Workspace option.

Next, right-click the *Robs Place* folder at the top left, select Android Tools, and rename the package to a string such as com.janedoedev.robsplace. Then edit the *strings.xml* file in *res/values*, changing the word Wrapper to Robs Place. As with the project name, you cannot rename the app to "Rob's Place" because the apostrophe is not allowed in the home screen icon name.

Copying the Rob's Place Files to the Project

Now open up the *Rob's Files* folder that you copied to your desktop and drag-and-drop the *index.htm* file into the *assets* folder in the left pane of the SDK. When prompted, ensure that the Copy Files and Folders radio button is selected and click OK. Also, click Yes when you are asked whether to overwrite the *index.htm* file.

Updating the Home Screen Icon

Now change the home screen icon by dragging-and-dropping *icon72.png* from the *Rob's Files* folder on your desktop into the *res/drawable* folder in the left pane of the SDK. When prompted, ensure that Copy Files is checked and click OK.

Now open the *res/drawable* folder, right-click the old icon (*icon.png*), and select Delete. Then right-click *icon72.png* and select Refactor | Rename, and rename the file to *icon.png*.

Compiling and Running the Application

You can now test the app by clicking the Build and Run button and then selecting either the virtual device you created before or an attached device for the target. After the app has been compiled and transferred to the device, it should display the screen shown in Figure 15-12.

Distributing Your Apps

You may not know it, but Android is a very open system. It enables you to distribute your apps by simply placing them on your website. But you do need to go through the process of signing them first, so that users can be sure that the app was created by you.

Figure 15-12 Rob's Place as a stand-alone app

To do this, open an app in the SDK, right-click it and choose Export, click Android | Export Android Application, and click Next to display the screen shown in Figure 15-13, in which (the first time you export an app) you should choose the Create New Keystore option.

Then click the Browse button and choose a suitable location to store it (such as the *workspace* folder) using a filename such as *janedoedev.keystore*. Enter a password (twice) and click Next to see the screen shown in Figure 15-14.

NOTE

After you create the *.keystore* file, the next time you export an app, you can select the Use Existing Keystore radio button, click the Browse button to select the app, and then simply enter its password to access it.

Figure 15-13 Creating a keystore file

Now enter an Alias (which could be your development ID), a password (twice), a value of 30 for the Validity (for 30 years), your first and last name, and click Next to see the screen shown in Figure 15-15, in which I have chosen to save the app to the desktop by clicking the Browse button and searching for it. Click Finish when you are done, and the app will be compiled and saved to the chosen location.

NOTE
The next time you export an app, you can choose the Use Existing Key option, then select the key from the pull-down menu and enter its password.

You can now upload this app to a website, although (for ease of entering its name for download) you may wish to remove the space in the filename and change it to all lowercase letters first, by renaming it to *robsplace.apk* (or whatever your app is called).

For example, I have uploaded all three examples in this chapter to the companion website, so if you point your Android device at the following URLs, you should be able to download the apps directly:

html5formobile.com/examples/helloworld.apk
html5formobile.com/examples/emlebook.apk
html5formobile.com/examples/robsplace.apk

Figure 15-14 Creating a key

Figure 15-15 Selecting a destination for the app

Ask the Expert

Q: I tried to download these apps from the website but my smartphone said I needed an SD card and it failed. What can I do?

A: When downloading an app via the Android browser, the android device may sometimes require you to have an SD card installed. This memory is used to store the download before it is then installed to the main storage. If you get this message, unfortunately, your only option is either to insert an SD card or to download the app from the Android Market (if it is also available there).

Downloading an App from a Website

To be able to download apps from websites as well as from the Android Market, you must first open the Settings screen on your Android device, choose Applications, and check the box next to Unknown Sources.

As mentioned in the Ask the Expert sidebar, some Android devices may also require that you have an SD card inserted, on which to store downloads.

Uploading Apps to the Android Market

Now that you have your signed and exported apps, you can upload them to the Android Market if you pay the $25 registration fee. To do this, go to *market.android.com/publish* (see Figure 15-16) and log in using your Google credentials. This will take you to the screen shown in Figure 15-17, in which you should enter your Developer Name and other details and then click the Continue link.

On the next screen, you must read the distribution agreement and then click the button to pay your $25 registration via Google Checkout. This brings up a long page on which you must enter all your billing details and agree to the terms.

Once you have completed the registration and paid your fee, you can go to the main Market screen, as shown in Figure 15-18, in which you can see that I have five apps already placed.

Now you are ready to upload an app, so let's go over this procedure with the Rob's Place app. Click the Upload Application link, which brings you to a new screen, the topmost part of which is shown in Figure 15-19, in which I have already uploaded the *robsplace.apk* file, two 480×800-pixel screen grabs, and the 512×512-pixel high-resolution icon that was also required by the iTunes Store.

On this page, you also have the opportunity to upload a 180×120-pixel promotional graphic for use in the Market (this is required if you entered any promotional text), along with

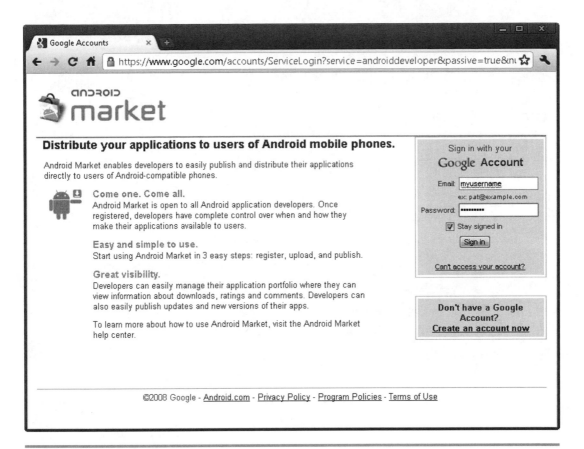

Figure 15-16   Logging into the Android Market

a 1024×500-pixel feature graphic to use in case your app is selected by Google to be featured. And you can even add the YouTube URL of any promotional video you have made.

All of these choices are optional, but you must scroll down the page and fill in the app's listing details, as shown in Figure 15-20, which I have filled in with basic information. I recommend that you use all the characters allowed, to really sell your app. You need to also select a price for your app, which (if not free) you will be paid via Google checkout—less 30 percent commission.

Finally, at the bottom of the page, you get to the publishing options and some other options (see Figure 15-21). Here you can choose whether to copy-protect the app, select a content rating, and choose in which countries the app should be available. You must also provide a website and e-mail address for queries about your app, and you need to check both boxes in the final section to confirm that the app meets the Android guidelines and that you have complied with all applicable laws.

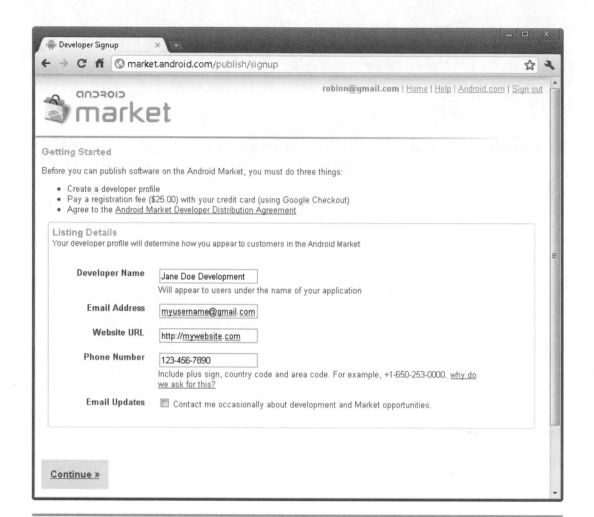

Figure 15-17 Creating an account

After you have provided all the details and are ready to publish your app, you can click the Publish button at the bottom of the page. You also have the option to save the details and complete the process at a later time, or delete the details and start over.

Once you click Publish, your app will be available instantly in the Android Market, and you can download and install it on any Android device from there.

Updating Apps

When you update an app, you must change its Version code if you wish to resubmit it to the Market (as described in the section "Updating the Manifest File," earlier in the

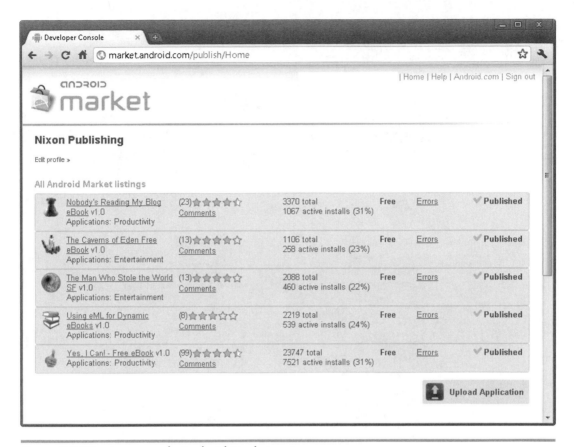

Figure 15-18 An example Android Market main screen

chapter); otherwise, it will be rejected by Google. Generally, this is simply a matter of incrementing the number. You may also wish to also update the Version name, too, though this isn't required.

Once you have changed the Version code and re-exported the app, you can use the Recent Changes field (see Figure 15-20) to tell people what's new in the app.

Clearly Labeling Test Apps

When uploading any of these examples to the Android market solely for testing purposes, please include in the description some text such as "This is a test - please don't download"; otherwise, users may unwittingly download it. After completing your testing, please also be a good participant of the Market and unpublish the apps if they are no-longer of use.

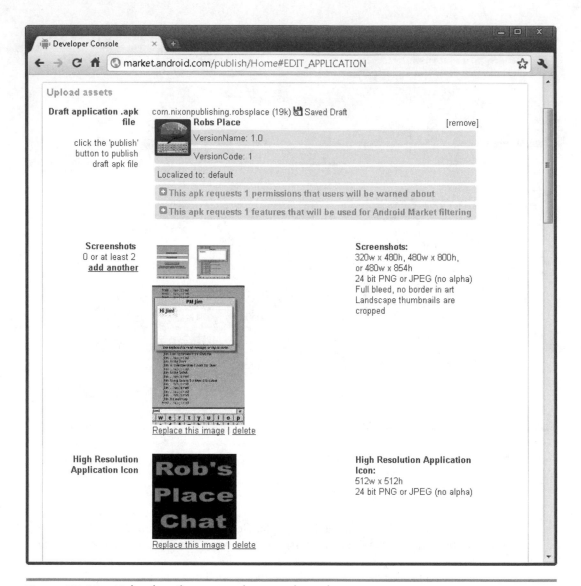

Figure 15-19 Uploading the app and assorted graphics

Figure 15-20   Filling in the listing details

Publishing options

Copy Protection
- ◉ Off (Application can be copied from the device)
- ○ On (Helps prevent copying of this application from the device. Increases the amount of memory on the phone required to install the application.)

The copy protection feature will be deprecated soon, please use underline{licensing service} instead.

Content Rating
[Learn More]
- ○ Mature
- ◉ Teen
- ○ Pre-Teen
- ○ All

Locations
Select locations to list in:

☑ **All locations**
(Includes more countries than those listed below. As the developer, you are responsible for complying with country-specific laws related to the distribution or sale of your application into that country, including your home country.)

Contact information

Website `http://myappwebsite.com`

Email `myusername@gmail.com`

Phone

Consent

☑ This application meets Android Content Guidelines

☑ I acknowledge that my software application may be subject to United States export laws, regardless of my location or nationality. I agree that I have complied with all such laws, including any requirements for software with encryption functions. I hereby certify that my application is authorized for export from the United States under these laws. [Learn More]

`Publish`   `Save`   `Delete`

Figure 15-21 Publishing options, contact information, and consent

Summary

You have now learned everything you need to know to be able to leverage the web technologies of HTML5, CSS3, and JavaScript, along with the server technologies of PHP and MySQL, to create advanced and professional web applications that you can then turn into stand-alone iOS and Android apps.

And you have learned how to do all of this (without needing to learn either Objective C or Java) by building your apps on top of the Wrapper projects available on the companion website. But once you have published some apps, I hope you'll take the opportunity to further investigate the Xcode and Eclipse SDKs to tailor your apps ever more closely to your exact specifications. If you do so, I believe you'll find that you start learning these languages almost by osmosis, and you may even decide to make the transition to developing native apps—but that's a whole other book (or two).

In the meantime, I hope you have found this book (which incorporates many tips and tricks that took me months to learn) to be a handy guide, and that it has helped you to successfully negotiate the minefield of iOS and Android development and publish your own web applications and stand-alone apps.

Index

References to figures are in italics.

T

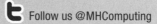

Practical Guides for Microsoft SharePoint 2010 Users of Every Level

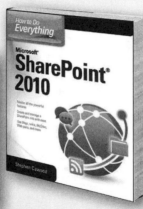
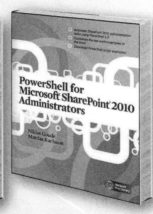